Coordination and Cooperation

Series on International Taxation

VOLUME 81

Series Editors

Prof. Ruth Mason, University of Virginia School of Law
Prof. Dr Ekkehart Reimer, University of Heidelberg

Introduction & Contents

The Series on International Taxation deals with a wide variety of topics in the global tax arena. The authors include many of the field's leading experts as well as talented newcomers. Their expert views and incisive commentary have proven highly useful to practitioners and academics alike.

Objective

The volumes published in this series are aimed at offering high-quality analytical information and practical solutions to international tax practitioners.

Readership

Practitioners, academics and policy makers in international tax law.

Frequency of Publication

2-3 new volumes published each year.

The titles published in this series are listed at the end of this volume.

Coordination and Cooperation

Tax Policy in the 21st Century

Edited by

Brigitte Alepin
Lyne Latulippe
Louise Otis

Wolters Kluwer

Published by:
Kluwer Law International B.V.
PO Box 316
2400 AH Alphen aan den Rijn
The Netherlands
E-mail: international-sales@wolterskluwer.com
Website: www.wolterskluwer.com/en/solutions/kluwerlawinternational

Sold and distributed by:
Wolters Kluwer Legal & Regulatory U.S.
7201 McKinney Circle
Frederick, MD 21704
United States of America
E-mail: customer.service@wolterskluwer.com

ISBN 978-94-035-3740-5

e-Book: ISBN 978-94-035-3760-3
web-PDF: ISBN 978-94-035-3781-8

Editors

Brigitte Alepin is a Harvard trained tax policy advisor and a professor in taxation at the Université du Québec en Outaouais. A Fellow Chartered Professional Accountant (Canada), she holds Masters degrees in taxation (Université de Sherbrooke) and tax administration with a concentration in microeconomics (Harvard University). As a tax specialist and tax policy advisor, she has led several major researches and projects for governments, Fortune 500 corporations and NGOs, in various fields, including environmental taxation, international taxation, oil and gas taxation and healthcare. She has both public- and private-sector experience that allows her to offer a rare multidimensional perspective on tax policies and public finances. She is a special advisor to politicians and political parties and also acts as an expert witness on various committees of the Canadian House of Commons and the Canadian Senate. Brigitte Alepin authored three books: *Ces riches qui ne paient pas d'impôt* [The Rich Who Do Not Pay Taxes], *Bill Gates, pay your fair share of taxes like we do!* and *La crise fiscale qui vient* [The Coming Fiscal Crisis] and also the award-winning documentary film *The Price We Pay*, directed by Harold Crooks and co-written by herself and Harold Crooks. She is also the director of the 2020 documentary film *Fast and Dangerous: A Tax Race to the Bottom*.

Lyne Latulippe holds an LL.B from the Université de Montreal and an LL.M. in Taxation from Université de Sherbrooke, as well as a Ph.D. in Political Science from Concordia University (Montreal). She worked for a large accounting firm for many before completing her Ph.D. As a professor at Université de Sherbrooke and principal researcher for the Research Chair in Taxation and Public Finance, she has been involved in numerous projects addressing tax fairness, aggressive tax planning, international taxation and transfer pricing. Her main research interests are the development and implementation of national and international tax policies, international tax governance and the actors involved. She has authored and co-authored articles and book chapters and she regularly speaks at conferences with a focus on political science and tax policy, in Canada and abroad.

Louise Otis is a civil and commercial mediator and arbitrator at the Canadian and international levels. She is a retired Justice of the Quebec Court of Appeal where she spearheaded the introduction of judicial mediation. She participated in over 3,000 judgments in civil, commercial, and criminal law. She has conducted over 700 mediation sessions in commercial and civil law. Louise Otis regularly participates in international governance and justice reform missions with the United Nations (UN), the International Monetary Fund (IMF), the World Bank (WB), and the International Finance Corporation (IFC) of the World Bank Group (WB). In 2020, Louise Otis was appointed by the United Nations secretary-general to a five-member panel of independent international experts given the task of redesigning the United Nations system of administration of Justice. She has also created a system of transitional justice for countries affected by armed conflicts and/or environmental disasters.

Contributors

Brian J. Arnold is a senior advisor at the Canadian Tax Foundation. He is a graduate of Harvard Law School (J.D., 1969) and taught tax law in Canada for many years. He has been a consultant to various governments, the Organisation for Economic Co-operation and Development and the United Nations. He has been a visiting professor at several universities including Harvard Law School (2005-2011), New York University School of Law (2005, 2012) and Sydney and Melbourne law schools in Australia.

Elena Belletti is an economist and advisor, specialized in green fiscal policies. She has been working at the United Nations Department of Economic and Social Affairs since 2015, supporting government officials to develop policies with the double aim to improve public finances and protect the environment. Among other achievements, she has been working with the UN Subcommittee on Environmental Taxation Issues to develop a Handbook on Carbon Taxation for Developing Countries and spearheaded the introduction of a yearly panel on environmental taxation in the Special Meeting on Tax of the UN Economic and Social Council. She previously worked for five years as a senior advisor and economist in the private energy sector (corporate and consulting). Ms. Belletti holds a B.Sc. and M.Sc. in Economics from Bocconi University and an MPA in Environmental Science and Policy from Columbia University.

Christina Dimitropoulou is currently a research and teaching associate and Ph.D. Candidate in the Doctoral Program in International Business Taxation of the Vienna University of Economics and Business (Wirtschaftsuniversität Wien). She is a tax lawyer and a member of the Athens Bar Association and has been previously worked with PwC Greece as a tax litigator and senior tax consultant. She specializes in robot taxation, digital taxes, and digitalization of tax procedures while she publishes articles and gives lectures regarding a broader range of tax policy issues and international and European tax law. She is a member of the European Artificial Intelligence (AI) Alliance and of the observatory legislative committee of the Greek Ministry of Justice regarding the implementation of Artificial Intelligence (AI) in justice. She has received papers' awards and has actively participated in tax law and technology conferences while she is also a reviewer in tax law journals.

Aimée Dushime is a chartered certified accountant (ACCA) and a chartered tax professional (ADIT) with seven years of tax and investment experience gained from working in Rwanda, Kenya, and Nigeria. She is well versed in Transfer Pricing and International Tax advisory and is passionate about tax policies and their potential to spur economic growth. She's also keen on tax research that focuses on international tax policy analysis, tax havens, and the relationship between taxation and economic development. Through her research, she aims to help in the ongoing fight against illicit financial flows, tax abuse, and inefficient tax systems.

Marie-Christine Esclassan is a professor of public finance and taxation at the University Paris 1—Panthéon Sorbonne at the Sorbonne Law School. She directs the French Journal of Public Finance. She is a member of the board of directors of the European Grouping of Public Finance. She is also a Chevalier of the Ordre of the Legion of Honor of the France Republic. She is the author of several books.

Vidushi Gupta is a tax lawyer and a policy professional. She was recognized by TaxCOOP as one of the thirty-five Leaders of the Future in Taxation. She is currently pursuing an LL.M. in Taxation from the London School of Economics as a Chevening Scholar. She previously led the tax law vertical at the Vidhi Centre for Legal Policy and worked at PwC India.

Simon Morin is a tax professional working at Revenu Québec (business audit, aggressive tax planning). Before joining Revenu Québec, Simon worked many years as a manager in the mergers and acquisitions tax team at PwC Canada. He obtained his Chartered Accountant designation (Quebec) in 2013 and his Master's in Taxation from the Université de Sherbrooke in 2014. He completed a B.B.A. (Accounting) with a major in Economics at Bishop's University, and a Diploma in Public Accountancy (Chartered Accountancy) at McGill University.

Richard Murphy is Professor of Accounting Practice, Sheffield University Management School and director of both Tax Research UK and the Corporate Accountability Network. He cofounded the Tax Justice Network. He is also a practicing chartered accountant.

Joy Waruguru Ndubai is currently pursuing a Doctorate in Law with a focus on international tax law at WU Vienna University of Economics and Business whilst carrying out research at the WU Institute for Austrian and International Tax Law, Global Tax Policy Center. Her research focuses on the interplay between tax transparency and corruption and the tools that could enhance inter-agency cooperative efforts to minimize tax evasion and other financial crimes; and the interaction between taxation, international investment agreements and trade agreements, amongst other pertinent areas concerning tax competition, digitalization and the digital economy and the African tax landscape, overall. She holds an LL.M. in Taxation from the London School of Economics and an LL.B. from SOAS (University of London). Prior to working in Vienna, she served as Global Tax Advisor at ActionAid Denmark and has previously worked with Oxfam GB (Kenya office) and Tax Justice Network Africa. She has also gained experience in the private sector working as a tax advisor at KPMG East Africa. She is a member of the BEPS Monitoring Group and a Tax COOP 35 leader of the future 2020.

Xavier Oberson is a Professor of Swiss and International Tax Law at the University of Geneva since 1994. After his studies at the University of Geneva where he obtained a law degree, a Master of Advanced Studies and a Doctorate (Ph.D.) in Law in 1990, he pursued his studies and research at the Harvard Law School where he finalized an LL.M. and also completed the International Tax Program (ITP) in 1992. He has published numerous books and articles, notably: "International Exchange of Information in Tax Matters. Towards Global Transparency," Edward Elgar Publishing, London 2015; "Droit fiscal Suisse," Basel 2021, 5th ed. (Helbing & Lichtenhahn); "Précis de droit fiscal international," Bern 2014, 4th ed. (Stämpfli); and, as a co-author, "Switzerland in international tax law," 4th ed., Amsterdam 2011 (IBFD Publications). He teaches regularly in various Universities abroad and, notably, was invited Professor at La Sorbonne (Paris) for many years. Since 2016, he has initiated a research on the potential taxation of robots. In this context, he gave the opening lecture at the University of Geneva in February 2017 and published: "Taxing Robots? From the Emergence of an Electronic Ability to Pay to a Tax on Robots or the Use of Robots," World Tax Journal 2017 (volume 9), No. 2. Recently, his book "Taxing Robot" has been published by Elgar Publishing (UK/USA) 2019.

Chuks Okoriekwe is a Graduate Student at the University of Florida's International Taxation (with Concentration in U.S. Law) program. He was previously an Associate at LeLaw (Barristers & Solicitors), Lagos, Nigeria where he advised clients on business, tax and transaction structuring. In addition to advising clients on complex legal issues, he also contributes thought leadership insights on topical issues in leading print and electronic media on the intersection of law, technology, and taxation. His publications can be found here: https://www.lexology.com/1166665/author/Chuks_Okoriekwe/ He was recently named among thirty-five Leaders of the Future in Taxation by TaxCOOP, a neutral and inclusive initiative dedicated to tax competition and tax cooperation. His proposal on Blockchain for Tax Compliance won the Innovation Award at the TaxCOOP Tax Responsible Society Innovation Contest held in Montréal, Canada in 2020. He is a Research Fellow at the African Academic Network on Internet Policy (AANoIP), Carrington and StartingBloc Institute Fellow.

Jeffrey Owens has led the OECD tax work for over twenty years, and now he is the Director of the WU Global Tax Policy Center (WU GTPC) at the Institute for Austrian and International Tax Law, Vienna University of Economics and Business (Wirtschaftsuniversität Wien, WU). He also serves as a Senior Policy Advisor to the Global Vice Chair of Tax at EY, and as a Senior Advisor to the United Nations Tax Committee, the Inter-American Development Bank (IDB) and UNCTAD and a number of regional tax administration organizations as well as being involved with a number of NGOs.

Natalia Pushkareva is a tax policy expert and a Ph.D. candidate in Global Studies at the University of Urbino where she studies the effects of institutional design on the inclusivity of tax policy fora. Having a background in law and finance, Natalia accumulated her experience at Big 4, policy think tanks and academia, and is particularly interested in using tax policy for development.

William Ross, is coordinator of Échec aux Paradis Fiscaux since 2020. Échec aux Paradis Fiscaux is a Québec based NGO advocating for the abolition of tax havens and other fiscal loopholes. He is also a Ph.D. student in Philosophy working in the fields of social theory, epistemology, and critical theory.

Gabriella Sobodker is a tax practitioner specialized in international tax law and policy. She has been working for TaxCOOP since January 2020, where she works on various projects related to tax cooperation and tax fairness. She holds a Master's in Taxation Law from HEC Montreal and Bachelor's in Accountancy from Concordia University.

Félix-Antoine Ste-Marie has completed his law degree at the University of Montreal and a master's degree in tax from HEC Montreal. He is a member of the Quebec Bar association since 2015. In the past few years, he has been working for Raymond Chabot Grant Thornton where his practice consists of helping and advising SMEs in navigating the Canadian tax system.

Vito Tanzi is a Ph.D. in Economics (Harvard, 1967) and was a Professor of Economics at The American University (1967-1974). He has also been the Head of Tax policy Division at the IMF (1974-1981), Director of the Fiscal Affairs Department at the IMF (1981-2000), Undersecretary for Economy and Finance, Italian Government (2001-2003). He is the author of twenty-five books and hundreds of articles in professional economic journals. An economic effect, "The Tanzi effect" was named after him.

Summary of Contents

Table of Contents

Acknowledgments

The late Kofi Annan, Secretary General of the United Nations (1997-2006), said "Reform is a process and not an event." When the time comes to reform international and even national taxation, there is nothing truer. International tax reform is a laborious process that requires time and dedication from all stakeholders, including governments, market actors and citizens.

The first stuttering moves toward international tax reform date back to 2008 when the G20 called for increased transparency and exchange of information to respond to the global economic crisis. In July 2012, the G20 Leaders in Los Cabos approved the work done by the OECD through the Global Forum on Transparency and Exchange of Information to increase tax transparency and also supported the launching of the base erosion and profit shifting project (BEPS) by the organization to address legal tax avoidance allowed by the international tax system.

TaxCOOP was founded in 2014 in Montreal, Canada, at a time when no global tax reform proposals tackled tax competition head-on, and the issue was practically being ignored in any discussions related to the modernization of tax regimes. For the founders of TaxCOOP, globalization was incomplete without reforming our tax regimes in order to address the problem of international tax competition in a globalized world. The objective of TaxCOOP was simple: To get the tax world to recognize the problem of international tax competition and the threat of a race-to-the bottom, and to promote cooperation as a replacement for this competition in the taxation area. Moreover, when launching TaxCOOP in 2014 on Canadian public television, the idea, then rarely mentioned, of a global minimum tax was raised as a possible solution.

Launched in 2015 at the Montreal Museum of Fine Arts in 2015, the first TaxCOOP conference innovated by reuniting a wide audience including experts, professionals, academics, policymakers, politicians but also citizens to make them aware of the issues at stake. With unique partnerships each year, the following TaxCOOP conferences have been presented at the World Bank in Washington in 2016, the UN in Geneva in 2017, the OECD in Paris in 2018, and in Madrid in December 2019 as part of COP25 under the theme of green taxation.

After this world tour, TaxCOOP's ultimate goal was to return to Canada in 2020 to present the World Tax Summit to reunite stakeholders from a variety of countries and take stock of advances with regard to tax competition and tax cooperation and discuss future challenges facing international tax policy. It is in this context that TaxCOOP2020 took place online in the midst of the COVID-19 pandemic from October 11 to 14, 2020. With 135 speakers and more than 2,300 participants from 80 countries, the World Tax Summit—TaxCOOP2020 proved a unique and innovative conference, open to the public. To further raise awareness about tax competition, the book *Winning the tax wars* inspired from TaxCOOP2017 has been published with Wolters Kluwer in 2018 and TaxCOOP produced and presented the film *Fast & Dangerous Race to the Bottom* on Canadian public television and in several countries.

TaxCOOP has now held six major free public events dedicated to tax competition and international tax cooperation, with hundreds of speakers and thousands of participants over the years, including a place for younger experts to express themselves. The organization reached an even wider audience through books and articles published in major newspapers, a contests and a film.

On June 7, 2021, the G7 committed to the goal of a minimum global corporate tax rate of at least 15%. The G20 and the 132 countries of the inclusive OECD framework followed in the following weeks. The list of leaders who now recognize the global race to the bottom in corporate taxation is long, including United States Treasury Secretary Janet Yellen, OECD Secretary-General Mathias Cormann, Minister of Finance of France Bruno LeMaire and Minister of Finance of Canada Chrystia Freeland.

International tax competition is being recognized and considered within global tax reform, and more than 130 countries and territories have adhered to the principle of a global minimum tax. The impossible has now become possible in the field of taxation and, these achievements are in line with the purpose of TaxCOOP.

In the words of Kofi Annan, reform is indeed a process and this process requires teamwork. Why have suddenly over 130 countries accepted the unimaginable, the establishment of a global minimum tax? Academics and historians will have a case to study and a story to tell, providing a lot of work for many years to come, in order to explain this evolution and to help future tax generations navigate through the changes of these uncertain times. But one thing is certain, the exceptional contribution of the OECD and other major international organizations, and the dedication of major tax leaders to the cause, has been a crucial source behind the great achievements to date.

Having been on this journey since 2014, the founders of TaxCOOP are satisfied to have participated in fueling the discussions about the race-to-the-bottom and the idea of the global minimum tax as well as pinpointing other important topics such as taxation and the environment and taxation of the ultra-rich. TaxCOOP would therefore like to thank the governments, international organizations, speakers, experts, authors of its books, the younger generation, its participants, and the media. In addition, TaxCOOP could not have accomplished all of this without being able to count on committed financial partners and a team of dedicated and brilliant people.

It is with well-grounded initiatives like this book that TaxCOOP has contributed in its own unique way to international tax reform. A big thank you to all the authors for sharing their valuable thoughts and their writing to make this a better world.

Introduction

Brigitte Alepin, Lyne Latulippe & Louise Otis

The more than a hundred years old corporate tax systems rose among the top priorities on the international agenda in the past decades. As fundamental problems with the international tax system emerged, such as the underlying inequity generated, and the inefficiency in dealing with avoidance and evasion, more people voiced their concerns to demand a reform.

Significant proposals are currently on the table to change international tax rules. While some policies were modified more recently, other proposals could lead shortly to a substantial reform of the international tax system, particularly in relation to the taxation of multinationals. This major reform will create a new international tax system that could very well be in place for decades. It is of the utmost importance to consider these reform proposals in a broader social, economic and environmental perspective in order to reach a global regime adapted to the current and future needs of both developed and developing countries.

This book offers a rare multidisciplinary overview with various perspectives expressed by actors from the private sector, academia, governments, international organizations, and non-governmental organizations (NGOs) on the topics surrounding the international tax reform agenda and other crucial issues with regard to tax policy. Also, this book is about reuniting experienced well-renowned experts and emerging experts to offer solid and innovative ideas on tax policy for future generations. It is hoped that in the book "Coordination and Cooperation—Tax Policy in the 21st Century" readers will find information and ideas not only useful but also thought-provoking and that they will be encouraged to pursue such studies further.

Among the topics covered are tax policies in times of crisis, wealth taxation, small- and medium-sized enterprises (SMEs) as well as multinationals taxation, environmental taxation, tax competition, tax administration, tax justice and many more. The book is inspired by the content of the World Tax Summit—TaxCOOP2020 attended by more than 2,300 participants and 135 high-level speakers, making it a unique tax conference in 2020. Some speakers who participated in the Summit have written chapters while other chapters are the result of a collaboration between speakers at the Summit and young tax leaders. The book offers food for thoughts to address the current challenges facing the international tax system, as well as reform proposals and related topics, such as the use of tax policies to achieve sustainable development goals.

Cooperation is more important than ever to achieve the major reform currently underway, to stop the adoption of non-coordinated unilateral measures and to act with regard to inequalities particularly in a pandemic and post-pandemic era. Inequalities have been high on the priority list of world leaders and the pandemic will make it rise even higher. Tax cooperation can also help support actions to fight climate change. Governments will need to make important decisions related to their tax system to ensure sufficient revenues and sound public finances while working on reducing inequalities and fighting climate change. Globalization makes it very difficult for most states to act unilaterally, and cooperation is key to develop an efficient international tax system.

The first section of the book is concerned with tax policy decisions in times of crisis, discussing experiences as well as lessons from the past or principles that should guide policymakers, particularly facing the pandemic's economic and social consequences. These lessons will also be valuable in addressing the economic and social impact of climate change. In Chapter 1, Vito Tanzi provides a historical overview of the economic and social role of taxation. He discusses the role tax policy has played and should play in governments' duty to predict, prepare for and manage random events, such as pandemics and natural disasters. In Chapter 2, based on ideas expressed by two renowned experts, namely Mariana Mazzucato and Arthur Laffer, Chuks Okoriekwe presents contrasting insights about fiscal and economic ideologies that can help shape governments' tax policy responses following global economic crises. Then, in Chapter 3, William Ross shares his thoughts on tax justice in times of crisis. By shedding light on the existing tension first between opacity and transparency and second between inequalities and justice, the author claims that tax justice is linked to social justice and that redistribution of wealth goes alongside a redistribution of capacities.

The second section concerns the international tax system, more particularly the current challenges and the reform underway. It examines the perspectives of developed countries, developing countries, tax havens, and international organizations. Joy Waruguru Ndubay addresses tax competition and the race to the bottom in Chapter 4. She discusses the progress made in minimizing the negative effects of tax competition, addresses whether new opportunities to engage in competition are emerging or already available and examines whether some of the most recent proposed solutions could end the race to the bottom for corporate income tax. In Chapter 5, Lyne Latulippe, Brigitte Alepin, and Louise Otis briefly present how the work of international organizations with regard to tax policy at the domestic and international levels has evolved. This chapter then presents the point of view regarding international tax cooperation and multilateralism of a tax leader from each of the international organizations. In Chapter 6, Brian Arnold and Gabriella Sobodker look at the impact of globalization and digitalization on international tax policy. They relate recent developments, particularly large multinationals taxation, as manifested in the form of unilateral, bilateral and multilateral measures, and analyze how these policy directions interact (or fail to interact) with one another. In Chapter 7, Aimee Dushime summarizes diverging points of view concerning the role of tax havens in the global economy, their impact on the international tax system and the international efforts to constrain the use of tax havens. Finally, in Chapter 8, Natalia Pushkareva summarizes key tax issues especially important to developing countries with regard to international tax policy and then discusses the challenges faced by lower-income jurisdictions when representing their interests at international tax policy fora.

The second section addresses the challenges of administering taxes in the 21st century. In Chapter 9, Vidushi Gupta summarizes the views of three high-level administrators within the Canada Revenue Agency about tax administration prior to the pandemic, the approach adopted by the tax administration in the first six months of the pandemic in order to face issues and challenges and the way forward for tax authorities. This provides a holistic picture of tax administration in these unprecedented times. Simon Morin explores the future of tax administrations in more detail in Chapter 10. The chapter summarizes major current and emerging trends that tax administrations must face in the 21st century. He exposes key challenges—in addition to the COVID-19 crisis—and opportunities for tax administrations in these times of technological and economic upheavals. In Chapter 11, Jeffrey Owens and Simon Morin explore more specifically how disruptive technologies, such as blockchain and artificial intelligence (AI), provide transformational opportunities and challenges to governments and tax authorities and are expected to fundamentally change the environment in which tax administrations evolve as well as the manner in which tax administrations interact with taxpayers.

The fourth section exposes future challenges that tax policy will need to address and that will likely require international cooperation. Chapter 12 is about the taxation of wealth. After a brief historical overview of the French policies to tax wealth, presented by Marie-Christine Esclassan, four experts from opposing sides debate the need, the efficiency and the feasibility of taxing wealth. In Chapter 13, Christina Dimitropoulou examines the role of tax policy in reaction to the new technologies and analyses the concept of robot taxation and the international tax competition concerns that might arise from the taxation of robots and the use of AI. The chapter concludes with comments by Xavier Oberson, who provides further context and elaborates on taxing robots as enterprises. In Chapter 14, Elena Belletti explores how tax policy can support a green economic recovery and provides a framework for thought and action by governments and the international community, including examples of both tax policy and expenditure strategies. She also analyses how the green transition can help create fairer, more inclusive societies. Concerning more particularly the taxation of SMEs, Félix-Antoine Ste-Marie in Chapter 15 questions the adequacy of actual tax systems with regard to SMEs. The author argues for the necessity to reform the tax system for SMEs more broadly to help these enterprises be more prepared to face other crises. Finally, pervasive in the tax field are ethical considerations. In Chapter 16, Richard Murphy offers a proposition to enhance tax ethics and suggests a universal approach to the ethics of taxation. Drawing from the perspectives of various actors in the taxation field, from taxpayers to tax academics and tax authorities, he elaborates on an inclusive code of ethics for taxation, intended to meet the needs of all stakeholders.

The conclusion reiterates the need for coordination and cooperation for efficient and equitable tax policies in the 21st century and as we are moving forward to modernize our tax systems, the editors share some thoughts on the necessary steps down that road.

In 2016, the book *Winning the Tax Wars* was published following TaxCOOP2016 conference at the World Bank to share information and insights more broadly. This new book takes stock of the recent but impressive progress to reform the international tax system while also insisting on necessary conditions for a successful reform. It also aims at fostering a discussion about highly relevant tax policy issues to consider when adjusting tax systems to the collective needs to face the challenges of the 21st century.

CHAPTER 1

Some History's Lessons

Vito Tanzi[*]

Taxation is a major policy instrument that governments use to promote collective needs.

The role of taxation changed in the past century, to reflect changing social needs and aspirations. It especially came to include the pursuit of economic equity and the promotion of growth and stabilization. The tax level considered desirable generally increased over the years, but it continues to be related to what were considered the needs of an economy in normal times. Taxes were to be efficient and sufficient for those times.

However, countries occasionally encounter unexpected and random damaging events, including pandemics and major natural disasters, that make countries' situations not normal. Major, random events make what might have been considered adequate tax levels and structures inadequate. Random events, such as pandemics and major disasters have occurred many times over the centuries. They are difficult to predict statistically, unlike statistically measurable "risks." Uncertain events have continued to be ignored by economic theory and by policies.

The paper argues that more effort should be made to prepare for major pandemics and disasters. They should influence economic theory and make the pursuit of equity in taxation more important when they occur.

* Valuable comments received from Andres Solimano, Partho Shome, Alex Tanzi, George Iden, and Nuri Erbas were much appreciated and helped to improve this chapter. These individuals are, of course, not responsible for any remaining errors, or for the views expressed.

§1.01 INTRODUCTION

Taxation is one of the major instruments available to governments to promote collective or national goals, and governments are the main institutions through which citizens pursue, or hope to pursue, collective goals. It is, of course, not easy to determine precisely what the collective needs of a country, or a community, are at a given moment, and how much taxation is necessary to finance their provision. However, for democratic countries with market economies, the usual assumption is that the collective needs can be determined democratically, and their determination will suggest a given tax level. The democratic process can, then, determines how the tax burden should be allocated among the citizens.

Naturally, there will always be some individuals, or some groups, who thought or will think that the tax level, whatever it is, is too high; and others who will think that it is too low and not sufficient to pay for the collective needs. Others are likely to think that the tax burden is not allocated fairly among the citizens, and others will think that the money collected in taxes is not spent efficiently. These make democracies exciting places to live in.

Over the last century, views about taxation changed significantly, as did those about what the desirable government economic role should be. Broadly speaking, and recognizing strong opposition that comes from libertarian, or conservative,

groups, the desirable government role was extended over the decades. It came to include especially: (a) the need to redistribute some income and wealth, from richer to poorer, deserving citizens, when the distribution generated by the market was not considered fair. It was recognized that in a market economy there are efficiency limits to this redistributive policy; and (b) attempts by governments to promote, with their policies, full, or fuller, employment of labor and capital, especially during economic slowdown and recessions.

The desirable, tax level and the use of tax revenue have been normally considered by tax experts and by governments to relate to normal times. Occasionally, during exceptional times, such as wars, some non-normal, exceptional revenue needs were created. During these times, the tax levels were pushed up, to finance the higher, military spending. However, in normal, peaceful times the tax level and the tax structure have been assumed to be consistent with the normal requirements of a market economy, one that is expected to operate efficiently; and with the requirements of a democratic, political system, that directs the government policies toward popular support, and towards winning the next elections. Therefore, the taxes are expected to be *efficient in their impact* and *sufficient* to satisfy the *routine and immediate* needs of the citizens. These, at least, have been the basic guiding principles (Tanzi, 2020).

In normal times and economic situations, governments are expected to keep the tax levels as low and as efficient as possible, and to focus public spending toward meeting the immediate, short run, needs of the citizens and the economy. Uncertain and contingent future needs attract little if any, attention and generally do not influence taxes and public spending. A government that has spent a significant amount of money to prepare for distant and uncertain needs, needs that might never materialize, would, likely, pay a high political price in popularity, and in the coming elections.

In markets, assumed to be competitive, private enterprises will focus on maximizing profits by minimizing the current use of labor and capital in their operations. They will also keep inventories low, in order to contain costs. Enterprises that allocated significant resources to deal with uncertain, future, events would become less competitive in the short run (Tanzi, 2020).

In conclusion, neither governments nor enterprises are likely to give much thought or pay much attention to potential, future, and highly uncertain events, such as pandemics and major natural disasters. The theories of taxation and of market behavior were developed for normal situations, not for crises. Those theories focused on equilibrium situations and on the achievement of short-run optimality, as Paul Samuelson stressed in his classic book (Samuelson, 1947).

§1.02 PROBLEMS CREATED BY RANDOM EVENTS

Normally, future crises, created by pandemics and by other major catastrophes, are considered anomalies. In normal times their future possibilities do not change the modus operandi of governments and of enterprises, in countries that are democratic and that have market economies. These uncertain future crises do not and cannot enter in the routine policy decisions of governments, or in the planning and behavior of private enterprises, as Keynes had theorized in his *Treatise on Probability*.[1]

Future crises are impossible to predict, in both *timing* and *severity*, in order to allow governments and private enterprises to allocate current resources to prepare for them, when they may come. The *timing* and the *severity* of epidemics, major hurricanes, earthquakes, fires, and tidal waves cannot be predicted to allow efficient preparation or to develop insurance markets to deal with them.[2] In an important book, published in 1921, Frank Knight, had elaborated on the importance of the distinction between *risk* and *uncertainty*. Insurance markets can be developed to deal with risk but no markets can arise to deal with uncertainty. Governments can develop programs to deal with risks faced by individuals but not for future events characterized by uncertainty as individuals and enterprises could buy insurance against risk but not against uncertainty because there are no markets for uncertainty.

Over the centuries, there have been major pandemics, including the Black Plague of 1347-1352 in Europe that killed at least a third of the European population, and the Spanish Flu of 1918-1919, that killed more people than had World War I (Garrett, 1994). There have also been other major natural disasters (major hurricanes, earthquakes, tidal waves, and others). They happened in the past, at times when governments' resources and their capacity to act had been limited. When the disasters came, few expected the governments to be able to do much.

1. *See also* Pindick and Wang, 2009; and Martin and Pindick, 2019, for recent analyses.
2. For some recent discussion of this "Knightian Uncertainty," *see* the recent book by Kay and King, 2020.

The pandemics and the other catastrophes had been considered "Acts of God," or even "God's Revenge" for the bad behavior of mortals. They had called for flagellation and repentance, and not for actions by the government. They could not be predicted and, in part because of this, it would have been difficult to prepare for their coming. Wars had been in a different category. They could not be considered Acts of God and, to some extent, they could be anticipated, and some resources could be allocated for them.

In more recent decades, business fluctuations, such as the Great Depression of the 1930s and the Great Recession of 2008-2009, attracted the attention of economists and policy makers. These fluctuations had more regularity, especially in timing, than other crises. This led to expectations that governments could and should adopt some policies to fight them when they came, and even that they could adopt some policies in anticipation of their coming. This led, first, to what came to be called the Keynesian Revolution, and later to the increasing use of the monetary policy.

The "Keynesian Revolution" called on governments to increase spending during recessions, and to finance the additional spending with fiscal deficits. It also led to calls for some other policies, such as to permanently increase public spending, and for the use of built-in stabilizers, to reduce automatically the severity of the recessions. This may have been the first call on governments to deal, on a permanent basis, with economic crises, which arrived with more regularity than other crises (Solimano, 2020).

There were no similar calls to prepare countries for other kinds of catastrophes. As mentioned earlier, their randomness, in time and in severity, prevented this preparation. The way economies and governments are expected to operate, in democratic countries with market economies, does not create incentives, for them, to adopt, in normal times, policies that would make it easier for the countries to deal with these future catastrophes. This preparation might involve spending more money for hospitals, for building more protections against floods, and for building stronger buildings against major earthquakes and hurricanes. This additional spending would inevitably require higher taxes, which would encounter taxpayers' resistance and have political costs.

For a democratic government worried about the next election, there would not be any political advantages, and only political costs, in doing so. The benefits from the extra spending would come later, and at times much later. However, the costs in higher taxes or in stricter regulations would be immediate. The frequency of political elections, that make the relevant time horizon of most democratic governments short, and political pressures to keep tax levels low and to use the revenue to satisfy immediate needs, would prevent democratic governments from allocating significant resources to provide better protection to citizens against future, random, and highly uncertain events. A government that invested large resources in protecting citizens against such events would be criticized for wasting taxpayers' money and it would run a higher risk of losing the elections. Uncertainty would play against future security.

Governments have occasionally relied on the use of *regulations*, rather than on spending, to promote better safety codes against some catastrophic events. For example, in areas subject to earthquakes, such as California or Tokyo, they have strengthened building codes. In areas subject to major hurricanes, they have imposed regulations to keep some distance from the coastline. However, by increasing the cost of housing, governments have, at times, been criticized for having strengthened these regulations. The prevalence of homeless people in California is at times attributed to these strict regulations, perhaps unfairly.

On the side of the private sector, the forces of competition also tend to promote actions, or behavior, that do not encourage enterprises to deal with future, uncertain crises or, even, with recessions, that might affect them more directly. Private enterprises, which operate in competitive markets, have strong incentives to keep costs low. They do so by squeezing real wages, minimizing their workforces, and keeping inventories low, relying on "just-in-time" systems of delivery. The CEOs of corporations have an incentive to maximize profits and to distribute the profits of the corporations to the shareholders, or to use the profits to buy shares of their own corporations. This increases the value of the shares, keeps the shareholders happy, and helps justify the CEOs' high compensation packages, that over the years have been increasingly tied to the values of the shares. It also reduces the taxes that the shareholders pay on their capital earnings, because of the non-taxation of unrealized capital gains that characterizes most tax systems.

Corporations are also encouraged, by the tax systems, to make greater use of debt to finance their investments or, even, to buy their own shares, especially when credit is cheap. The deductibility of the interest paid on the debt, in the calculation of the taxable profits, makes the use of debt attractive. When the cost of borrowing is kept low by central banks' policies, as it has been kept in recent years, borrowing is further stimulated. This leads to high shares of private debt (and to lower tax revenue) (Tanzi, 2016a).

These and other actions contribute to conditions that make corporations more vulnerable to crises when the crises come. If the enterprises are "too big to fail," they can hope that the government will come to their rescue, as it did during the Great Recession of 2008-2009. Workers are often the ones who bear the major costs of economic crises because they lose their jobs, their incomes, and, often, even their health insurance. As Milton Friedman argued, in a famous and influential essay, published on September 12, 1970, in *The New York Times Magazine*, "The Social Responsibility of Business is to Increase Its Profits." He stated that enterprises do not have "social" responsibilities, only the responsibility of generating profits for their owners. That position leads to an obvious question: who has social responsibilities? It would be logical to assume that if a business does not have social responsibilities, the government must be responsible. However, market fundamentalism made it difficult for the United States and some other governments to do so.

The above discussion moves the focus from what governments and enterprises should have done but did not do in anticipation of future, random crises, including pandemics, to what they should do when the crises become a reality. This question is addressed in the next section, with special reference to the current pandemic, using, especially, the United States current situation.

§1.03 POLICIES DURING THE PANDEMIC

When everything seems to fail, as it does during major catastrophes, citizens in modern countries inevitably turn to the government to intervene. The first and rather obvious observation, concerning governments' interventions, is that, when major catastrophes are realistic even though still future, random events, as to timing and severity, they should provide an additional reason for modern governments to keep their fiscal houses in order and to maintain some fiscal space. This fiscal space would make it easier for them to step in quickly, when the time calls for it, with additional spending and with less concern about the sustainability of the public debt. Governments that are already burdened by high debts and by running fiscal deficits, and are already relying on distortive taxes, will have less degrees of freedom to act when intervention is needed. This initial fiscal condition is always important, but it is systematically ignored.

The above initial condition is, of course, an argument against the views expressed by some leading economists (Krugman, Stiglitz, and others) who, in recent years, have complained about what they have called "austerity policies" (i.e., presumably conservative spending policies adopted by some governments), in what were, largely, normal times, and not crises periods. These economists have criticized some governments for spending too little, even when the latter were already spending high shares (in some cases 50% or more) of their countries' GDPs. It is also an argument against other economists (Blanchard, Kelton, and others) who have argued that there is almost no limit to the use of government debt and that public debt, especially when contracted in a country's own currency, cannot create economic difficulties.

Similar observations can be made concerning the behavior of private enterprises. In this context, a comparison between the behavior of American and Japanese enterprises may be of some interest. Japanese enterprises, in normal times, tend to hold larger shares of their profits as precautionary balances. They use these profits to retain their workers during recessions when sales and profits fall. American companies do not hold their profits and, when crises come, they do not hesitate to lay off their workers. The consequence is that the unemployment rate fluctuates much less in Japan than it does in the United States. Following Friedman's view, many American economists have considered the Japanese behavior as less conducive to longer-term economic growth. In several European countries, businesses also tend to hold on to their workers during downturns, to a much greater extent than the United States, thus again violating Friedman's guideline.

In this context, it should be pointed out that most workers save litter and normally depend on their current wages to sustain their current standards of living. Many of them do not have precautionary balances. When they lose their jobs, they lose their incomes, and many face immediate, economic, difficulties, including the loss of health insurance. These difficulties may be partly reduced, in the short run, by governments, temporary, unemployment compensation programs. On the other hand, many owners of corporate shares, normally, have some, or much, accumulated wealth distributed among shares of different corporations, to fall on in bad times. Wealth provides an important buffer against negative shocks. It is a major shock absorber.

With the popularity of the corporate form of business organization, that, over the years, replaced what used to be enterprises owned by single or few private owners, many richer individuals now allocate their total wealth on shares of different corporations, they spread their proverbial eggs among many baskets, reducing their total risk. The poor performance of a single or of a few corporations is likely to affect less the total purchasing power of many shareholders, than does the loss of jobs for workers.

Furthermore, because of the impact of "market fundamentalism" on policies since the late 1970s, the tax treatment of capital income and of some other sources of income became significantly lighter compared with that of the wages of dependent workers. Some studies (Saez and Zucman, 2019) have estimates that, in the United States, the tax burden of normal workers is now similar to that of the richest families. Others have found that, after the 2017 Tax Cuts and Jobs Act, in 2018, billionaires paid a lower effective tax rate, 23%, than the working class, 24%. The above important aspects are often ignored in discussions of the desirable tax burdens of workers and owners of capital and managers.

Let us now deal more directly with the current pandemic and with the use of taxes at this time. The pandemic has been hardly neutral in its impact on different sectors of the economy and on income distribution. During the ongoing pandemic, millions of workers lost their jobs and their incomes. Many of them did not have assets to fall back on, and they might remain unemployed for a long time. Unemployment claims have been high (many millions) and are expected to remain high for an unknown period. Political debates continue to rage as to how much and for how long to help, with government assistance, the unemployed workers and many of the small enterprises (restaurants, barbershops, gyms, etc.) that are facing economic difficulties because of the pandemic.

The future impact of the pandemic on the real economy remains uncertain and worrisome. The longer the pandemic lasts, the greater will be the consequences for countries' economies and for many citizens. The pandemic will change permanently some economic arrangements. Consumer confidence has continued to be low. Global trade has suffered. The debt of governments has exploded and, in the United States, the Federal debt now exceeds USD 26 trillion. According to the latest estimates by the Congressional Budget Office, the Federal debt which was 79% of GDP in 2019 rose to 98% in 2020 and is now expected to reach 195% in 2050. The US Federal deficit will be a record 16% of GDP in 2020 and will remain high for years to come. In some other countries, the public debt has increased even more. The tax revenues of US subnational governments that depend significantly on sales taxes have collapsed. Many American states will find it impossible to meet their constitutional, balanced-budget, obligations without sharply cutting spending, or without getting large Federal assistance. Especially, many small enterprises will not recover, and their owners and employees will continue to face difficulties.

A remarkable aspect of this crisis is that the US stock market, that should have collapsed to accompany the sharp fall in output and the rise in unemployment, has been doing very well. Its level in mid-September 2020 has been at a historical high, at a time when the number of those infected by COVID-19 was exceeding six million and the deaths had already exceeded 200,000 while still forecasting a sharp rise. The real estate market has also been doing well because of the low mortgage rates and the desire of many city dwellers, who can afford it, to have more space during lockdowns. In sum, those who own wealth, or have high and safe incomes, are doing very well economically, in spite of the pandemic.

This great disconnect between what is happening to those who own most wealth and have safe jobs and, especially, what is happening to workers who are in occupations ironically called "essential" (health care and personal service workers, food supply workers, farm workers, and others) is nothing short of extraordinary. It is almost obscene. It seems that it helps if one's occupation is not "essential." The less "essential" an occupation seems to be, the more it is being valued by the market. The workers in the "essential" activities are the ones who are paying a high price, in both health and income, for the pandemic. They are not only exposed more to the effects of the virus but, many of them have lost their jobs and their income (Torpey, 2020). Individuals who do not need to work, because they have accumulated assets, or because they can work in safer environments, are in privileged positions. The stock market is compensating many of them with its rise. These developments cannot be seen as a complement to the ethic and the fairness of the market economy and perhaps also to that of the government.

§1.04 SOME REASONS FOR THE DISCONNECT

There may be several reasons for the disconnect between the real economy and the stock market but two may be particularly important. They are: (a) the tax policies followed by the United States and by some other countries in recent decades; and (b) the monetary policies followed by central banks in more recent years. The above policies have combined, over the decades, with the process of globalization and with the coming into existence of large, global, and technologically based monopolies, which now account for a significant share of the total value of the US stock market. These monopolies have continued to make large profits and to pay little in taxes on their profits during the pandemic.

The current crisis has shown what may be considered a shortcoming of *market fundamentalism,* and of the limitation of the *trickle down* assumption, that had been used to justify it by its advocates. The view that a free market resembles a favorable tide that "lifts all boats" has been shown to be naïve. The current shortcomings have made it more obvious than it had been in the past that the spontaneous *trickle down* must be aided by adequate government tax and spending policies that promote a more equitable income distribution. Significant trickle down has not emerged spontaneously from the free work of the market. The government must play a complementary role. The assumption that "market fundamentalism" and low taxes (especially low taxes on high incomes and on incomes from capital), that were promoted by supply-side economists, would benefit everyone has been shown to be an illusion. Only adequate social policies can make a market fair.

It is not possible in this paper to discuss in detail past policies, and how they may have played a role in the current dichotomy. We will limit our observations to a few, rather general points, starting with the statement, as several studies (including some by the US Federal Reserve System and by the Census Bureau) have shown, that over the past four decades the share of total income and total wealth received by a small share of the population (the top one or 0.1%) increased remarkably. These individuals benefitted the most from the economic growth and many of them are benefitting from the current behavior of the stock market. There has been little "trickle down" in recent decades, mostly "trickle up." Since the 1980s, government policies, and the manipulations of some of those policies by well-placed individuals, played a major role in this trend (Tanzi, forthcoming). These policies have included tax, regulatory, and, in more recent decades, monetary policies. We shall ignore regulatory policies, which also played a major role, in the following discussion.

[A] Tax Policy

Many people may not be fully aware of the changes in tax policy since World War II, and especially since the 1970s. Some basic data are provided for the United States of America. In 1944-1945, the tax rate on the highest tax bracket of the Federal personal income tax was 94%. The rate was reduced to 91% in 1950, to 70% in 1965, to 50% in 1982, and to 28% in 1988. Because of concerns about rising fiscal deficits, in the late 1980s, the rate rose a little in later years. It is now 37% on the highest, reported taxable incomes.

These reductions in tax rates have meant that individuals who had very high taxable incomes (millionaires and billionaires) benefited enormously from the reductions. They experienced huge drops in their average tax burdens. Those in the middle class, and especially dependent workers without stable, long-term work contracts, benefited far less. Furthermore, while in 1965 the average compensation of the CEOs of the largest corporations had been about 20 times that of average workers, it grew to 58 times in 1989, and to 312 times in 2017. The tax reductions were not limited to the United States.[3]

Over the same decades, the main tax rate on the profits of US corporations also fell significantly. Until 1969, it had been 52%. It was reduced to 46% in 1979-1981, to 34% in 1988, and then to 21% in 2018. This was an enormous reduction, but some US observers have continued to complain that 21% is still too high, and President Trump has suggested that it could be further reduced if he remained in power.

In addition to the fall in the main statutory tax rates reported above, rates that are the visible tips of the iceberg, there were many other, less visible, structural changes in the tax treatment of income from capital, in the tax treatment of the compensations of CEOs and of other high-income individuals. These changes are more difficult to

3. For data on other OECD countries, *see* Messere, 1993 and Tanzi, 2011.

describe. They have included the favorable treatment of some incomes, such as those from "carried trade," changes in depreciation rules, shift of the compensation of executives toward lower-taxed stock options, and several others that have further reduced the effective tax rates on high incomes. At the same time unrealized capital gains, which in the 1950s and 1960s had attracted much attention by tax experts, have remained untaxed, during a period that has seen great market capitalization. The above changes have been described as "corporate welfare."

The globalization of economic activities, that took place in the past four decades of financial and trade deregulation, opened many, new channels, for both high net worth individuals and global corporations, to avoid paying taxes. They have done so by shifting (and often hiding), income and wealth in foreign jurisdictions (tax havens and low-tax countries) where they could enjoy low or even tax-free status, and could also maintain anonymity.[4] Tax planning has become a major global activity and it is now assisted by a growing supply of clever and well-paid tax advisors who can design tax-avoiding strategies, exploiting the many tax complexities that have grown in many countries' tax systems, and aided by tax competition among countries.

A large and growing literature has provided much information on the tax-avoiding schemes made possible by global activities and by tax complexity.[5] Governments have been unable to deal successfully with these schemes. Published estimates indicate that several trillions of US dollars in wealth are now hidden in foreign accounts and that hundreds of billions of dollars have been beyond the reach of national tax authorities.

The architecture of the taxation of global corporations, and of global economic activities in general, is in clear need of redesign. That architecture had been largely created before the world became highly globalized, and before much world production became multi-country. It has now become clearly anachronistic. There is still no *truly global* organization with the skills, the resources, and the authority to try to do the job of redesigning and monitoring new tax rules for the whole world, and of selling those rules to all the governments of the world, as has tried to do the World Trade Organization for trade relations. Such an authority would exercise a direct, surveillance function on the tax behavior of each member. Such an organization would need to be truly global to be effective, as suggested by Tanzi, in 1988, 1998, and 2016.

Over the years, there have been various proposals made by the OECD—an organization that represents mainly richer countries, and that inevitably reflects, or is seen to reflect, the interests of its members—to deal with some of these problems. A current OECD proposal is to require that corporations be subjected to some minimum taxes, to reduce tax competition between countries. It remains to be seen what will happen to this proposal. Past attempts by the OECD, to deal with some of these problems got nowhere, because of technical difficulties and because of lack of needed

4. *See* the work by Zucman, by Henry, and by several other experts on the quantitative importance of this factor.
5. *See*, for example, some papers, including Henry's, in Pogge and Mehta, 2016.

international cooperation. The objectives of different countries remain widely different, and these differences continue to defy global solutions. The OECD does not have the power of coercion. It can only propose.

[B] Monetary Policy

Perhaps more controversially, it can be argued that the monetary policies that have been followed by the US Federal Reserve Bank, by the European Central Bank, and by some other major central banks in recent years, have made large and increasing amounts of cheap credit available not to everyone, as would the classic "helicopter money." It did so mainly to governments and to large economic actors, many in a shadow banking sector, a sector that has significantly replaced traditional banking in recent decades. Thus, monetary policy has increasingly drifted into fiscal policy, without the political controls that exist for tax policy.

Many large, financial, and economic actors are better placed and more able, than average citizens and small enterprises, to access the cheap credit made available by policies, such as quantitative easing and other recent, unorthodox monetary instruments. These actors have used cheap credit to promote their own economic interests, which are not necessarily identical with the public interest. In addition, the very low or, at times, negative interest rates, promoted by the central banks, have boosted the prices of assets, such as stocks, bonds, and real estate, helping the better-to-do, who save more and own large shares of these assets.

Recent data, compiled by economists Emmanuel Saez and Gabriel Zucman, on saving rates by wealth classes, indicate that while those in the top 1% of the wealth distribution save about 40% of their income, those in the bottom 90% save almost nothing. The 9% in between save about 10%. If correct, these data, do not point toward a future with less inequality.[6]

The central banks have largely ignored the possible and significant distributive or equity aspects of their monetary policies, because they have considered those aspects as being outside the scope of their mandates and, therefore, not their concern. The share of total profits and incomes that has been going to those who operate in the financial sector has increased significantly over the years. For example, finance now takes about one-third of all profits, up from 10% thirty-five years ago and even less before. This dramatic change has raised questions, by some economists and financial commentators, about the impact of that sector on the public interest (Zingales, 2015; Wolf, 2008).

Most citizens and small enterprises do not have access to the cheap credit made available by the central banks. They have continued to depend on commercial banks for their borrowing and to pay high, and at times very high, interest rates on the money they borrow. Exceptions have been loans given by special institutions (mortgage banks and car dealers), to borrowers who post valuable collaterals, such as houses and new

6. The data come from Financial Samurai: https://www.financialsamurai.com/.

cars, against the loans, and that can borrow in transactions that have low administrative costs. The above dichotomy has created two monetary universes: one for the normal, middle, and lower class, citizens and small enterprises, and the other for large actors and major institutions, including governments and corporations.

Billion-dollar compensations have become common for some well-placed individuals. Especially in the United States, in recent years, cheap loans to governments, to some extent, have replaced the taxes that the rich had been paying in the past. This has led to the large growth in the public debt and to lower taxes on the rich.

This important aspect of monetary policy has been largely ignored in recent discussions and requires more attention and analysis.

§1.05 IS THERE A ROLE FOR TAXES AT THIS TIME?

The role of taxes in normal times should differ from their role in exceptional times. In exceptional times, including during wars, pandemics, and other major catastrophes, the focus of taxation should be mainly on fairness and on what the tax system could do to alleviate and spread the costs of the crises, by taxing more those who have more, rather than pursue exclusively longer-run objectives. These long-run objectives might include: (a) promoting green policies; (b) redistributing income worldwide; (c) dealing with global warming; (d) helping economies grow with fairer income distribution and others. While these and similar longer-run objectives are always important for taxation, changing tax systems to promote them, in the presence of other more immediate, urgent needs, is likely to bring complexity in the policies and to be counterproductive. For example relying more on a value-added tax to get more revenue may not be desirable during a pandemic (Bird, 2020). The first recipient of the Nobel Prize in Economics, Jan Tinbergen, seven decades ago, had argued that it is always better to direct the use of policy instruments towards well-specified, single objectives, whenever this is possible, rather than to pursue multiple objectives with single instruments. This helps to keep policies simple and improves the chance of achieving the desired objective.

During a major crisis, which affects different groups differently, such as pandemics, it would seem more natural to ask how the tax system can make all citizens share in the costs of the crisis in proportion to their ability to do so. The better-to-do should contribute more to the government spending than they would in normal times when efficiency considerations and other objectives are likely to be more important. It should be recalled that, during past wars, some countries introduced *excess profit taxes* on enterprises that, because of the war, were making exceptional profits. The countries also raised the highest tax rate of the personal income tax.

Given the dichotomous impact that the pandemic is having on the economy and on the citizens, it would seem fair to impose exceptional and clearly time-limited taxes on individuals who have high incomes and wealth, and who are paying a low price, or are even benefiting, from the pandemic. These taxes would remain in place while the pandemic continued to have its impact. The simplest options might be:

(a) an increase in the highest, marginal income tax rate on individuals;
(b) a tax on wealth ownership above some given high level; and
(c) a financial transaction tax on the trading of corporate shares.

The temporary nature of these taxes would reduce or minimize whatever disincentive effects they might be assumed to have when imposed in the long run. Various technical and political problems would need to be addressed, including the levels at which they would become effective, and the rates. Therefore, there should be some careful analysis of how high these additional taxes would be, and of the revenue that they should generate. The revenue from these taxes would replace some of the public debt that the governments have been contracting, to reduce future debt-sustainability problems.

Especially for the taxes on wealth, there may be technical issues that arise.[7] A clear definition of the wealth that would become part of the tax base would be needed. A simple option might be the taxation of wealth held in corporate shares, for which information should be easily available. As mentioned earlier, the value of this particular wealth has grown significantly in the most recent years, in part due to the tax reduction of 2017 and that wealth has continued to grow significantly during the pandemics. Therefore, the taxes paid might come largely out of the higher market evaluation (out of "excess profits"). The additional, higher personal income taxes would be paid out of the highest incomes of individuals who have more ability to pay.

The financial transaction tax, also recommended in the past by Keynes and, in more recent years, by the late James Tobin, would be levied at a very low rate (e.g., 0.25%) on the value of the stocks traded. Such a tax could raise large tax revenue with a very low rate. Being a *temporary* tax it would not lead to maneuvers to avoid it, as this tax would over the long run. Should the stock market continue to boom the tax would hardly be felt by those taxed.

§1.06 CONCLUDING COMMENTS

The current pandemic has raised uncomfortable questions about the fairness of the market economy when that economy works without some government correctives. Those questions are especially pertinent in times of major crises. It must be recognized that the correctives (progressive taxes and public spending programs), that often significantly reduce the Gini coefficients that the free market generates, are the ones that increase the market legitimacy and its fairness in a democratic country. Only the existence of these correctives would justify Friedman's view, that corporate leaders should focus on maximizing shareholders' returns and should ignore social responsibilities. Without those correctives, Friedman's view makes no sense.

Popular attitude about the fairness of the uncorrected, or little corrected, market economy has become less favorable over the years. It is likely to continue to become even more negative if current conditions and policies do not change. Growing

7. *See*, for example, Oh and Zolt, 2020.

populism could become a serious challenge for the future of market economies, leading to less attractive alternatives.

Bibliography

Bird, Richard M. 2020. "VAT During and After the Pandemic", *Tax Notes International* (September 28).

Garrett, Laurie. 1994. *The Coming Plague; Newly Emerging Diseases in a World Out of Balance* (New York: Farrar, Straus, and Gioroux).

Henry, James S. & David L. Lighton, 2020. *Distribution of Suffering Relief and Greed in the Pandemic*, American Interest, available at https://www.the-american-interest.com/2020/05/13/the-distribution-of-suffering-and-greed-in-the-pandemic/.

Kay, John & Mervyn King. 2020. *Radical Uncertainty: Decision Making Beyond the Numbers* (New York: W.W. Norton and Company).

Knight, Frank. 1921. *Risk, Uncertainty and Profit*. Vol. 31. (Houghton Mifflin).

Martin, W.R. & Robert Pindyck, 2019. "Welfare Costs of Catastrophes: Lost Consumption and Lost Lives", *NBER Working Paper*, No. 26068, July 2019.

Messere, Ken C. 1993. *Tax Policy in OECD Countries: Choices and Conflicts* (Amsterdam: IBFD Publications BV).

Oh, James & Eric M. Zolt. 2020. "Wealth Tax Design: Lessons from Estate Tax Avoidance" *UCLA School of Law, Law-Econ Research Paper* 20-01.

Pindick, Robert S. & Neng Wang. 2009. "The Economics and Policy Consequences of Catastrophes", *NBER Working Paper*, No. 15373, September 2009.

Samuelson, Paul. 1947. *Foundations of Economic Analysis* (Cambridge Mass.: Harvard University Press).

Solimano, Andres. 2020. *A History of Big Recessions in the Long Twentieth Century* (Cambridge UK: Cambridge University Press).

Tanzi, Vito. 1988. "Forces that Shape Tax Policy" in *Tax Policy in the 21st Century*, edited by Herbert Stein (New York: John Wiley and Sons) pp. 266-277.

Tanzi, Vito. 1999. "Does the World Need a World Tax Organization?" in *The Economics of Globalization*, edited by Assaf Razin and Efraim Sadka (Cambridge UK: Cambridge University Press).

Tanzi, Vito. 2011. *Government Versus Markets: The Changing Economic Role of the State* (Cambridge UK: Cambridge University Press).

Tanzi, Vito. 2016a. "Pleasant Dreams and Nightmares in Public Debts Scenarios," CIF Ifo Institute (Munich, Germany).

Tanzi, Vito. 2016b. "Lakes, Oceans and Taxes: Why the World Needs a World Tax Authority" in *Global Tax Fairness*, edited by Pogge Thomas and Krishen Mehta (Oxford, UK: Oxford University Press).

Tanzi, Vito. 2021. *Perfect Markets, Perfect Democracies and Pandemics*. Transformation, Integration and Globalization Economic Research.

Thomas, Pogge & Krishen Mehta, editors. 2016. *Global Tax Fairness* (Oxford, UK: Oxford University Press).

Torpey, Elka. 2020. "Essential Work Employment and Outlook in Occupations that Protect and Provide," Career Outlook, US Bureau of Labor Statistics, September. United States.

Wolf, Martin. 2008. *Fixing Global Finance* (Baltimore, United States: Johns Hopkins University Press).

Zingales, Luigi. 2015. "Presidential Address: Does Finance Benefit Society?" *Journal of Finance*, 70 (4), pp. 1327-1363.

Zucman, Gabriel. 2015. *The Hidden Wealth of Nations: The Scourge of Tax Havens* (Chicago: The University of Chicago Press).

CHAPTER 2

Contrasted Insights about Fiscal and Economic Ideologies

Chuks Okoriekwe

The chapter captures the thoughts of renowned tax policy experts, Mariana Mazzucato and Arthur Laffer as they explored, through a historical perspective, how countries in the past have navigated economic crises using tax policy as an effective tool. Mariana Mazzucato focused on the theory of value and wealth creation while also emphasizing that tax policy can be a veritable tool to incentivize investment and stimulate growth. In times of crises where businesses are withdrawing their investment, the government could use grants, loans, procurement, and tax policy to optimize its growth rate and keep the economy on track. Additionally, the government could stimulate the economy through investments in new areas such as biotech, nanotech, etc. Drawing from a historical perspective on tax policy and economic crises, Arthur Laffer examined the basis of optimal taxation. Accordingly, governments were enjoined to adopt a low rate, broad base, and flat tax approach which serves as a disincentive to taxpayers to evade, avoid or not report their taxable income. Using the United States, he also drew history's lessons from President Richard Nixon to the Coronavirus Aid, Relief, and Economic Security (CARES) Act under President Donald Trump. The chapter concludes on the note of recommendation to governments to understand their economic peculiarities before adopting any tax policy.

§2.01 INTRODUCTION

The world is currently at a crossroad, experiencing a global pandemic and induced economic recession owing to a lockdown on economic activities to slow down the spread of COVID-19, which has put pressure on global public revenue. This chapter presents contrasting insights about fiscal and economic ideologies that can help shape tax policy responses following global economic crises based on the views of two renowned experts: Mariana Mazzucato and Arthur Laffer.

§2.02 THE THEORY OF VALUE AND HOW WEALTH CREATION COMES ABOUT[1]

The design of tax policy in any country affects the rate of growth and direction of the economy (Gale and Samwick, 2014). It is however important to define basic concepts such as the economy, market, and business. Oftentimes, these concepts are confused with business. What then is the economy? The economic system comprises the production, distribution, and consumption of goods and services (Kenton, 2020). Markets are outcomes of the co-creation of value by various types of actors in the economy (Haro, Martínez-Ruiz, and Martínez-Cañas, 2014) and the regulation of the corporate sector.

Additionally, it is important to distinguish the role of the state in a market economy (Tanzi, 1997). In economics, for instance, it is often assumed that the public sector simply intends to fix market failures. Therefore, governmental action reacts to market failure and intervenes either through taxation or expenditures. Some advocate that a more interesting way to govern public institutions is through an explicit admission that public actors are co-shaping and co-creating markets beyond merely fixing them (Mazzucato, 2016). Other actors in the system such as the civil society, trade unions, labor unions, etc. have also been fundamental in shaping market outcomes throughout the history of capitalism (ILO, 2005). Thus, weekends, eight-hour workdays amongst others seen in a capitalist society did not occur due to the direct government or business actions but as a result of struggles and social movements; in particular, the trade union movement. (ILO, 2005)

How then can tax policy become an effective tool in steering the direction of an economy? For Mazzucato, tax policy can be instructive in designing a system to create an inclusive economy that is ambitious and more sustainable. For instance, to promote a green economy, the government could focus on imposing more taxes on materials than labor. Also, emphasis should be on fostering long-term growth over short-term growth, especially long-term growth that leads to a more sustainable type of production structure. This could also be in the form of offering tax incentives to companies committed to carbon emission reduction.

In creating an inclusive economy, there is the need to introduce more progressive taxes and reduce the use of regressive taxation such as the border adjustment tax (BAT) or a flat rate tax which prescribe greater penalties for those with lower incomes as opposed to those with higher incomes (Joumard, Pisu and Bloch, 2012). More so, Mazzucato opines that a reduction in the top marginal income bracket will not achieve

1. This section is based on the speech from Mariana Mazzucato at the World Tax Summit—TaxCOOP2020, on October 13, 2020.

inclusive growth. Thus, emphasis should be on designing a tax policy that focuses on co-creating and co-shaping with a view to leveling the playing field for all actors. This will eventually bolster inclusion, sustainability, etc., and achieve the targets under the sustainable development goals (Long and Miller, 2017).

Redesigning the global tax system cannot be overemphasized given the inadequacies of the current system.

§2.03 TAX POLICY AS A TOOL TO INCENTIVIZE PRIVATE INVESTMENT AND STIMULATE GROWTH

The rate of economic growth largely depends on the business investment approach adopted. However, to optimize growth rate, grants, loans, procurement, and taxation are some of the key levers that government could utilize to crowd in business investment. According to John Maynard Keynes, the big problem with national output to GDP is that business investment is very volatile, unstable across the business cycle but also procyclical; too much during good times and too little during bad times (Long and Summers, 1988). One of the key points for government is therefore to be counter-cyclical so that when businesses are withdrawing their investment in bad times, the government should be in a position to increase its investment in order to get the economy back on track. Notwithstanding, where business investment is too low, the government needs strategies to increase it in order to make up for lost business investment but also stimulate and catalyze investment.

In terms of tax policy, are there options for the government when business investment is limited? There is the notion that businesses already want to invest and all that is required is for governments to make it cheaper, for example through the reduction in corporate income tax or introducing different types of indirect tax incentives, such as tax credits on research and development (R&D). Nonetheless, there is little evidence that supports this notion that tax incentives will increase investment, however, what it surely does is increase profits, which is not the direct aim of government (Meinzer, Ndajiwo, Etter-Phoya and Diakité, 2019). Generally, governmental bodies are not in the business of increasing profit but increasing investment to support jobs and potential growth, such as employment, productivity, and so forth. The real issue, however, is how to ensure that the government can increase output and not only profit, especially in difficult periods such as the current pandemic where we need more business investment.

Despite the lack of unequivocal evidence that tax incentives increase private investment, Mazzucato notes that government should stimulate the economy through more ambitious investment in new areas. This provides innovative opportunities, whether it is by developing a whole new technology area such as biotech, nanotech, the internet (which came out of government's investment), etc. Businesses often follow the direction/flow of money. Thus, "crowding in" strategies use direct and ambitious public investments—not indirect tax incentives—in high-risk, high-growth opportunity areas, to attract private investments.

Once the business perspective is supported by these direct government investments and well-designed tax incentives, an increase in marginal investment becomes more likely. For example, R&D tax credit would have a better impact when it is complemented by or preceded by, government investment in high-risk early stages of R&D projects.

Similarly, a patent box tax policy—a tax policy which provides a lower effective tax rate on profit generated by patents—arguably denies the government necessary revenue given that patents are already monopolies for twenty years. Patents are a monopoly granted by the government to the private sector and thus, should not further enjoy reduced taxes on monopoly profits. The incentive has already been given to the companies through a twenty-year monopoly of the patents.

It is also noteworthy that R&D tax credits and the patent box policy when not complemented by direct government investments, tend to simply increase profits and not investment. This does not however imply that R&D tax credits are not important. A whole portfolio of different instruments needs to be evaluated to ascertain what actually works and the importance of direct government investment to create the perception in the business community.

Mazzucato emphasizes that public investments have been instructive in the development of new technology such as GPS, touch screen, etc., all of which were developed using public investment or funded businesses that developed the technology. Ultimately, these inventions were made possible through tax funds. In the same vein, Mazzucato states that around 75 % of new molecular entities with priority ratings in the health innovation areas are outcomes of a variety of public investments across the globe. More so, in the United States, the government spends more than USD 40 billion a year on health innovation through the national institutes of health while in the U.K, the government and charities spend a lot too. This underpins the fact that value is co-created by both the private sector and public entities.

§2.04 DO SHARED RISKS LEAD TO SHARED PROFITS?

It is essential to ensure that the public sector gets its fair share from the invested public funds and the risks it incurred. That is, private companies which are beneficiaries of these public investments in technology, such as the Internet, GPS, should not employ tax evasion tactics and thus, pay back their fair share. For instance, Apple transferred one of its subsidiaries from its headquarters in Cupertino, California to Reno, Nevada where there is a zero tax rate to avoid its tax bill and save a huge amount of money (Duhigg and Kocieniewski, 2012). Similarly, in the health sector, according to Oxfam report "*Prescription for Poverty,*" big pharmaceutical companies including Johnson and Johnson, Pfizer, American Co., etc., have utilized different types of tax dodging maneuvers to save close to USD 4 billion a year (Oxfam, 2018). These are companies that have benefited and continue to benefit massively from public investments. When governments use public funds to support private businesses in these cases, citizens suffer when these companies are not contributing their fair share of taxes to the public purse. This is even more accurate today, given the global economic strain caused by the pandemic. Thus, in these circumstances, the taxes companies pay to countries, from which they massively benefit through public investments made through different actors in the economy, are essential for building a strong global health system (Mazzucato, 2020).

As it was reiterated in the Oxfam Report (2018), public education, public transportation, and public health suffer the most when companies evade taxes. Interestingly, some countries are taking measures that not only curb tax evasion but tie recovery funds to conditionality. For instance, in Denmark, the recovery funds being provided by the government to businesses during the pandemic are upon the condition that the companies are not associated with tax evasion activities (including registration in a tax haven) (Quicke, 2020). Consequently, using a tax haven makes the funds inaccessible to these categories of companies. President Emmanuel Macron of France also introduced conditionality in shaping the country's direction of growth by stating that companies, including Renault in the automotive sector, and Air France in the airline industry, will not have access to the country's recovery funds unless they commit to reducing their carbon emission footprint (AFP, 2020).

The issue of conditionality is quite important in not only navigating the grueling financial and economic situation but also building a better, more sustainable, and inclusive type of economy. Also, conditionality could be examined from the angle of public and private sector partnership towards the development of COVID-19 vaccines (or treatments) especially in terms of innovation in vaccine development and deployment. Vaccines must be universally available and accessible to all. Therefore, the process should ensure the optimal use of public funds as well as intellectual property rights.

In summary, rethinking tax needs to be accompanied by rethinking the narrative of where wealth comes from, where value comes from, and, most importantly, by accepting that value is collectively created and markets are outcomes of how different organizations in the economy are interrelated. Designing a progressive taxation system must be underpinned by a real belief that the ability to foster the capabilities and opportunities across the whole economy and across many different actors in the economy contributes towards building a better system.

§2.05 HISTORICAL PERSPECTIVE ON TAX POLICY AND ECONOMIC CRISIS[2]

For Arthur Laffer, there are three basic things to consider when discussing the role of government in the economy: how they spend, how much they spend; how they tax, how much they tax; and the total level of government spending.

2. This section is based on the speech from Arthur Laffer at the World Tax Summit – TaxCOOP2020, on October 13, 2020.

[A] Optimal Taxation

This approach lies on the assumption that all taxes are bad but some taxes are worse than others (Tax Policy Center, 2020). While generating revenue through taxation, emphasis ought to be on collecting revenue in the least damaging fashion possible, which is usually through a low rate, broad base, and flat tax (Gale, 2001). This provides taxpayers with the least incentive to evade, avoid or otherwise not report their taxable income and also gives them the least places in the tax code where they can place their income to avoid paying taxes. Regarding expenditure, the government's focus should be on spending public revenue in the most beneficial fashion possible, which includes helping the poor, social spending, etc. (Herrmann, Tausch, Heshmati and Bajalan, 2008).

To achieve an optimal level of governance, governments should stop when the "damage" done by the last dollar of taxes collected is a little less than the benefit conferred by the last dollar of money spent. Any spending that requires raising tax revenues is inadequate if the taxes applied create more damages than the benefit conferred by the spending. This is how governments should determine the ideal level of tax spending in the economy.

While taxes are important, spending restraint is much more important. According to Laffer, there are five pillars of prosperity: taxation, spending restraint, sound money, free trade, and minimal regulation. These pillars propel any economy. One of the things that has the potential to cripple any economy is hyperinflation in a nonsound currency. Minimal regulations are equally important; however, overregulation that goes beyond a specific purpose may have a counter effect and thus create collateral damage on the economy. Free trade is underscored by the interdependency of countries. For instance, there are commodities better produced in the United States than in some foreign countries and vice versa. These goods are then better exchanged amongst countries under terms mutually agreed which is where the World Trade Organization (WTO) comes in under General Agreement on Trade and Tariffs (GATT).

[B] History's Lessons from the United States

Governments across the globe are often faced with economic crises. The United States is not an exception, and a lot could be gleaned from the reactions of America's former presidents to economic crises. Arthur Laffer provides a brief historical overview of the United States tax policy responses when faced with crises, starting with the Nixon shock in 1971.

First, the panic situation in President Nixon's White House in 1971 typifies the reaction of an average politician when faced with a crisis; the consequences of which are rarely attractive. On August 14, 1971, President Nixon valued the U.S. dollar and stopped its conversion to gold at a fixed value. He also imposed a 10% tax surcharge on all products while introducing what he called the "job development tax credit" which was an investment tax credit. At the same time, he put on wage and price control. These decisions were arguably very bad and ultimately caused a lot of damage to the U.S. economy (Amadeo, 2000).

After President Nixon left office, Gerald Ford became president. He introduced what was called the "whip inflation now" program to address the inflation caused by the 5% tax surcharge. It is instructive that the introduction of a 5% surcharge tax did not result in 5% more revenue. An increase in tax rate by 5% may result in 4% or 2% more revenue but not 5% more revenue. In actual fact, there may be revenue loss. This is represented by the Laffer Curve (Laffer, 2004).

During the administration of President Jimmy Carter, he introduced the national energy plan that had price controls leading to the reduction in American pumped oil (Eugene, 1978). It also put the price of oil and gas below market, which resulted in huge disruption in the U.S. economy while also introducing a tax surcharge on excess profit tax of companies that ultimately caused enormous distortion of the economy.

However, Laffer considers President Ronald Reagan to be one of the only presidents with the right response when facing an economic crisis with his 1981 tax code, which was based on tax cuts. Interestingly, before the tax cut took effect in January 1983, many companies deferred their income to take advantage of it. By deferring the tax cuts, Reagan caused a real decline in the U.S. economy in 1981-1982. Regardless of the plea to abandon the proposed tax cuts in the third year, President Reagan maintained these cuts and for the next year and a half, the U.S. economy grew by 12% at 8% per annum. The right decision was to do nothing in that circumstance (Wessel, 2017).

In 1987, President Reagan was again faced with a huge collapse in the stock market. He was advised to make some panic moves to stabilize the market. Instead, he did nothing. The stock market eventually recovered, recoupled its losses and the economy continued on its trajectory of prosperity. Laffer affirms that President Reagan can be arguably described as the only President who truly followed the correct dictate of what a policy leader should do in times of economic crisis.

The Latin phrase "*primum non nocere*" means "*first, do no harm.*" This philosophy should be at the heart of tax policy decisions: a policy response must not do any harm to the economy. Another philosophy employed by President Reagan was his belief and practice of "*vis medicatrix naturae*" which is the healing power of nature exemplified by his approach of "*do not just stand there, undo something.*" During the Reagan era, this approach translated into getting rid of taxes, cutting government spending, and reducing regulations.

Prosperity was associated with the Reagan administration and then Clinton's presidency. According to Laffer, President Bill Clinton also did a fantastic job running the economy. While President H.W. Bush had decided to raise taxes, Clinton presented the bill to repeal retirement tax on social security, which was a unique tax on elderly workers. He also initiated welfare reforms. Additionally, he cut government spending as a share of the GDP by more than the next three peace-time presidents combined.

Lastly, Presidents W. Bush and Obama also faced major economic crises starting with the tail end of Bill Clinton's administration. However, both made huge mistakes by thinking that government could solve the problem—the government is often not the solution but the problem. By invoking stimulus spending and Obama's administration raising taxes throughout the process, the United States experienced the worst recovery in its history. Oftentimes, the main challenge with those in the government is that they want to take action even in times of crisis. Indeed, Laffer believes that the best approach has always been to take a deep breath, remain calm and collected. In responding to an economic crisis, composure is important. For Laffer, almost all real crises in the U.S. have been as a result of bad responses to things happening outside the country.

The situation is not much different with the current COVID-19 pandemic. The United States panicked and made a provision of USD 3.6 trillion through the Coronavirus Aid, Relief, and Economic Security (CARES) Act. Understandably, some of its provisions are arguably good while others are arguably worse. Stimulating medicine research, payroll protection plan, underwriting by the U.S. Federal Government to guarantee loans were good provisions of the Act. In times of crisis, it is important to make sure that liquidity problems do not morph into solvency issues, which was what the U.S. Federal Government did by guaranteeing loans of solvent companies. However, Laffer considers that the CARES Act went too far, for example by offering protection to companies that were already insolvent beforehand, essentially giving away substantial taxpayers' money; a panic response that went too far. Nonetheless, the government perhaps retraced its steps and became even more careful. It has cut tax rates and dramatically proposed additional cuts in tax rates (York, 2020).

In summary, in times of crisis, the government should take a step back and not rush policy actions. Government should also consider the five pillars of prosperity; tax policy, government spending, monetary policy, trade policy, and regulatory policy while the aim should be to achieve a low rate, broad base, flat tax, spending restraint, sound money, free trade, and minimal regulation.

§2.06 CONCLUSION

To facilitate navigating through an economic crisis, the government should understand its economic environment and its peculiarities taking a cue from previous reactions will aid in navigating such crisis. Notwithstanding the opposing views of the role of government, it seems a tax policy that takes cognizance of government spending and provides direction to the economy through government investment can support the recovery process of the economy in times of crisis.

Bibliography

Agence France-Presse (AFP). 2020. "French Government Announces 'Historic €7 Billion Aid Package for Air France-KLM'". France 24. <https://www.france24.com/en/20200424-french-government-announces-historic-%E2%82%AC7-billion-aid-pakage-for-air-france-klm> (accessed January 26, 2021).

Amadeo, Kimberly. 2020. "President Richard M. Nixon's Economic Policies: How Nixon Destroyed the Dollar". The Balance. < https://www.thebalance.com/president-richard-m-nixon-s-economic-policies-3305562 > (accessed January 28, 2021).

Bradford De Long, J. and Summers, Lawrence H. 1998. 'How Does Macroeconomic Policy Affect Output?', Brookings Papers on Economic Activity, 2:1988 < https://www.brookings.edu/wp-content/uploads/1988/06/1988b_bpea_delong_summers_mankiw_romer.pdf > (accessed January 17, 2021).

Duhigg, Charles and Kocieniewski, David. 2012. "How Apple Sidesteps Billions in Taxes: Funneling Earnings to Low-Tax Regions". New York Times. < https://www.pulitzer.org/files/2013/explanatory-reporting/04ieconomy4-29.pdf > (accessed January 21, 2021).

Eugene J. McAlister, 1978. "An Analysis of the Carter Anti-Inflation Program". The Heritage Foundation. < https://www.heritage.org/jobs-and-labor/report/analysis-the-carter-anti-inflation-program > (accessed January 29, 2021).

Gale, William. 2001. "Tax Simplification: Issues and Options", Brookings Institute. < https://www.brookings.edu/testimonies/tax-simplification-issues-and-options/ > (accessed January 23, 2021).

Gale, William and Samwick, Andrew. 2014. "Effects of Income Tax Changes on Economic Growth" Brookings, September 9, 2014 < http://dx.doi.org/10.2139/ssrn.2494468 > (accessed December 28, 2021).

Herrmann, Peter, Tausch, Arno, Heshmati, Almas and Bajalan, Chemen S.J. 2008. 'Efficiency and Effectiveness of Social Spending', IZA Discussion Paper No. 3482. < http://ftp.iza.org/dp3482.pdf > (accessed January 24, 2021).

International Federation of Accountants. 2001. 'Governance in the Public Sector: A Governing Body Perspective', International Public Sector Study (13). < http://www1.worldbank.org/publicsector/pe/befa05/Study_13_Governance.pdf > (accessed January 10, 2021).

International Labour Organization. 2005. 'The Role of Trade Union in the Global Economy and the Fight Against Poverty'. being background paper at the International Workers' Symposium. < https://www.ilo.org/wcmsp5/groups/public/---ed_dialogue/---actrav/documents/meetingdocument/wcms_111311.pdf > (accessed January 12, 2021).

Jacobs, Jim. 2020. 'Taxpayers Helped Make it, So Why Does Remdesivir Cost $3,200 a Patient?'. GV Wire. < https://gvwire.com/2020/08/04/taxpayers-helped-make-it-so-why-does-remdesivir-cost-3200-a-patient/ > (accessed January 27, 2021).

Jensen, Michael C., 'Value Maximization and the Corporate Objective Function', *Business Ethics Quarterly*, 12(1), pp. 235-256.

Joumard, Isabelle, Pisu, Mauro and Bloch, Debbie. 2012. "Tackling Income Inequality: The Role of Taxes and Transfers". OECD Journal: Economic Studies, published online first. < http://dx.doi.org/10.1787/eco_studies-2012-5k95xd6l65lt > (accessed January 15, 2021).

Kenton, Will. 2020. 'Economy', Investopedia. < https://www.investopedia.com/terms/e/economy.asp > (accessed 19 December 2020).

Laffer, Arthur. 2004. 'Executive Summary: The Laffer Curve: Past, Present, and Future', The Heritage Foundation <https://www.heritage.org/node/17780/print-display> (accessed 28 January 2021).

Laffer, Arthur. 2020. World Tax Summit—Taxation in Times of Crisis—History's Lessons, Montreal (online), October 13, 2020.

Lenain, Patrick and Bartoszuk, Leszek. 2000. 'The Polish Tax Reform', OECD Economics Department Working Papers No. 234. <https://doi.org/10.1787/18151973> (accessed 18 January 2021).

Long, Cathal and Miller, Mark. 2017. 'Taxation and the Sustainable Development Goals: Do Good Things Come to Those Who Tax More?'. ODI Briefing Note. <https://www.odi.org/sites/odi.org.uk/files/resource-documents/11695.pdf> (accessed 29 January 2021).

Mazzucato, Mariana, Chow, Heidi, Fitzpatrick, Saoirse, Laplane, Andrea et al. 2018. 'The People's Prescription: Re-imagining Health Innovation to Deliver Public Value'. UCL Institute for Innovation of Public Purpose. <https://www.ucl.ac.uk/bartlett/public-purpose/sites/public-purpose/files/peoples_prescription_report_final_online.pdf> (accessed 30 January 2021).

Mazzucato, Mariana. 2015. 'From Market Fixing to Market-Creating: A new framework for economic policy'. Science Policy Research Unit Working Paper Series. <https://poseidon01.ssrn.com/delivery.php?ID=573003097124109024096017028106073102004031054052030066103127101126127086090027072007006034063101028059032066030097005127072096046016071077042066007084090079125078096068080057089028002089067083002081125065123082072027107024016024006121081102010105082104&EXT=pdf&INDEX=TRUE> (accessed 10 January, 2021).

Mazzucato, Mariana. 2020. World Tax Summit—Taxation in Times of Crisis—History's Lessons, Montreal (online), October 13, 2020

Meinzer, Markus, Ndajiwo, Mustapha, Etter-Phoya, Rachel and Diakité Maïmouna. 2019. 'Comparing Tax Incentives across Jurisdictions: A Pilot Study'. Tax Justice Network. <Comparing-tax-incentives-across-jurisdictions_Tax-Justice-Network_2019.pdf> (accessed 17 January 2021)

Oxfam. 2018. Oxfam Report 'Prescription for Poverty: Drug Companies as Tax Dodgers, Price Gougers, and Influence Peddlers'. <https://s3.amazonaws.com/oxfam-us/www/static/media/files/Prescription_for_Poverty_Full_Report.pdf> (accessed 24 January 2021).

Quicke, Audrey. 2020. 'Denmark Bars Tax Haven Companies from Covid-19 Financial Aid', Nordic Policy Centre. <https://www.nordicpolicycentre.org.au/denmark_bars_tax_haven_companies_from_covid_19_financial_aid> (accessed 25 January 2021).

Tanzi, Vito. 1997. 'The Changing Role of the State in the Economy: A Historical Perspective'. International Monetary Fund (IMF) Working Paper (WP/97/114). <https://www.imf.org/external/pubs/ft/wp/wp97114.pdf> (accessed 7 January 2021).

Tax Policy Center. 2020. Briefing Book, 'How Do Taxes Affect Income Inequality'. <https://www.taxpolicycenter.org/briefing-book/how-do-taxes-affect-income-inequality> (accessed 23 January 2021).

Wessel, David. 2017. 'What we Learned from Reagan's Tax Cuts'. Brookings. https://www.brookings.edu/blog/up-front/2017/12/08/what-we-learned-from-reagans-tax-cuts/ (accessed 29 January 2021)

York, Erica. 2020. 'President Trump Outlines Second Term Ideas'. Tax Foundation. <https://taxfoundation.org/president-trump-tax-plan-2020/> (accessed 20 January 2021)

CHAPTER 3
Tax Justice in Times of Crisis

William Ross

This chapter argues that the COVID-19 global pandemic and the socio-economic transformation it implied revealed social possibilities for tax justice that were previously hindered. Mobilizing the notion of a citizen's perspective, the argument follows the line of two major problems linked to tax justice: opacity of economic activities and information, on the one hand, and socio-economic inequalities, on the other. By shedding light on the existing tension, first, between opacity and transparency, and second, between inequalities and justice, this chapter suggests a reflection on the way we, as a society, are able to experience our own capacities and possibilities. The claim is that tax justice is linked to social justice under the aspect that redistribution of wealth goes alongside a redistribution of capacities by which it is possible to reconfigure our self-understanding and our collective will.

§3.01 INTRODUCTION[1]

Tax justice, along with all other 'tax' and fiscal related topics, easily becomes an abstruse and technical domain seemingly reserved for experts or an initiated elite. An internal tension, however, runs through tax justice: the justice in question is the concern of the many and not of the few. In this sense, the question of democratizing

1. This chapter was originally conceived as a critical summary of TaxCOOP2020 citizens' discussion' – 'Tax Justice in Time of Crisis' – that took place at the World Tax Summit on 15 October 2020, between Huguette Labelle, Former Chair of the board of Transparency International, and Toby Sanger, Executive Director of Canadians for Tax Fairness and myself, William Ross, as moderator. I am deeply indebted towards them and the ideas they have shared in this discussion. I would like to express my gratitude to both of them.

access to tax justice is one that needs to be addressed. In this chapter, I will present this point in light of the current crisis – the global pandemic and the economic turmoil that emerged with it – ordinary citizens experiencing a reality that revealed a new order of possibility: the actualization of tax justice as redistribution of wealth and redistribution of capacities.

In order to do so, I propose a philosophical analysis of the situation: not only one in which tax justice is the answer to the challenges imposed upon us by the pandemic but also one in which the pandemic itself reveals an aspect of our own societal, economic and political modes of organization, which were already impinging our own capacity to realize tax justice. The aim of such a philosophical perspective is to be able to show tendencies that go beyond the grasping of the facts; it is not meant to be read as a correction of any facts, nor is it just an interpretation which one would be free to accept or to reject. What is at stake is an attempt to engage differently with the objects, concepts and ideas that make up what we call tax justice, in view of gaining another perspective on that which we are capable.

Defending the idea that the current crisis is pregnant with the possibility that, as a society, we acquire a better understanding of our own spheres of action requires a few building blocks. First, it demands the portrayal of the notion of a citizen's perspective. From there, it will be possible to assess the state of affairs concerning tax justice. In a third step, I will present that the experience of the pandemic can help us redefine our collective ambition.

§3.02 THE NOTION OF A CITIZEN'S PERSPECTIVE

It is essential to introduce the notion of a citizen's perspective, for if misunderstood can create a misconception on the scope of the judgments that are portrayed therein. To create the sharpest contrast possible, let's compare the 'scientific approach' and the 'citizen's perspective' with one another.

Scientific knowledge depends on the validity and adequacy of its own classificatory system. This means that in order for scientific knowledge to have any value, it must first make sure to carve out the real and semantic space that it delimits as the scope of its own validity. Inside this 'space', notions have to be able (1) to explain situations and answer questions and (2) to be classified in such a way that the notions don't impinge on one another.

The citizen's perspective can be understood in contrast with this approach for its aim is different. The citizen's perspective's goal is not merely to achieve an adequate categorization of reality. It is by no means a denial of the scientific categorization of which it uses. Rather, its ultimate aim is to challenge the way reality *is* by pitting it against the moral standard that the members of a society – its citizens – expect their reality *should be*.

Therefore, instead of working from a classificatory standard, the citizen's perspective has to come up with new ways of organizing the relations between notions. For example, in order to get a clear understanding of a complex situation, it is sometimes better to create a focal point toward which every single element can converge rather than, by the use of a classificatory approach, to put every element inside the categorial drawer in which they traditionally belong. It is such a 'focal point' that this text will build around the idea that COVID-19 created the conditions under which it is possible to loosen the shackles of our own socio-economic categories and think beyond the immediacy of the given condition in order to contemplate the possibility that things could be otherwise.

This has a major consequence: the citizen's perspective is unapologetically political for it addresses our collective capacity to change collectively.

Let's sketch a model of what a citizen's perspective is not. From a liminal perspective, it could seem that such a perspective simply conveys a bunch of information, facts and data that are juxtaposed together in a more or less rhapsodic fashion. If this were the case then, specialists of these questions could simply say that a citizen's perspective on these topics confuses different levels of reality and therefore puts the interlocutors in a situation in which 'they do not know what they are talking about'. This kind of interpretation is what this text hopes to prove wrong, not because the author claims to be right. What I wish to defend here is more nuanced; citizens in a discussion not only 'know what they are talking about', but they also produce a type of knowledge that is albeit different from the 'traditional' knowledge of the specialists, but that is nonetheless knowledge. The question is: what kind of knowledge is produced from this perspective and what are its aims? Unless the focal point that I briefly introduced earlier is made explicit, this specificity of a citizen's discussion can be overlooked.

The implicit focal point that is presupposed is that, as a society, we have access to possibilities of change that we deny to ourselves when we fail to see that we can act not as individuals but as a society. By acting as a society, I mean that we can act politically in a way that is not determined by pursuing individual interests, but by creating structural conditions in which individuals can strive and reach a fuller life. The question remains: on what ground are we able to build such possibilities? The content of the answer will be available once we unfold the content of the state of affairs. However, I can already hint toward one unifying theme: the experience of the pandemic creates a privileged locus from which we can observe our reality from a renewed perspective.

§3.03 THE STATE OF AFFAIRS BEFORE AND DURING THE PANDEMIC: WHAT EXACTLY IS BLOCKING FISCAL JUSTICE?

From a strict perspective of tax justice, the pandemic as such is not the crisis. It merely revealed new aspects of an ongoing crisis: the amounts parked in – and flowing through – tax havens have a major impact on security, on peace, on the rule of law and contribute to massive inequalities around the world, feeding terrorism, conflict and corruption. On the one side, according to the World Bank, 70% of grand corruption cases are the result of anonymous companies moving financial assets undetected (World Bank, 2011). On the other side, global wealth is in the hands of very few as the 1% richest own 40% to 50% of the global wealth (Frank, 2017). The capacity for corporations and individuals to accumulate such a delirious amount of private wealth relies heavily on tax evasion. This situation precedes the pandemic but continued to flourish within it. The problem is that opacity governs these schemes and it renders us unable to state the actual causes of the rising inequalities and injustices we witness.

[A] Opacity and Transparency

One of the main challenges facing our capacity to address the question of tax evasion relies on the fact that it is incredibly difficult to obtain a definite amount of how much money is involved within something whose main purpose is to remain hidden. Yet, the numbers estimated by different organizations are simply staggering. The Tax Justice Network gives the gigantic amount of USD 3.1 trillion a year that evades tax systems (Shaxson, 2014), which represents roughly USD 427 billion missing in public funds around the world or, as their last campaign states, the yearly salary of one nurse every second (Mansour, 2020). The International Monetary Fund's (IMF's) data match these numbers by estimating that tax avoidance for Organisation for Economic Co-operation and Development (OECD) countries alone is USD 400 billion per year (Shaxson, 2019). In terms of trade mis-invoicing, Global Financial Integrity presented that 'the sum of the value gaps identified in trade between 135 developing countries and 36 advanced economies over the ten-year period 2008–2017' is the astronomical figure of USD 8.7 trillion (Global Financial Integrity, 2020).

This has a clear socio-political consequence and citizens are aware of it: the overall losses undermine the ability of governments around the world to serve public interest. Governments turn to salaried employees as well as small and medium businesses to make up as much as possible for the losses. When one of the biggest questions that governments are facing in regard to the COVID-19 crisis is how to be able to pay back the exceptionally high debt contracted in order to maintain economic stability, subsidize the sectors that are endangered and plan for the economic recovery, it becomes clear that to let tax evasion continue without restraints is not only completely immoral but also very dangerous. There is no legal nor economic justification by which someone could be able to cheat the tax systems while people are suffering and dying because of the underfunding of public institutions and services.

When we know that the World Economic Forum estimates that the entire 'COVID-19 pandemic will likely end up costing between USD 8.1 and USD 15.8 trillion globally' (Schwab, 2020), we should not act as if nothing has happened. Crises are a form of exceptional situations that allow for two types of responses: first, they prompt exceptional measures in order to overcome the crisis in question; second, they can trigger persistent and in-depth transformations of society to prevent the crisis from repeating itself. In other words, there is an opportunity here: the social benefactors of government help can be nudged in order to improve their societal imprint and be asked to trade subsidies for transparency. But this opportunity is what should always have been the ground level of public responsibility: making sure that public money is used for its intended purpose. The fact that companies can practise tax evasion while also receiving public money is not only an economical aberration – it is the funnelling of rationality outside of its own boundary: it is theft squared.

Unfortunately, as we have seen, in times of crisis, when governments want to apply such measures to improve their public institutions and the state of their economy as well as promote transparency and accountability (Chown, 2020), they are usually unable to do so. The reason is that they did not act earlier to counteract the opaque corporate and tax structures whose origin goes back to the 19th century. This consequently created, over time, a drastic asymmetry between multinational enterprises (MNEs) and large corporations on the one side, and authorities on the other. This asymmetry has to be understood both in terms of power and exchange of information. The concentration of capital and the tendency towards stronger and completely integrated globalization gave birth to a new world where ubiquitous corporations rival nation states in a struggle for power. Extraterritorial entities, such as MNEs, can subjugate the rule of law simply by threatening to 'take their business' somewhere else. This, in turn, created the condition in which states are competing against one another in a race to the bottom to create 'legislation of convenience' that bends head over heels to comply with the desires of the few giants of the economy. This situation thus gives us the confirmation that the law of concentration of capital and the tendency toward monopolization are not only an economic phenomenon but also a socio-political reality that impedes the capacity of citizens around the world to exercise their citizenship as a form of meaningful political participation.

To add another layer of opacity and go beyond the mere juridical structure of the problem, we also have to acknowledge that the role of facilitators in illicit financial flows and state capture is one factor that contributes to the intensification of the problem. These facilitators are bankers, lawyers, notaries and real estate agents that promote the use of tax loopholes for their clients (Medina, 2021). They use their professional reputation and the financing of political parties to acquire privilege access to the legislature in order to increase loopholes, both presently and in the future.

In relation to the problems described, a toolbox of solutions already exists to create a shift of perspective. Instead of seeing transparency as a cost without benefits, we should act according to the idea that *transparency builds trust*. The first item of this toolbox is the well-known country-by-country reporting for companies, which would give a detailed account of where actual economic activities occur, rather than only where such activities are declared as revenues. The second tool would be to enhance the national and international cooperation between tax authorities and investigating bodies. On an international scale, tax evasion, money laundering, grand corruption and criminality go hand in hand. This combination creates a grey area where culprits are able to act in the blind spots of what is regulated by the fiscal authorities and the investigating bodies. The third tool is designed for traceability and accountability. It is the implementation of beneficial ownership registries of companies, subsidiaries and trusts in all countries. Countries also have to introduce appropriate measures to eradicate the practice of facilitators. Finally, a global solution must be found in order to make sure that stolen assets are recovered and transferred back to the state that they were removed from, when and where it is safe to do.

These solutions do not work independently from one another; it is only together that they will produce a stable result, for the problem of fiscal justice is a problem of tracing, sanctioning and recovering the losses created by fiscal injustice.

If this toolbox is not to be a mere incremental step in reform but a radical change in the approach of our tax systems, it should be understood that countries and governments allow themselves to claim back some of the political power they have lost to the hands of MNEs and to the globalized capitalist process. The idea that 'transparency builds trust' makes it clear that transparency is not an end in itself but rather one component to create striving economic, social and political relations because of the trust with which they are granted. Trust is a value inasmuch as it is linked with the idea of truth: corporations and governmental institutions will inspire trust only to the extent that they will not hide crucial elements from the public judgment or act in the shadows as they are accustomed to. In other words, before considering transparency as having intrinsic market value, the statement should be understood as a strong argument toward a political understanding and valorization of the notion of transparency.

[B] Inequalities and Justice

Transparency conceived in such a fashion can therefore act as a powerful political notion in order to address the other aspect of tax justice: reducing inequalities by seeing them as having an intrinsic cause inside our economic and tax system. Regressive tax policies do not only block wealth redistribution (Stirling, 2020), they also leave the State chronically underfunded, therefore breaking apart the social fabric that could help struggling individuals and communities.

However, the COVID-19 pandemic, on the one hand, gave people a new understanding of why we pay taxes. On the other hand, people have noticed that the crisis resulted in an acceleration of trends of inequality that had already existed for decades. Both the necessity of taxes and the feeling of accelerating inequalities were experienced simultaneously in order to create a merging of horizons: the necessity of tax reform. This necessity may have been hidden by the catchphrases used during the crisis, by which some feigned solidarity that did not and does not, in fact, exist. Even if 'we are all in this together,' as many claimed, we do not live through this together and some people have better chances than others, not only to succeed but also to turn the crisis into an opportunity to increase their own wealth. This trend is not new. In the past decades, the 1% wealthiest have increased their wealth so much so that it is now estimated that around the world the twenty-six richest billionaires own as much wealth as the poorest 50% of humanity (Oxfam, 2019). The acceleration that we witness at this level is simply appalling: over the first six months of the pandemic, the wealth of the US billionaires has increased over USD 800 billion (Alcorn, 2020), while the top forty billionaires worldwide have increased their wealth by 27% in the same period (Read, 2020).

Of course, these trends are closely related to the impoverishment of the lower and middle class of our societies. In the last four decades, we have witnessed the erosion of the middle class, the stagnation of income alongside the hike of living costs and the staggering indebtedness of families and individuals. In the recent crisis, those with the lowest incomes have suffered the most, not only from job loss and the high rates of unemployment but also from the incapacity to face their indebtedness and provide for themselves. This distress was always lurking in the current system, but the crisis deepened the wound and exposed it for the world to see. For instance, the Aspen Institute estimates that between 30 and 40 million Americans, which represent between 7.9% to 10.5% of the US population, are at risk of being evicted from their houses or apartments (Benfer and al., 2020). The same trends apply to the business world where corporation concentration is also accelerating while smaller main street businesses are struggling and closing, one after the other.

All these trends are not only related but have common causes, the main one being regressive tax policies. Lower tax rates on corporations, tax deductions, cuts in business taxes, tax loopholes, lower taxes on capital and wealth and the ability for rich individuals and corporations to avoid taxes are all working together to maintain inequality. These regressive policies create a great concentration of wealth and power – a large concentration of corporations – which creates in return, the conditions necessary for the existence of oligarchy, for the public cult of 'strong men,' the public appeal for autocratic measures and the whittling away of our democracies. The current situation in which wealth begets wealth creates individuals and corporations that gain so much economic, social and political power that they are able to subjugate our juridical and political institutions. In every situation where, through lobbying or corruption, the wealthy are able to tilt the tables toward themselves, our democracy is in danger. If not addressed correctly, these trends can fuel authoritarian and violent politics.

More often than not, the advocates of the wealthy will rehearse the orthodox economic mantra that in order to distribute more wealth, we have to create more wealth, meaning that lower tax rates are necessary in order to stimulate investment funds. This kind of justification and rationalization for the aforementioned trends is not only disturbing and dangerous – it is detrimental for the economy itself. The indirect government help through low tax rates for businesses and top income individuals has been used widely used to stimulate economic growth and favour trickling down policies. However, these measures have never shown the expected results: disparities continue to expand (Hope and Limberg, 2020).

Reality therefore contradicts the theory. The result of continuing to act according to false theory is the creation of more suffering and more inequalities: trickle-down economics is not only false but harmful for the vast majority of the population. Nowadays, even the IMF, the OECD and the broad majority of mainstream economists recognize this mistake and agree that economic growth goes hand in hand with greater equality. The IMF already said before the pandemic, in January 2020, via their managing director, that governments could consider raising progressive taxes on more affluent individuals via measures such as wealth taxes, alongside ensuring that MNEs pay taxes that are commensurate with their profitability inside the territory controlled by a jurisdiction (Wood, 2020).

Put all together, this situation points to one conclusion: we need fundamental reform of international corporate taxation accompanied with broad progressive domestic tax reform. During the pandemic, priorities should be to introduce an excess profit tax just like during the two World Wars. For example, in the Second World War, the excess profit tax generated more revenue than the general corporate income tax. This increase happened because times of crisis are abnormal times in which the economy is concentrated in only a few sectors. This contingent concentration should not imply that the vast majority of the population suffer from the temporary rearrangement of the economic institutions and structures. Another aspect that gained a lot of traction recently is the introduction of a wealth tax for the wealthiest. This is important in hard times and should also be considered an essential tool against the piling up of inequalities (Giridharadas, 2021).

§3.04 THE PANDEMIC AS AN EXPERIENCE: FROM NEOLIBERAL INCAPACITATION TO COLLECTIVE AMBITION[2]

As said above, to take the portrayal of the state of affairs as a mere factual or descriptive presentation of the current situation would miss the target. On the contrary, we already were able to extract something else. By using a series of elements, facts, information and data in order to portray a focal point that usually resists its own presentation, a blind spot of our own understanding of the problem of tax justice emerged. In one sentence, this blind spot is none other than our own societal possibilities. The crux of the circumstances goes as follows: the collective and shared experience of the pandemic can act as a privileged locus from which we can observe our reality from a renewed perspective and therefore see that some of the capacities that we thought we were deprived of are actually available. In other words, we are able to go way beyond what we have been led to believe and expect. The main shift of perspective that can be operated from this experience is an expansion of the meaning of tax justice, understood not only as a redistribution of wealth but more essentially as a redistribution of capacities.

To portray this expansion to the full extent of its meaning, it is important to sketch the contrast that is created by such an experience. There is a common threat in the history of civilizations that transforms socially produced inequality and socially produced suffering as a form of necessary natural state of affairs. One of the main roles of what is known as ideology is to provide a narrative that justifies the conservation of an inequality beyond the need for its historical existence. Neoliberal politics and economic regimes that overtook the western world over forty years ago acts as such a

2. The following section presents the philosophical contribution that I wish to bring to the debate. For the sake of clarity, I have not included a list of references in this instance. This seemed reasonable to me, to the extent that the application of a theory to a particular situation is rarely straightforward and, in the present case, I have allowed myself to freely adapt various ideas from the history of ideas. A complete list of references would have been required in an academic context, but in this instance, I think it would only have served to obfuscate the point and to hinder the readability of the argument.

justification among many others that existed before. Even though we have produced many times over the proof that the idea that one person is poor because they do not work hard enough is not true, it still prevails as a form of accepted social discourse, but also as a form of political justification when the time comes to create social security policies.

These neoliberal policies in turn act as a self-fulfilling prophecy: the regressive tax policies that accompany the neoliberal worldview force government austerity as a 'necessity'. Of course, this 'necessity' is not at all necessary, for it is dependent on the totally contingent choice to adopt the neoliberal understanding of reality. Unfortunately, this austerity has devastating consequences for our public institutions and services starting with education and health, which have been chronically underfunded over the last decades.

One of the most pernicious results of these policies is, however, not as perceptible: decades of neoliberalism has instigated the idea that we are, as a society, in a deep-rooted state of incapacity, of being incapable of doing differently, for the success of ideology is to bestow a 'natural veil' over a historically and socially produced situation. How many times have we heard that improvements and even incremental reforms are impossible because we lack the capacity to execute them properly? How many times have we been served the same argument that the economy will crash or deeply suffer if we increase the minimum wage? Who has not heard that inequalities are present in nature, that they are natural, and therefore are outside the scope of social and political solutions? It is on this particular aspect that the COVID-19 pandemic can be perceived as a pivotal moment. Let me unfold this thought through an example.

As was said earlier, the pandemic accelerated trends that were already present before, just as the concentration of wealth in the hands of fewer and fewer people, the raising of inequalities, the erosion of the middle class, etc. What is important to underline is what becomes perceptible under the experience of acceleration. Within a limited amount of time, acceleration gives a societal and collective experience of the deep tendencies that animate the social process. This does not mean that what becomes perceptible now was not already present; it just means that through its collective and temporally dense conditions, acceleration, as a form of experience, renders the possibility of portraying things more clearly. For instance, it was already a known social reality that workers who have difficulty making ends meet are also often the ones cumulating jobs. As a result of the precariousness of the employment market and the preponderance of the minimum wage, part-time, retail jobs an ever-growing number of people are continually living only a few pay cheques away from a life on the streets. To be clear, people often experience their own social position not as a choice, but as a fate. For this reason, even when it is not made explicit in their own words, they have an experience that the economic narrative of the 'free market' is a lie and that their economic situation is an aberration: they know they create and contribute to the national wealth to a larger extent than the 'social contract' leaves it to be understood.

This aberration became clear with the beginning of the pandemic: when everything started closing as precautionary measures, all of a sudden, these *same workers* were now *essential workers*. From quasi-outcasts that did not deserve a decent minimum wage, they promptly became *the backbone of our economy and of our country*. It was now clear, for everyone who is not completely blinded by ideology, that these people were the *condition of possibility of wealth and of our collective well-being*. To bring this point to its full-fledged consequence, it became clear that wealth does not stem from investment but from labour in general, and from the labour of these essential workers in particular. Investments are, in this respect, a social capacity to buy a labour force that will, in turn, create more wealth. The biggest implication from this shift of perspective is the following: wealth is therefore not in, and by itself, a private property. On the contrary, wealth is a *social product* that can be bought and turned into a private property.

To make a short story around a debate that is at least bicentennial, there are two major camps surrounding the notion of the origin of wealth. The first one, and the historically dominant one, could be framed as the liberal understanding of wealth. This view sees wealth as an attribute of the individual self that results from its own productive activity of valorization inside a network of other economic agents. The other paradigm takes a step back from what seems to be so obvious i.e. the fact that valorization is a result of an individual being at work. In this context, to take a step back means to not immediately consider what is given to experience – individuals at work – as being what is first in a logical and historical order. From this perspective, the economy has always been, not an individual activity based solely on the additions of actions of every economic agent, but rather a social institution constructed and organized as a way of responding to the needs of individuals. Therefore, wealth is not an individual result, but the result of a complete societal process. In other words, wealth is the surplus that a whole society is able to create beyond its immediate needs. This surplus therefore does not belong to one individual or the other but to the collective itself. Wealth is the treasury of social capacities stocked until they are needed for social purposes.

This has major implications on the way we understand tax justice. First, let's propose the following working definition: taxes are a way of creating an equilibrium between the contribution of the individual and the societal needs for which the societal economic activity exists in the first place. When one speaks about tax justice as a question of redistribution of wealth, one expresses the following idea: the wealth that was created as a result of a total social process ends up being concentrated in the hands of individuals that have a legal obligation, through tax laws, to give some of this wealth back to society – under the guise of the state, which is the political and legal representative of society as a whole. What is in question here is not prima facie a question of redistributing wealth qua wealth but redistributing wealth as a form of the capacities that society has already produced for itself. Portrayed as such, it implies that when corporations and individuals avoid paying taxes, they deprive society of its capacity to understand its own real potential.

This is the tragedy that belongs to the coupling of existing neoliberal domination and the ideology that tags along with it: through the concentration of wealth in the hands of a few corporations and individuals, society is deprived of the capacities that it has produced for itself. As if it was not enough, through the convincing form of the narrative imposed by ideology, the individuals that make up society are deprived of the experience and the consciousness of having ever created these capacities. Tax justice, therefore, is not only the redistribution of wealth but the act of reclaiming the possibilities that belong not to particular individuals but to society itself. Poverty in a world of plenty is not a fate: it is a socially produced reality. This reality can change when we consider how much power we actually own and build together.

All of this means one simple thing: the possibility for a more egalitarian society in which the economy works for the common good and not only for private interest is a possibility that already exists in our own world. It is not a frivolous utopia, even if we lacked the collective consciousness to express it until now. This is how and why the COVID-19 crisis can act as an opportunity: over the last year, we have experienced, in a very short period of only a few weeks, that we can construct a new social framework. In Canada, for instance, in the span of three weeks, governments and revenue authorities designed a program that was not perfect, but that prevented significant, yet unnecessary, suffering and prevented the beginnings of an economic depression. This was possible in part because we realized that while working together, we have a greater power of action. It was also possible because all the elements needed to establish such a program already existed as a form of latent possibility within our social organization. Something that no one would have thought to be available just a year ago did not just appear out of nowhere. As much as we would like to believe in miracles, there is no magic at work here. The only thing that happened is that the crisis revealed something about us and our collective capacities that were blocked for our consciousness. These capacities are now written in our collective experience and we now know that with a good sense of urgency we can transform a lot. This is especially important in regard to another crisis that we have to face: climate change and the ecological crisis. If we can channel the 'sense of urgency' and nudge our collective ambitions accordingly, we have a chance to imprint lasting solutions that can save us from the catastrophe.

The question of tax justice therefore can become the collective consciousness of our own capacities and the political action needed to claim them back as something which belongs to all and escape the realm of private ownership. What the crisis did in this situation is to unveil some of the essential social structures beyond narratives that normally blind us to them. Such unveiling implies the honesty of calling the more exploited individuals of our society for what they are: *essential workers*. Once this is said, the reality must change, we have to take action in order to change *their* lives for the better: one cannot be at the same time essential to society and be maintained in the margin of that same society.

On this specific point, what is true at the level of the minimum wage earners in our economy is also true at the macro level of international politics. The scale of the crisis gives us an opportunity to address the question of international economy, not as a globalized unitarian process, but as the result of a historical network of unequal exchanges in which entire countries, if not continents, were literally robbed from their own capacities to act for and by themselves. So much so, that what I portrayed as a form of tax justice inside one nation-state economy, also holds for international relations: the capacity of the richest nation in the world resides in the fact that they have deprived other nations of their capacities. This is also a question of tax justice for which the idea that I have presented in this text can serve as a pivotal moment: giving back to the societies the capacities that they have been producing for themselves.

§3.05 CONCLUSION: OUR FRAGILE POSSIBILITIES

In conclusion, it is important to note that the crisis is only an opportunity. This opportunity is fragile. I have argued that the weakness that has been exposed during the crisis can act as a foundation for our future strengths. Unfortunately, this citizen's perspective is not the only political perspective on the field. Right-wing populism, autocratic fantasies and corporatocracy are alive and well; they will also target the same weaknesses that were unfolded by the crisis with very different objectives in mind. Therefore, the overture created by the circumstances is not fate and our optimism must be tamed by the seriousness of our desire to create a better collective future. In this perspective, it has been suggested that a referendum on what could be done to improve tax justice in all countries be published. This could be a strong first step to give a strong and democratic voice to all citizens who are, after all, the subjects of tax justice.

Bibliography

Alcorn, Chauncey. 2020. 'US Billionaires' Fortunes Have Skyrocketed $845 Billion since March,' *CNN*, 17 September 2020, URL: https://www.cnn.com/2020/09/17/business/us-billionaire-wealth-increase-pandemic/index.html.

Benfer Emily, David Bloom Robinson, Stacy Butler, Lavar Edmonds, Sam Gilman, Katherine Lucas McKay, Zach Neumann, Lisa Owens, Neil Steinkamp and Diane Yentel. 2020. 'The COVID-19 Eviction Crisis: an Estimated 30–40 Million People in America Are at Risk,' *Aspen Institute*, 7 August 2020, URL: https://www.aspeninstitute.org/blog-posts/the-covid-19-eviction-crisis-an-estimated-30-40-million-people-in-america-are-at-risk/.

Chown Oved, Marco. 2020. 'Justin Trudeau's Position on COVID-19 Bailouts for Tax-Haven Companies Gets Murkier,' *Toronto Star*, 29 April 2020, URL: https://www.thestar.com/politics/federal/2020/04/29/justin-trudeaus-position-on-covid-19-bailouts-for-tax-haven-companies-gets-murkier.html.

Frank, Robert. 2017. 'Richest 1% Now Owns Half the World's Wealth,' *CNBC*, November 2017, URL: https://www.cnbc.com/2017/11/14/richest-1-percent-now-own-half-the-worlds-wealth.html.

Giridharadas, Anand 2021. 'Warren Buffet and the Myth of the "Good Billionaire"', *New-York Times*, 13 June 2021, URL: https://www.nytimes.com/2021/06/13/opinion/warren-buffett-billionaire-taxes.html.

Global Financial Integrity. 2020. *Trade-Related Illicit Financial Flows in 135 Developing Countries: 2008–2017*, March 2020, URL: https://gfintegrity.org/report/trade-related-illicit-financial-flows-in-135-developing-countries-2008-2017/.

Hope, David & Julian Limberg. 2020. 'The Economic Consequences of Major Tax Cuts for the Rich,' *International Inequalities Institute from The London School of Economics and Political Science*, December 2020, URL: http://eprints.lse.ac.uk/107919/1/Hope_economic_consequences_of_major_tax_cuts_published.pdf.

Huguette Labelle, William Ross & Toby Sanger. 2020. World Tax Summit – TaxCOOP2020, Tax Justice in Times of Crisis, Montreal (online), 15 October 2020.

Mansour, Mark Bou. 2020. '$427 Bn Lost to Tax Havens Every Year: Landmark Study Reveals Countries' Losses and Worst Offenders,' *Tax Justice Network*, November 2020, URL: https://www.taxjustice.net/2020/11/20/427bn-lost-to-tax-havens-every-year-landmark-study-reveals-countries-losses-and-worst-offenders/.

Medina, Brenda. 2021. 'How the World's Richest Defend Their Wealth, with Help from a Dedicated Industry,' *ICIJ*, 1 June 2021, URL: https://www.icij.org/inside-icij/2021/06/how-the-worlds-richest-defend-their-wealth-with-help-from-a-dedicated-industry/.

OXFAM. 2019. *Public Good or Private Wealth?*, executive summary, 2019, URL: https://oxfamilibrary.openrepository.com/bitstream/handle/10546/620599/bp-public-good-or-private-wealth-210119-summ-en.pdf?utm_source=indepth.

Read, Simon. 2020. 'Billionaires See Fortunes Rise by 27% During the Pandemic,' *BBC*, 7 October 2020, URL: https://www.bbc.com/news/business-54446285.

Shaxson, Nicholas. 2014. 'Cost of Tax Abuse, 2011,' Tax Justice Network, April 2014, URL: https://www.taxjustice.net/2014/04/01/cost-tax-abuse-2011/.

Shaxson, Nicholas. 2019. 'Tackling Tax Havens' in *Finance & Development*, September 2019, Vol. 56, No. 3, URL: https://www.imf.org/external/pubs/ft/fandd/2019/09/pdf/tackling-global-tax-havens-shaxon.pdf.

Schwab, Jeremy. 'Fighting COVID-19 Could Cost 500 Times as Much as Pandemic Prevention Measures,' in *World Economic Forum*, URL: https://www.weforum.org/agenda/2020/08/pandemic-fight-costs-500x-more-than-preventing-one-futurity/.

Stirling, Craig. 2020. 'Fifty Years of Tax Cuts for Rich Didn't Trickle Down, Study Says,' *Bloomberg Wealth*, 15 December 2020, URL: https://www.bloomberg.com/news/articles/2020-12-16/fifty-years-of-tax-cuts-for-rich-didn-t-trickle-down-study-says.

Wood, Vincent. 2020. 'Raise Taxes on the Rich to Tackle Inequality, IMF Says,' *The Independent*, 8 January 2020, URL: https://www.independent.co.uk/news/imf-tax-rise-rich-trickle-down-economics-kristalina-georgieva-a9275386.html.

World Bank/UNODC. 2011. 'Stolen Asset Recovery Initiative', *The Puppet Masters*, October 2011, URL: https://star.worldbank.org/resources/puppet-masters.

CHAPTER 4

The Tax Race: The Current Situation

Joy Waruguru Ndubai

This chapter evaluates the progress made in minimizing the negative effects of tax competition, addresses whether new opportunities to engage in competition are emerging or already available, and examines whether some of the most recent proposed solutions could end the race to the bottom for corporate income tax. It does so by evaluating some of the common characteristics of tax competition, assessing how to define harmful tax competition whilst acknowledging the broader aspect of spillover effects; providing an overview of recent developments in multilateral efforts to minimize competition; and highlighting the potential for competition in other aspects of taxation.

§4.01 INTRODUCTION

A major constraint in trying to limit tax competition is that the policies that may contribute to it vary in their nature and have continued to change over time. In order to center global coordination in this area, policy proposals have focused on the aspects of tax competition that have harmful consequences. However, considering the overall constraints, there are expected difficulties in identifying an acceptable definition of what constitutes harmful tax competition. Indeed, "not only is the definition a subject of debate but so too is everything else related to tax competition" (Faulhaber, 2018). While a number of organizations have tried to identify the common features, it remains the case that "tax competition can take various forms" (Devereux & Loretz, 2013).

What could be considered competitive behavior in the tax space may include the use of special economic zones (SEZs), tax holidays, patent boxes, headquarter regimes, interest or loss deductions, large treaty networks, golden passport regimes, exemptions from personal income tax, no taxes on dividends or interest or even wealth tax exemptions, amongst others. This non-exhaustive list is expanding and has implications beyond the corporate income tax (CIT), signaling the innovation amongst policymakers to increasingly attract a variety of mobile aspects of the global economy, mobile aspects that are also expanding. Although some of these policies may often share some common features and give rise to similar outcomes, the policy options emerging today—particularly those relating to high-net-worth individuals (HNWIs)—reveal that remedies focused on eliminating the undesirable tools whilst permitting others will no longer be sufficient. This is because a tax competitive policy introduced in one country can have unintentional effects in another. As a result, as the IMF pointed out in 2014, the spillover effects on corporate tax bases can be significant and sizeable (IMF, 2014), the main challenge is whether or not countries are willing to limit these adverse spillovers.

The most significant effort to first determine the factors that give rise to harmful tax competition, the OECD[1] 1998 report on Harmful Tax Competition, raised concerns about "tax policies aimed primarily at diverting financial and other geographically mobile capital" that could "induce potential distortions in the patterns of trade and investment and reduce global welfare" (OECD, 1998). The report identified that these actions could erode national tax bases of other countries by shifting burdens from mobile to relatively immobile factors, hamper redistributive objectives, and pressure countries to modify their tax systems in response (OECD, 1998). However, the OECD equally recognized that countries were at liberty to introduce low rates of tax while broadening bases, and this interaction between differing domestic policies and the ensuing tax competition could have effects that only some countries would view as negative or harmful (OECD, 1998). By identifying the characteristics of tax havens and harmful preferential tax regimes that lead to tax base erosion in other jurisdictions, the OECD was able to negotiate how to deal with the most harmful features whilst conceding that tax competition as a whole was still desirable. The result was that countries agreed to engage in enhancing transparency and exchange of information efforts to minimize secrecy and anonymity. However, dealing with these factors, both in the early 2000s and later via the Base Erosion and Profit Shifting (BEPS) project,[2] did not reduce the spillover effects of tax competition and the race to the bottom has persevered. Thus far, despite the efforts to combat profit shifting, "there is little evidence that [it] is subsiding; in 2019 data, US [Multinational Corporations] reported the same share of their foreign direct investment earnings in havens as they did in recent years prior." (Clausing, Saez & Zucman, 2020).

Alongside the ever-present likelihood that MNEs will continue to take advantage of the systems that provide the most convenience, a number of factors in the field of tax competition emphasize the implications of continued uncertainty or lack of consensus regarding how to identify and deal with harmful tax competition. First, the tools adopted by countries to engage in competitive behavior continue to change and respond to the changing policy environment. Whereas secrecy and anonymity were

1. Organization for Economic Cooperation and Development.
2. Particularly Action 5 on Harmful Tax Practices.

previously common tools, today, the widespread adoption of transparency and exchange of information frameworks have made them less attractive. Second, the tools being used or those being prepared for future use will continue to compete for different mobile aspects of the economy, for instance, the growing prevalence of golden passport regimes and personal income exemption programs demonstrates more interest in attracting HNWIs and remote workers. Third, since these tools continue to be adapted, their impact will continually raise new challenges for other jurisdictions and there will remain a need to scrutinize their negative or harmful impacts on an ongoing basis. Fourth, this will entail continuing engagement in determining which activities to limit and to what extent and this will likely create more complexities for tax authorities seeking to minimize the outcomes of competitive policies. Finally, there are now higher stakes in evaluating how to limit some competitive tax policies and, given the challenges of cooperation in international taxation, countries may consider (where they are capable) the use of trade mechanisms to challenge specific policies[3] or adopting defensive mechanisms (that may still have trade implications):

> "Throughout the world policymakers have been put in an impossible position, facing serious pressures from international tax competition while also attempting to protect the corporate tax base. At the same time multinational companies are more powerful than they have ever been. They command larger profits and larger market shares than in prior decades, control a large part of the economy, and undertake the vast majority of all international trade ... In many countries policymakers have responded to tax competition pressures by slowly and steadily lowering corporate tax rates and shifting more of the tax burden onto labor and consumption." (Clausing, 2020b)

Overall, it may appear as though only limited progress can be made in managing tax competition if the focus continues to be on curbing the use of specific policies rather than limiting their effects. Countries will, likely, continue to face the same challenges with new tools that provide preferential tax treatment beyond corporate income taxes. A major area for analysis, considering recent developments regarding cooperative efforts to introduce a global Minimum Effective Tax Rate (METR), is whether countries will continue to be stuck in a race to the bottom and how prevalent tax competition will continue to be if a consensus is found. For this reason, this chapter tries to address and evaluate the progress made in minimizing the negative effects of tax competition, determine whether new opportunities emerge, and examine whether some of the proposed solutions could end the race to the bottom. It does so by evaluating some of the common characteristics of tax competition, assessing how to define harmful tax competition whilst acknowledging the broader aspect of spillover effects; providing an overview of recent developments in multilateral efforts to minimize competition, and highlighting the potential for competition in other aspects of taxation.

3. This is especially evident based on the EU State Aid cases and ongoing subsidies cases relating to tax measures at the WTO Dispute Settlement Body.

§4.02 WHAT IS TAX COMPETITION?

Since "competitiveness is an elusive concept" (Clausing, 2020b), identifying the tax elements of competitiveness can be an equally challenging process:

> "In everyday usage 'competitive' is a relative concept. When applied to a business, it means that a firm is able to produce its output at the same or lower cost than other firms in the same line of business, or that it has some other advantage over them such as the quality of its product. In most industries a competitive firm (as a result of its costs or other advantages over its rivals) would be able to earn returns in excess of its cost of capital. It is more difficult conceptually to apply the term competitive to an economy as a whole rather than to a particular firm." (Owens, 2012)

The difficulty is that countries are concerned about their competitiveness as locations for economic activity (Clausing, 2020b) but this is often dependent on a number of factors including tax. Owens (2012) has discussed this extensively, highlighting not only the variety of factors that influence competitiveness but also identifying the impact that taxation may also have on these factors. For instance, the effectiveness and fairness of institutions (including the legal and administrative frameworks that back them) in a country that facilitates good governance and certainty for investors should also prioritize the fair raising of tax revenue and transparent, evidence-based tax policy making (Owens, 2012). Another notable factor is that of technological readiness and innovation, or "the ability of economies to adapt existing technologies and innovation to the development and application of new technologies and products" (Owens, 2012). While, "there is some evidence that a favorable tax regime for R&D increases the amount of such expenditure," there is "less clear evidence on the best design of any tax relief or the appropriate degree of tax privilege" (Owens, 2012). Not only is the contribution of a tax competitive policy difficult to quantify, but it is also complex to evaluate the most ideal design to attract investment whilst raising revenue. As a result, countries adopt a variety of policies with specific objectives, but often unpredictable outcomes:

> "In practice, the range of empirical estimates of the responsiveness of FDI to corporate tax rates is quite wide and this makes clear cut policy recommendation difficult. Nevertheless, this elasticity appears to have increased over the last decade and international competition for FDI thus reinforces the wider competitiveness arguments ... for a tax regime that fosters a conducive climate for investment and innovation." (Owens, 2012)

A variety of policies have the capability to enhance the "competitiveness" of a tax system relative to other jurisdictions. The 1998 report recognized that "globalization and the increased mobility of capital have promoted the development of capital and financial markets and has encouraged countries to reduce tax barriers to capital flows and to modernize their tax systems to reflect these developments" (OECD, 1998). A majority of those reforms "also addressed the need to adapt tax systems to this new global environment" (OECD, 1998). This process of adaptation to the changing global environment (which continues even now) gave rise to new challenges for tax authorities:

> "Globalization has, however, also had the negative effects of opening up new ways by which companies and individuals can minimize and avoid taxes and in which countries can exploit these new opportunities by developing tax policies aimed primarily at diverting potential distortions in the patterns of trade and investment and reduce global welfare ... these schemes can erode national tax bases of other countries, may alter the structure of taxation (by shifting part of the tax burden from mobile to relatively immobile factors and from income to consumption) and may hamper the application of progressive tax rates and the achievement of redistributive goals. Pressure of this sort can result in changes in tax structures in which all countries may be forced by spillover effects to modify their tax bases ... ." (OECD, 1998)

As stated above, the OECD acknowledged that there was no reason for countries to have the same level and structure of taxation and, while differences could affect other countries, that remained a domestic policy matter. The 1998 Report focused its attention on the use of preferential tax regimes and tax havens. Tax havens were characterized by no or nominal taxes; a lack of effective exchange of information; lack of transparency; and no substantial activities (OECD, 1998). Preferential tax regimes, on the other hand, were defined by no or low effective tax rates; ring fencing; a lack of effective exchange of information; and lack of transparency (OECD, 1998). Indeed, these two tools were meant to represent the major policy instruments that countries were concerned about, but they are not the only ones that could make a tax system more competitive. The introduction to this chapter identified a number of these tools and there are a number of others with differing characteristics and objectives. However, the outcome is almost always the direct or indirect lowering of the effective tax rate for the taxpayer. This can be further driven down by a taxpayer engaging in aggressive tax avoidance which has not been effectively countered by a country (Owens, 2012). Multinationals or individuals may engage in aggressive tax avoidance taking advantage of the preferential rules or rates; the mismatches in national regulation; the ability to engage in transfer mispricing; or through other means.

The implication of this could be that countries opting not to introduce measures to counter aggressive tax avoidance are also, implicitly, engaging in tax competitive behavior. Faulhaber recognizes that the converse should also be included:

> "Since anti-avoidance measures target international tax competition, and measures targeting international tax competition are efforts to shift competition in favor of the country or countries passing the anti-tax-competition measure, both recent anti-tax-competition and anti-avoidance measures are themselves forms of tax competition. In other words, even when countries seem to be trying to limit tax competition, they are in fact competing ... highlighting that anti-tax-competition measures are in fact their own form of competition complicates the idea that only some countries are involved in tax competition and underscores the need for more nuanced conversations about what countries intend to achieve with their tax systems." (Faulhaber, 2018)

There are also administrative aspects that could facilitate tax competition. This can be the case for instance, where administrations agree to engage in sweetheart deals or comfort letters providing preferential tax treatment to a company that will often not be transparent or available to other taxpayers or countries.

The discussion so far seems to suggest that tax competition involves a number of actions, omissions, and elements of policy design. We may then better identify tax competitive policies if we better understand the most common consequences or outcomes:

- Lowering of effective tax rates.
- Facilitates tax avoidance or evasion.
- Fails or restricts efforts to counter tax avoidance or evasion.
- Succeeds in or assists in the countering of tax avoidance or evasion.
- Encourages certainty, simplicity, or fairness in a tax system.

There may be additional elements, but the intention here is to capture the category of outcomes that can result from varying policies. It is also important to note that countries may adopt a mix of policies that give rise to contradicting outcomes. This chapter takes a broad approach in focusing on the outcome rather than the type of policy because the nature of tax competition has changed since 1998, and it could be more useful to focus on the shared characteristics of common policies or practices and identify which ones are more or less desirable. More importantly, this approach may also anticipate the spillover effects on other countries.

§4.03 HARMFUL TAX COMPETITION OR SPILLOVER EFFECTS?

Having briefly discussed the various aspects of tax competition, it is useful to address its harmful effects. Efforts to establish global consensus about harmful tax competition through intensified cooperation after the publication of the 1998 report focused on eliminating the harmful features of preferential regimes and on identifying the jurisdictions that met the tax haven criteria (OECD, 2000). Just over fifteen years later, the final report on Action 5 regarding *Harmful Tax Practices* re-emphasized the concerns raised in the 1998 report and highlighted new concerns about the risk of preferential regimes being used to facilitate artificial profit shifting and the lack of certainty and transparency in specific rulings (OECD, 2015). The work of the OECD Forum on Harmful Tax Practices (FHTP) focused on establishing substantial activity requirements, compulsory exchange of information, and reviews of preferential regimes to determine if they are harmful. In addition, the OECD now sought to engage non-OECD member countries, "in order to achieve a level playing field and avoid the risk that the work on harmful tax practices could displace regimes to third countries" (OECD, 2015).

The final report on Action 5 largely reiterated the criteria[4] set out in 1998 to determine whether a regime could be considered harmful, however, eight other factors were also included (OECD, 2015):

- An artificial definition of the tax base.
- Failure to adhere to international transfer pricing principles.
- Foreign source income is exempt from residence country taxation.
- Negotiable tax rate or tax base.
- Existence of secrecy provisions.
- Access to a wide network of tax treaties.
- The regime is promoted as a tax minimization vehicle.
- The regime encourages operations or arrangements that are purely tax-driven and involve no substantial activities.

No or low effective tax rates must apply as a gateway criterion to a regime being considered potentially harmful, the additional factors are then applied as part of an overall assessment (OECD, 2015). Action 5 also considers that where a regime may have harmful economic effects, then it will be categorized as a harmful preferential regime. To make this assessment, the report provides three questions (OECD, 2015):

- Does the tax regime shift activity from one country to the country providing the preferential tax regime, rather than generate significant new activity?
- Is the presence and level of activities in the host country commensurate with the amount of investment income?
- Is the preferential regime the primary motivation for the location of an activity?

If a regime is found to actually be harmful, "the relevant country is given the opportunity to abolish the regime or remove the features that create the harmful effect" (OECD, 2015). In contrast, the work on tax havens focused on the development of the list of uncooperative jurisdictions that would eventually be the subject of "a coordinated approach to defensive measures, comprised of jurisdictions meeting the tax haven criteria that choose not to eliminate their harmful tax practices" (OECD, 2000). By 2001, the OECD had listed thirty-five jurisdictions that met the tax haven criteria a process that has, together with the European Union (EU) list, consistently been brought to question as one focused on coercing non-OECD countries to comply with a process they had minimal opportunity to contribute to.[5]

The criticisms about the efforts to minimize what the OECD and its member countries categorized as harmful tax competition arose from a variety of actors in the

4. Four key factors identifying a preferential tax regime: no or low effective tax rates on income from geographically mobile financial and other service activities; regime is ring-fenced from the domestic economy; regime lacks transparency; and there is no effective exchange of information with respect to the regime.
5. *See*, for instance, Annet Wanyana Oguttu, *A Critique on the OECD Campaign Against Tax Havens: Has It Been Successful? A South African Perspective*, Stellenbosch Law Review (2010), Vol. 21, 172-200; or Oxfam, *Off the Hook: How the EU Is About to Whitewash the World's Tax Haven*, Oxfam, 2019.

early 2000s. From the perspective of countries that qualified as tax havens per the 1998 criteria, as vulnerable and developing economies their reliance on competing as offshore financial centers had supported at least some measure of financial independence and the OECD effort posed a threat to this.[6] Luxembourg expressed that it did not "share the Report's implicit belief that bank secrecy [was] necessarily a source of harmful tax competition" or "accept that an exchange of information ... be considered a criterion to identify a harmful preferential tax regime and a tax haven" (OECD, 1998). The United States also scaled back its support for the initiative in 2001 when the then-Secretary of the Treasury, Paul O'Neill, stated that "the United States does not support efforts to dictate to any country what its own tax rates or tax system should be, and will not participate in any initiative to harmonize world tax systems" (Morriss & Moberg, 2012). This weakened OECD efforts to get offshore tax havens to comply with the standards set and facilitated multilateral (rather than bilateral) negotiations between the OECD and these jurisdictions (Morriss & Moberg, 2012) and particularly silenced any effort to address low tax rates. The offshore jurisdictions pulled the wider Commonwealth into the debate and "poked significant holes in the OECD's arguments on substantive tax issues and undercut the effort to build an international consensus around the OECD's proposed standards" (Morriss & Moberg, 2012).

However, "the lack of agreement on harmful tax competition has not prevented countries from trying to stop it" (Faulhaber, 2018). There were indeed merits to the entire initiative discussed in section §4.04 below, and although the process was slowed by the criticisms it faced, efforts undertaken under the frame of Action 5 have had some impact. The question of what should be considered harmful has, however, remained under debate. When the work picked up momentum again in the form of Action 5, other actors had begun to carry out similar analyses of the problem of tax competition, only this time taking into consideration the context in developing countries. In particular, the IMF Report on Spillovers in International Corporate Taxation explored "the nature, significance and policy implications of spillovers in international corporate taxation—the effects of one country's rules and practices on others" (IMF, 2014). The report found that "the potential economic implications of international tax spillovers ... go well beyond tax revenue, with wider implications for the broader level and distribution of welfare across nations" (IMF, 2014). In addition:

> "The pervasiveness of the tax incentives that the IMF and other have long stressed as significantly undermining revenue in developing countries may to a large extent be a spillover reaction to policies pursued in other countries: a clear instance of tax competition. As a share of all revenue, the corporate income tax (CIT) is actually more important in low and upper middle-income countries than in advanced, so that their overall fiscal performance is more vulnerable to pressures on these receipts" (IMF, 2014).

6. For more on this discussion, *see* Richard A. Johnson, *Why Harmful Tax Practices Will Continue After Developing Nations Pay: A Critique of the OECD's Initiatives Against Harmful Tax Competition*, Boston College Third World Law Journal (2006), Vol. 26, Issue 2; and George M. Melo, *Taxation in the Global Arena: Preventing the Erosion of National Tax Bases or Impinging on Territorial Sovereignty (A Critique of the OECD's Report: Harmful Tax Competition: An Emerging Global Issue)*, Pace International Law Review (2000), Vol. 12, Issue 1.

The report found evidence of "strong strategic spillovers" particularly for the most mobile elements of the tax base and this confirmed the existence of "deliberate competition" (IMF, 2014). In addition, in the perspective of the IMF, "in designing specific measures, the notion of 'harmful tax practices' remains ill defined" (IMF, 2014). Indeed, existing reforms only addressed some spillovers and the overall institutional framework for addressing them was weak (IMF, 2014). According to the IMF, the approach needed to be more inclusive.

The process of determining whether a specified policy falls within the domain of tax competition and, whether it may be considered harmful is certainly dependent on a number of factors, how those factors have been established is important. The introduction to this chapter already identified some of the conceptual difficulties in economic and legal literature, the primary challenge with identifying which tax policies can contribute to harmful tax competition is that this determination is reliant on the outcome. This outcome may be ascertained either by way of the detection of misuse of a specific policy by the very multinationals it is designed to attract (this misuse may or may not have been known by the policymakers that introduced it); objections raised by other jurisdictions to the introduction of a specific policy (for instance through disputes raised concerning subsidies at the World Trade Organization (WTO) or state aid investigations); or where a policy does not meet the standards of multilateral institutions like the OECD FHTP. One way of developing an understanding of what may fall within the sphere of harm may be to evaluate the rules and proposals being designed by governments and multilateral initiatives and what they target (Faulhaber, 2018). To a certain extent, the FHTP has tried to evaluate the preferential regimes of countries to determine whether they are harmful or not, however, the underlying criteria are based upon the exclusive process undertaken between OECD member countries and the EU. This means that even where a regime may be found to be acceptable by the FHTP, it may have significant spillover effects on other jurisdictions that can be considered harmful. This brings us to the next consideration, in light of the prevailing constraints and weaknesses of the current framework to address harmful tax competition, have multilateral efforts produced some merit for countries?

§4.04 HOW PREVALENT IS TAX COMPETITION TODAY AND HOW SUCCESSFUL HAVE MULTILATERAL EFFORTS BEEN IN ADDRESSING HARMFUL ELEMENTS?

This section will focus mainly on the experiences of countries post-2010 since some of the criticisms and challenges faced have been partly covered in previous sections. As mentioned above, countries chose not to deal with low tax rates, particularly due to the sentiments raised by the United States at the time, and they were therefore put aside at least for some time. The OECD listing process in 2000 led to all the listed countries agreeing to make commitments to comply between 2001 and 2009 and this begun to expand the framework for exchange of information and overall transparency. The importance of these developments, despite the problematic political implications of listing processes, for tax administrations and their ability to detect tax evasion and avoidance were significant and they certainly established the foundations of the work on transparency today.

Later listing efforts, including the EU list of non-cooperative jurisdictions established in 2017, have coerced countries to comply with OECD minimum standards at the risk of facing coordinated sanctions. The reaction to the use of this tool to induce cooperation was immediate criticism from listed jurisdictions for "being arbitrary and overly punitive and from nonprofits fighting for international tax justice for being too limited in scope and for giving European territories a pass" (Collin, 2020). This did not stop the EU from claiming real gains in global tax transparency were being made, where formerly non-cooperative jurisdictions agreed to comply with the requirements set by the Code of Conduct Group on business taxation (European Commission, 2020). In 2021, Members of the European Parliament (MEP) adopted a resolution "pushing for the system used to draw up the EU list of tax havens to be changed, as it is currently 'confusing and ineffective'" (European Parliament, 2021). The changes proposed are intended to make the listing or delisting process more transparent, consistent, and impartial, and "criteria should be added to ensure that more countries are considered a tax haven" (European Parliament, 2021). In particular, MEPs are pursuing the widening of the criteria:

> "to include more practices and not only preferential tax rates ... Among other measures proposed, the resolution therefore, says that all jurisdictions with a 0% corporate tax rate or with no taxes on companies' profits should be automatically placed on the blacklist. Being removed from the blacklist should not be the result of only token tweaks to that jurisdiction's tax system ... all third countries need to be treated and screened fairly using the same criteria, MEPs say, stressing that the current list indicates that this is not the case." (European Parliament, 2021)

The outcome of this resolution is yet to be seen; however, it will be important to evaluate whether future lists will also include EU jurisdictions and their territories. It signals the importance of low tax rates as a gateway factor to facilitating harmful practices and may well be aligned with recent developments concerning the adoption of a global minimum tax, discussed further below.

The threat of sanctions has certainly pushed listed jurisdictions to comply with the requirements, whether in substance or only in form. However, the application of sanctions at a national level could have implications beyond the desired coercion. The 2016 decision of the WTO Appellate Body concerning the distinctions introduced by Argentina to treat cooperative and uncooperative countries differently found that this treatment did not violate the General Agreement on Trade in Services (GATS). The initial Panel found that the measures introduced for non-cooperative jurisdictions by Argentina, were inconsistent with the most-favored-nation obligation because they "accord less favorable treatment to services and services suppliers of non-cooperative countries in comparison to those from cooperative countries" (WTO, 2016), this was in addition to a number of other violations found. The Appellate body overturned this finding. Questions were also raised regarding the prudential carve-out provided by GATS Annex on Financial Services and the United States argued that the exception could preserve the discretion of national authorities to protect the financial system. It remains to be seen whether or not future defensive tax measures could give rise to similar claims of discrimination or fall under the GATS prudential carve-out. This decision does, however, indicate that taxation measures will have increasing trade implications.

Regarding preferential regimes, by 2006, the OECD Committee considered that the work "had fully achieved its initial aims and that the mandate given by the Council ... [had] therefor been met" (OECD, 2006). The future work would, therefore, focus on monitoring any continuing and newly introduced preferential tax regimes identified by member countries (OECD, 2006). Since the finalization of the BEPS Action Plan reports, the work on preferential regimes began to focus on those providing "benefits to geographically mobile business income ... which present a risk of BEPS activity" (OECD, 2019). One more key factor was also included in order to assess whether the regime may be harmful, whether "the regime encourages operations or arrangements that are purely tax-driven and involve no substantial activities" (OECD, 2019). In addition, the FHTP now reviews regimes adopted by members of the Inclusive Framework on BEPS. The work has, over time, resulted in the abolishment and acceptance of specific regimes submitted by countries.

In 2021, the IMF published its report on Corporate Income Taxes Under Pressure, which provides an evaluation of the need for reform and potential solutions. In this publication, they aptly analyze whether tax competition has become less harmful and determined that "tax competition has intensified in the last decades, despite international efforts to contain it" (De Mooij, Klemm & Perry, 2021). "Following a relatively flat trend from 2007 to 2012, statutory corporate income tax rates continued to decline in advanced and developing economies, reaching 22.3 and 24 percent, on average," and "the level of the headline corporate income tax rate—no matter how low—thus far remains unconstrained by these initiatives" (De Mooij, Klemm & Perry, 2021). Moreover, without further reforms to international corporate income taxes, it is unlikely that tax competition will stop or become less harmful (De Mooij, Klemm & Perry, 2021). Where preferential tax regimes continue to be provided, no matter how modest they may be, they will still trigger "strategic action" by other countries and affect the investment location decision (De Mooij, Klemm & Perry, 2021). This should signal to countries and international organizations alike that even where preferential regimes are categorized as not harmful, they will still give rise to tax competition that could potentially still have harmful consequences.

The main challenge in the last few years is that "tax competition ... has not been thus far at the fore of international initiatives" (De Mooij, Klemm & Perry, 2021). Although Action 5 sought to address harmful preferential tax regimes, this effort has only been in so far as they facilitate tax avoidance. Overall, the BEPS Project itself has been an initiative to address different aspects of tax policies and the practices of MNEs that give rise to tax avoidance, in particular. In recent months, however, countries that are part of the Inclusive Framework on BEPS have re-engaged in a consultation that is now determined to address one of the most important features of competition for corporate income taxes—low or no tax effective tax rates. The OECD Inclusive Framework Pillar Two blueprint of the proposal to address the Tax Challenges Arising from Digitalization includes the global minimum tax proposal intended to address the remaining BEPS challenges. While countries continue to engage in negotiations regarding the most ideal global minimum effective tax rate, a new proposal from the United States has challenged the current agenda. In April 2021, the Biden administration published the Made in America Tax Plan, intended to, amongst other things, strengthen the global minimum tax for U.S. multinationals (U.S. Department of the Treasury, 2021). The stated objective is:

> "Ending the race to the bottom around the world. Countries too often compete for multinationals' business by reducing corporate tax rates which makes it difficult for the United States and other countries to meet revenue needs. The President's plan provides a strong incentive for nations to join a global agreement that implements minimum tax rules worldwide through the denial of US deduction on related party payments to foreign corporations residing in a regime that has not implemented a strong minimum tax. This aspect of the plan is designed to help level the playing field between foreign and US companies." (U.S. Department of the Treasury, 2021)

The United States will, in order to ensure that large profitable MNEs pay a baseline amount of taxes, "impose a minimum tax on firms with large discrepancies between income reported to shareholders and that reported to the IRS" (U.S. Department of the Treasury, 2021). Recognizing that countries "will not stop the race to the bottom unless enough large economies adopt a minimum tax on foreign earnings," to "bring nations to the bargaining table," the United States will introduce SHIELD (Stopping Harmful Inversions and Ending Low-tax Developments) (US Department of the Treasury, 2021). It will deny U.S. tax deductions for MNEs subject to a low effective tax rate defined by reference to a multilateral agreement, or if this has not been arrived at, 21% (U.S. Department of the Treasury, 2021). In addition, where countries agree to adopt Pillar Two, the United States would switch off the SHIELD regime for entities resident in those jurisdictions This measure has led to a significant focus on a new floor for tax competition and the potential for consensus at the Inclusive Framework:

> "If current international corporate income tax arrangements were to be reformed, for example by introducing a (preferably internationally coordinated) minimum tax or multilateral destination-based tax, then tax competition would be alleviated or even eliminated." (De Mooij, Klemm & Perry, 2021)

Indeed, a minimum tax could establish a floor that would, at a minimum, ensure that the race to the bottom would become a race to the minimum. However, whether or not this initiative by the United States would be the answer to consensus, needs to be analyzed and that is beyond the ambit of this chapter. Concerns have already been expressed about the threshold of EUR 750 million for qualifying MNEs and whether these reforms as well as Pillar One and Two "are meant to support the super structure of developed countries" (Tandon, 2021).

§4.05 SOME PROPOSED SOLUTIONS

In reality, despite the shift in perspectives and the growing acceptance of a minimum tax in limited circumstances, lasting solutions must be supported by reform in the behavior of governments and taxpayers through cooperation (Owens, 2013). A floor for tax competition certainly provides a renewed understanding of the unacceptable aspects but will require genuine engagement in identifying the acceptable aspects and limiting the potential for new mechanisms to attract new mobile factors either by way of emerging golden passports or even remote worker exemption regimes.

The nature of tax competition, particularly the tools it involves and the reasons behind it, will continue to evolve and our understanding of it must follow. The ability to facilitate free trade and movement of capital and labor remains desirable, however, the main conflict is aiding or subsidizing free movement from a tax perspective which could have harsh consequences for national welfare (Wilkie, 2016). Moreover, as digitalization continues to change the business models available to legal entities and individuals alike, increasing complexity should be expected and there will be, inevitably, implications for the willingness of countries to find solutions based on consensus. Indeed, the adoption of digital service taxes by a number of countries has demonstrated a willingness to go against the grain, particularly for developing countries where current solutions may not effectively respond to their contexts. As mentioned above, these actions which qualify as defensive tax measures, also contribute to the framework of tax competition and should raise the alarm that unilateralism remains an option where consensus is not an inclusive process.

Overall, the current response to the harmful aspects of tax competition has not been enough to end or stop it altogether mainly due to the spillover effects that the acceptable competitive policies ultimately give rise to in other countries. A minimum tax has the greatest potential to limit tax competition, harmful or not. Even where tax competition for corporate income tax bases is limited, there remains the potential that other aspects of taxation will then be utilized for similar policy objectives. Perhaps it is time to redefine the underlying objectives or intended outcomes of tax policy in all its forms to simplicity, certainty, and fairness—objectives that are more aligned to national welfare from a broader perspective. By doing so, what could be viewed as a competitive tax system may shift away from minimizing rates to establishing more navigable systems for both domestic and foreign investors. In addition, with the impending adoption of minimum taxes worldwide, it is imperative that whatever approach is taken, it should be inclusive, simple, and fair.

Bibliography

Ates, Leylah, Moran Harari & Markus Meinzer, *Chapter 10: Negative Spillovers in International Corporate Taxation and the European Union*, in ed. Irma Mosquera Valderrama, Dries Lesage & Wouter Lips, *Taxation, International Cooperation and the 2030 Sustainable Development Agenda*, United Nations University Series on Regionalism, 2021, Vol. 19.

Avi-Yonah, Reuven & Kimberly Clausing, *Towards a 21st Century International Tax Regime*, Tax Notes International, August 2019, 839-849.

Clausing, Kimberly, *Does Tax Drive the Headquarters Locations of the World's Biggest Companies*, UNCTAD Transnational Corporations Journal, 2018, 25(2), 37-65.

Clausing, Kimberly, *Five Lessons on Profit Shifting from the US Country by Country Data*, Tax Notes Federal, November 2020a., 169(6), 925-940.

Clausing, Kimberly, *The Nature and Practice of Capital Tax Competition*, in ed. Peter Dietsch & Thomas Rixen, *Global Tax Governance*, ECPR Press, 2016.

Clausing, Kimberly, *Taxing Multinational Companies in the 21st Century*, in ed. Jay Shambaugh & Ryan Nunn, *Tackling the Tax Code: Efficient and Equitable Ways to Raise* Revenue, The Hamilton Project & Brookings Edu, 28 January 2020b, 237-283.

Clausing, Kimberly, Emmanuel Saez & Gabriel Zucman, *Ending Corporate Tax Avoidance and Tax Competition: A Plan to Collect the Tax Deficit of Multinationals*, UCLA School of Law, Law & Economics Papers No. 20-12, 2020.

Collin, Matthew, *Did the EU's Attempt to Name and Shame Tax Havens into Behaving Better Work?* Brookings, June 25, 2020. Accessed on April 30, 2021, available at: https://www.brookings.edu/blog/up-front/2020/06/25/did-the-eus-attempt-to-name-and-shame-tax-havens-into-behaving-better-work/.

De Mooij, Ruud A., Alexander D. Klemm & Victoria J. Perry, *Corporate Income Taxes under Pressure: Why Reform Is Needed and How it Could Be Designed*, IMF, 2021, available at: https://www.elibrary.imf.org/view/books/071/28329-9781513511771-en/ch006.xml.

Devereux, Michael P. & Simon Loretz, *What Do We Know about Corporate Tax Competition*, National Tax Journal, September 2013, 66(3), 745-774.

European Commission, *Fair Taxation: EU Updates List of Non-cooperative Tax Jurisdictions*, European Commission Press, February 18, 2020. Accessed on April 30, 2021, available at: https://ec.europa.eu/commission/presscorner/detail/en/ip_20_262.

European Parliament, *EU tax haven blacklist is not catching the worst offenders*, European Parliament Press release, January 21, 2021. Accessed on April 30, 2021, available at: https://www.europarl.europa.eu/news/en/press-room/20210114IPR95631/eu-tax-haven-blacklist-is-not-catching-the-worst-offenders.

Faulhaber, Lilian V., *The Trouble with Tax Competition: From Practice to Theory*, Tax Law Review, 2018, 71(2), 311-366.

Habimana, Pie, *In Search of the Boundaries Between Harmless and Harmful Tax Competition*, Amsterdam Law Forum, 2021, 13, 31.

IMF, *Spillovers in International Corporate Taxation*, IMF, 2014.

Littlewood, Michael, *Tax Competition: Harmful to Whom?*, Michigan Journal of International Law, 2001, 26(1).

Morris, Andrew P. & Lotta Moberg, *Cartelizing Taxes: Understanding the OECD's Campaign Against Harmful Tax Competition*, Columbia Journal of Tax Law, 2012, 4.

OECD/G20 Base Erosion and Profit Shifting Project, *Action 5: Final Report—Countering Harmful Tax Practices More Effectively, Taking into Account Transparency and Substance*, OECD, 2015.

OECD, *Harmful Tax Competition—An Emerging Global Issue*, OECD, 1998.

OECD, *Harmful Tax Practices—2018 Progress Report on Preferential Regimes: Inclusive Framework on BEPS—Action 5*, OECD, 2019.

OECD, *The OECD's Project on Harmful Tax Practices: 2006 Update on Progress in Member Countries*, OECD, 2006.

OECD, *Towards Global Tax Co-operation: Report to the 2000 Ministerial Council Meeting and Recommendations by the Committee on Fiscal Affairs*, OECD, 2000.

OECD, *Tax Challenges Arising from Digitalisation: Report on Pillar Two Blueprint: Inclusive Framework on BEPS, OECD/G20 Base Erosion and Profit Shifting Project*, OCDE, 2020.

Owens, Jeffrey, *The David H. Tillinghast Lecture Tax Competition: To Welcome or Not*, Tax Law Review, 2012, 65(2), 173-198.

Owens, Jeffrey, *The Taxation of Multinational Enterprises: An Elusive Balance*, Bulletin for International Taxation, 2013, 67(8).

Piantavigna, Paolo, *Tax Competition and Tax Coordination in Aggressive Tax Planning: A False Dichotomy*, World Tax Journal, November 2017, 9(4).

Tandon, Suranjali, *Why the US Treasury's Call for a Global Minimum Tax Is Unfair to Developing Economies*, The Indian Express, April 19, 2021. Accessed on May 11, 2021, available at: https://indianexpress.com/article/opinion/columns/why-the-us-treasurys-call-for-a-global-minimum-tax-is-unfair-to-developing-economies-7279387/.

US Department of the Treasury, *The Made in America Tax Plan*, US Department of the Treasury, April 2021, available at: https://home.treasury.gov/system/files/136/MadeInAmericaTaxPlan_Report.pdf.

Wilkie, Scott, *Aiding and/or Abetting: Tax Competition in the Light of State Aid*, University of Calgary, School of Public Policy, April 29, 2016.

WTO, *DS453: Argentina—Measures Relating to Trade in Goods and Services*, WTO Dispute Settlement, May 9, 2016, available at: https://www.wto.org/english/tratop_e/dispu_e/cases_e/ds453_e.htm.

CHAPTER 5

International Organizations and Tax Cooperation: Context and Points of View

Lyne Latulippe, Brigitte Alepin & Louise Otis

This chapter outlines the involvement of international organizations (IO), namely the Organization for Economic Co-Operation and Development (OECD), the International Monetary Fund (IMF), the United Nations (UN) and the World Bank (WB) at the international and domestic level in some countries over time concerning tax policymaking. It sets out the complementarity and the required coordination and cooperation between these IO to improve tax regimes. In a second part, this chapter relates the point of view expressed by a tax leader from each of these organizations concerning international cooperation and multilateralism in taxation.

§5.01 INTRODUCTION

The involvement of the Organisation for Economic Cooperation and Development (OECD), the United Nations (UN), the International Monetary Fund (IMF) and the World Bank (WB) in the tax policy area led to important tax reforms and essential tax coordination over the past century. The work of international organizations (IO) in some instances has been scrutinized and sometimes criticized over the years. Nevertheless, projects and processes of these organizations evolved, among other things, to be in line with their commitment towards the Millennium Development Goals (MDGs) and the Sustainable Development Goals (SDGs) more recently. Furthermore, recently required adjustments to tax policy, and more particularly international tax policy, would have been impossible without the work and commitment of IO.

The aim in the first part of this chapter is to provide some context about the involvement of IO with regard to tax policy and highlight their role and its evolution in this domain. The second section presents the current positions regarding tax policy from four tax leaders at the OECD, UN, WB and the IMF and their views about the challenges and the future of international tax policy as expressed at the World Tax Summit – TaxCOOP2020. The convergence among the objectives of these IO is noticeable and by building upon the coordination of their projects and working with complementary approaches, their involvement remains essential to continue to improve tax policy to face global challenges such as climate changes, inequality, and protecting the tax base and therefore states' resources and capacity. Also noteworthy is the fact that the speeches of these leaders took place not only in October 2020 at a tumultuous moment in the middle of the pandemic but also in the middle of very important work in progress to reform the international tax system that has continued to evolve since then.

§5.02 CONTEXT

[A] The Involvement of IOs in Tax Policy, Tax Reform and Tax Administration

IO have a long history of being involved with tax policy in many countries. Particularly, the mandate of the OECD, the WB, the UN and the IMF led these organizations to participate at different levels and through a variety of actions in domestic and international tax policy over the past century. Their work includes support, advice, data, research, assistance, evaluation and review. They perform these activities in coordinated, distinct or complementary projects, however, towards common goals of facilitating the administration and collection of taxes to secure economic and social development in different countries in a global market economy, achieve sustainable economic growth and reduce poverty.

The involvement of these international institutions in economic reform generally leads them to play a key role in taxation, since 'tax reform projects formed part of [a post-war] program from the beginning'. (Stewart, 2003, 154). The UN provided overall context and its agencies have participated in tax reform since the 1950s. Experts, sometimes in conjunction with the UN or the WB projects, led the work in the field and '[s]ince the 1980s, the WB has increased its technical assistance and policy advice on taxation in response to increased request from developing countries' in particular in relation to tax administrative reform (Stewart 2003, 160).

As for the IMF, given its role in global economic governance, advising Member States about tax reform has always been part of its mandate. More particularly, the institutions have provided support to borrowing member countries to implement reforms that secured revenues and sound public finance.

Also, the Committee on Fiscal Affairs of the OECD, replacing the Fiscal Committee in 1971, has a mandate to investigate the use of taxation to promote improved allocation and use of economic resources, both domestically and internationally and for proposing ways of increasing the effectiveness of taxation as a policy instrument for achieving governmental objectives (CFA, 1971).

The mandate of IOs is complementary and sometimes overlaps; coordination and collaboration among these organizations are essential to reach an optimal outcome.

[B] Fostering Coordination of the International Tax System

More specifically, international tax policy and coordination is a field in which the work of IO generated norms and standards over the years. The case of the bilateral tax treaty (BTT) network is illustrative of this involvement and its impact.

Acknowledging the autonomy and sovereignty of each state and government, these organizations are crucial in fostering the required cooperation among countries to ensure an adequate and efficient international tax system. As early as the beginning of the 20th century, the League of Nations identified a growing problem of double taxation and was eager to solve it to encourage economic recovery (Kolm, 2005). The beginning of the 20th century was a period of rapid industrial growth and internationalization of trade and following World War I, countries resorted to taxation to finance expenses. At this time, the League of Nations was to work on solving two different but connected problems, double taxation and tax avoidance and evasion.

The technical experts proposed models for a bilateral tax convention recommending the creation of a network of bilateral agreements that could eventually form the basis of a single multilateral convention eventually (Avery Jones, 1999; McIntyre, 2003). In 1928, the League of Nations published the first model treaty and developed and developing countries reached an agreement on the Mexico Draft several years later and the London draft in 1946. The London draft, which continued to generally attribute taxing rights to the residence country and limit the rights of the source country (McIntyre, 2003) has put in place the standards that have dominated since then.

The UN founded the Fiscal Committee in 1947 to continue the work of the League of Nations, including the tax treaty model with the objective to reconcile the interest of developed and developing countries and to find a common ground between the residence-principle and the source-principle. This committee was dissolved in 1954 (Kolm, 2005) and the OEEC and then the OECD took up this role and became the leader in this matter (McIntyre, 2003; Aubrey, 1967). The Fiscal Committee took the responsibility for tax policy with a clear mandate to facilitate the expansion of BTT networks between member countries. The first OECD model published in 1958 relied heavily on choices made by the League of Nations (Easson, 2000).

The work of the UN on BTT stopped because of problems of the East-West Cold War, the North-South divide and the fledgling UN's financial problems (Vann, 1991, 103). The UN resumed its work on the issue of double taxation in 1967 and established the United Nations Group of Experts on Tax Treaties between Developed and Developing Countries (UN Group) in order to look into this issue (Surrey, 1978). This Ad Hoc group based its analysis and discussion on the OECD model to see what changes could be made in order to better represent the interests of developing countries and published its BTT model in 1979. The UN group has produced much information on the particular topic of treaties between developed and developing countries (reports, guidelines and so on) at that time.

The international tax system is made up of a network of more than 3,000 bilateral tax treaties based on the OECD model. In the early 2010s, when it became clear that reform was needed to better take into account the globalization and digitization of the economy, the OECD has taken the lead in analysing the gaps and problems through the Base Erosion and Profit Shifting (BEPS) project and proposing solutions.

[C] SDGs and Taxation: Working Towards Common Goals

While the four IO have their own objectives that centre on increasing well-being, reduce poverty and provide better social and economic conditions around the world, they all support and work towards the implementation of SDGs (previously MDGs). In 2000, UN members adopted the MDGs to inspire and drive progress for the next fifteen years. The MDGs helped focus projects with real positive outcomes improving the life situation of many citizens in a variety of countries, and SDGs were adopted in 2015 to continue this endeavour. The commitment of IO to the same 'universal goals that meet the urgent environmental, political and economic challenges facing our world' (SDG) facilitates the coordination and collaboration to make the world better.

Taxation allows to raise funds, develop programs and decide on expenses that are in line with SDGs. IO collaborate with countries and with each other to support domestic resource mobilization in all countries. Each country should be able to design a tax policy that concurs to achieving these goals domestically. Furthermore, these organizations raise awareness about the impact of domestic policy decisions on reaching these goals globally.

[D] Cooperation Is Key

IO offer support to their members and beyond and facilitate cooperation among these member countries. The UN, WB and IMF membership is broad with around 190 countries. The OECD's membership now comprises thirty-eight members. While it has been working with non-member countries since the 1960s, from the late 1980s and more particularly in the 1990s, the OECD intensified its relationship with many non-OECD countries, generally or more specifically concerning tax policies and tax treaties. Launched in 2016, the G20/Inclusive Framework is the latest tax-related outreach initiative of the OECD to provide a forum for the participation of interested countries and jurisdictions, including developing economies in the elaboration of international tax standards.

To ensure proper responses to issues and challenges, a coordinated effort among IO is a necessary condition. A continual effort to coordinate international tax policy for example ensures the system does not allow for avoidance, evasion and the erosion of the tax base for all countries. It remains also essential to pursue the work and the collaboration on domestic tax policy and administration to facilitate the implementation of rules at the domestic level. To that end, the launching of the Platform for Collaboration on Tax (PCT), a joint initiative of the IMF, Organization for Economic Co-operation and Development (OECD), UN, and the WB Group is noteworthy.

In the past years, IO innovated with regard to cooperation and initiative such as the inclusive framework of the OECD and the PCT are interesting steps that improve the process to design required global solutions. A consensus among more than 130 countries on the principles for an international reform would have been highly unlikely without such a renewed cooperation.

Since 2015, we have had the great pleasure and opportunity at TaxCOOP to work with these IO more or less closely throughout the years and we have witnessed up-close their hard work and dedication to improving the tax systems. These organizations share the same ambitious goals of addressing the challenges that globalization and digitalization have brought to the tax system in every country and ensuring tax policy supports the advancement of SDGs and reduce inequality. It is important to mention that, while they may hold different opinions and expertise and may challenge each other, individuals involved in tax matters in each of these organisations interact and cooperate to advance workable solutions that can be beneficial to all. Cooperation among people holding different perspectives and openness towards diverging opinions are essential ingredients to develop solutions to global problems and the four large IO each plays an essential role in fostering global cooperation.

§5.03 POINTS OF VIEW FROM THE TAX LEADERS IN THE IO[1]

[A] Point of View: Pascal Saint-Amans – Director of the OECD Center for Tax Policy and Administration

Should we move to more multilateralism or less multilateralism in the international tax system? The answer I would like to provide, given where I come from, given my responsibilities, is pretty obvious: more multilateralism. However, what is interesting is that we come from a time where international tax has almost been exclusively bilateral. It's only recently, around 10–15 years ago, that multilateralism has become significant in the development of the international tax system.

The history of international tax is that it started with tax treaties and there was a model that operated by the League of Nations. This has been the box within which all the players; tax administrations, tax policy-makers and taxpayers have been playing within. And it's only recently that we have started thinking out of the box, and out of the box means that we have seen collectively, I think, that there was a need for multilateral action to regulate, from a tax perspective, globalization. The past 12 to 15 years has been about introducing a circle of tax regulation of globalization. Some would say that countries are getting more protectionist, are getting more concerned about their own sovereignty, and that this move towards more multilateralism in the tax system, could be in contradiction with this more recent move towards unilateralism

1. The following section is based on the transcript from speeches of these four experts, presented at the World Tax Summit – TaxCOOP2020 on 15 October 2020, https://taxcoop.org/en/taxcoop2020-archives/.

and more centric policies. But actually, and that's the tax paradox there, tax sovereignty, not to be only nominal, but to be real, requires tax cooperation and tax cooperation in the globalized environment can only be carried out through multilateralism.

This explains the change of paradigm for the past fifteen years, which started with enhancing tax cooperation in the field of exchanging information, meaning the end of bank secrecy. In 2008-2009, the G20 emerged at the leader's level and decided to take action. The shortcut for the political speech there was 'let's tackle tax havens', tax havens being bank secrecy jurisdictions. Then, we've moved to address the tax avoidance of multinational companies, which was the BEPS project for BEPS. And we're now moving to the next phase, which is trying to find the right regulation, the right sharing of the taxing rights between the emerging economies, developing countries, but also between developed countries, and that has been about addressing the tax challenges of the digitalization of the economy. In doing so and implementing the BEPS project, countries realize that they really needed to go a step further. The extra mile is addressing tax competition, which for a long time has been considered as very beneficial and it was only the harmful tax competition, the harmful tax practices, which were considered as being negative. There has been a shift there, initiated by the United States. Quite paradoxically or surprisingly, the US Senate, held by the Republicans, who were very much in favour of tax competition, decided to position the United States pretty well in the tax competition field by cutting the rate to 21% while they also broaden the base and put a floor to the race to the bottom: the global intangible low-taxed income (GILTI) provision for global intangible low-income tax. That has triggered a broad move by many countries, which said, well, we want to benefit from the same type of limit by putting an end to the race to the bottom.

So, if you look at the overall picture, what do we have? We have decades of bilateralism through tax treaties with old rules, based on the arm's-length principle to decide how companies would price internal transactions with limited tax cooperation. Attempts to reform the system with the G7 and the OECD in the 1990s were not very successful, and changes really comes to fruition in the aftermath of the global financial crisis, 2008–2009, until now. In this new phase, we have the end of bank secrecy, tax cooperation, then some form of regulation of the aggressive tax planning of multinational companies, and now the ultimate step, which is still in the making with the two-pillar approach on addressing the tax challenges of the digitalization of the economy.

Pillar 1, determining a new nexus, which is going beyond the initial definition of the permanent establishment and a new rule to reallocate profits, especially where there is a rent, an excess return. The detailed blueprint would be quite fast to turn into a consensus-based solution. We finally have the pillar 2, the global minimum tax, the Globe proposal, which is a kind of multilateralizing GILTI, which also has not yet been fully agreed [*see* 1 July Statement]. What is needed is a political agreement on the right, on the carve-out, on the subject to tax rules for developing countries and finding the balance between source and residence? But we are almost there.

What's next? There is appetite, still, by all countries to move together with the one hundred and thirty-seven countries of the global forum.[2] Will this be enough? We hope so. There may be some hiccups, some unilateral measures taken here and there, but I think we are moving towards an agreement in 2021 because the fundamentals are there. And the COVID crisis makes it even more necessary that we reach an agreement on taxing the digital companies and the digitalization of the economy, adapting the rules to allow that countries would tax their fair share of profit and, on the other hand, putting [an end] to the race to the bottom. When the wages have been nationalized by many governments, the least governments can expect is that companies, which have benefited from furlough, 'chômage partiel' and others, would not locate in the future their profits in zero-tax jurisdictions.

The last word is about the overall context, the background. The background is domestic resource mobilization, which is a universal principle, agreed by all the countries in the UN and which puts the emphasis on the need for developing countries, for emerging economies to better mobilize their domestic resources. That's where we are so proud to work with the UN, with the IMF, with the WB, through the PCT to make sure we mobilize the international resources to support the domestic resources.

[B] Point of View: Vitor Gaspar – Director of the Fiscal Affairs Department of the IMF

The story of international tax cooperation started about a hundred years ago in the context of the League of Nations, and at that point in time, the main goal, the dominant goal was to facilitate international financial and commercial relations. Already at that time, there was potential for tax competition and currently, there is much more potential for tax competition given the importance of globalization and the rise of multinational enterprises. In particular, the ability of multinational enterprises to shift profits towards lower tax jurisdiction has intensified with digitalization, but also with the increased importance of intangibles. International taxation originally focused on reducing or eliminating double taxation. Now, there is an increased emphasis on avoiding profit shifting. In that context, there was a change in emphasis, and at this point in time, we want to avoid double non-taxation, and that's the emphasis of the G20, OECD, BEPS initiative, and it represents very important progress, and it has achieved a lot in addressing profit shifting.

Cooperation in tax is intrinsically difficult. The more countries manage to cooperate and coordinate their tax policy, the stronger the incentive for other countries to defect on the agreement and therefore outcompete them. Global minimum taxes offer the promise to put a floor on tax competition. We, at the IMF, discussed minimum taxes in a 2019 policy paper, along with other reform options for the international corporate tax system. Minimum taxes are now under consideration in the context of the inclusive framework, specifically in the context of its work on digitalization. The recent proposals for minimum taxes should not be confused with proposals to have a

2. The Global Forum now reunites 163 members and the Inclusive Framework has 140 members.

minimum tax rate. Instead, they are taxes aimed at compensating for under taxation in another country. They come in two forms. A minimum tax on outward investment is applied in the country of residence if the source country does not tax profits generated at a sufficient level. A minimum tax on inbound investment is the alternative and is applied if profits are shifted out of the source country and not adequately taxed when they are received. These minimum taxes potentially reduce the gains from profit shifting, and therefore are an important instrument for international tax coordination.

In general, the problems faced by advanced economies and developing countries are similar. Two aspects typically should be taken into account, especially from the viewpoint of developing countries. First, many of them are source only rather than resident countries. Very few, if any, multinationals have headquarters in developing countries. Second, many developing countries depend strongly on the export of natural resources to capture corporate income taxation at source and inbound investment. Minimum tax can allow these countries to safeguard this tax base related to foreign multinationals, even where they have limited capacity to enforce complicated transfer price regulations. In the ongoing discussion about how to allocate taxing rights between resident and source countries, it will be important for the sake of developing countries to give high priority to those rules that ensure minimum taxation at source. There are many other complications and interesting issues to address. However, I want to end on an optimistic note. While globalization and digitalization have created tremendous challenges for the existing international tax system, this can be overcome with a combination of global cooperation and unilateral policy action. I, therefore, welcome very much events like TaxCOOP2020 that contribute to an international exchange of ideas and experiences.

[C] Point of View: Navid Hanif – Director of Financing for Sustainable Development Office at the UN Department of Economic and Social Affairs

The UN stands for a fair and transparent international tax system, a system that takes into account the interests of all stakeholders and countries and is especially focused on sustainable development of least developed countries and others in special situations. We particularly see as key stakeholders in tax systems, the wider citizenry, including those below taxing thresholds. They rightfully expect tax systems to promote sustainable development. Advancing such a tax system is not for us a question of multilateral or unilateral action. Rather, it is about an effective, multilayered approach.

Let me illustrate this perspective in three ways, which also helps point us toward the best paths forward. Firstly, in our work, multilateral approaches inform regional, bilateral, and unilateral responses and vice versa. An example is the work of the UN Committee on International Cooperation in Tax Matters. In one of its major focus areas, this representative group of experts takes a multilateral approach to develop guidance on international tax treaties and on domestic tax law. The last point is important because treaties only preserve taxing rights that already exist in domestic law. They do not create new taxing rights. The UN Model Double Taxation Convention helps inform bilateral treaty negotiations, but it also is informed by them. The 2017 update to the UN Model drew upon developing country practice in seeking a special provision on taxing fees for technical services, more specifically, Article 12(a). It systematized discussion on such provisions, including pros and cons, and provided drafting aimed to reduce the presence of differently worded provisions that benefit taxpayers and administrators. Important current and emerging committee guidance on issues, such as carbon taxation and extractive industry taxation, also represent examples of the value of multilateral discussion of domestic and bilateral tax matters.

Second, multilateral effort needs to be built on sound foundations. Effective multilateral approaches depend on a certain degree of agreement, on what the key issues are and how to deal with them fairly. It can take some time to establish this minimum level of agreement. The convening power of the UN, along with other bodies such as the OECD and the IMF, can certainly facilitate this. For instance, agreeing on what the issues are before you agree to negotiate a solution, which means negotiating about negotiations. The world faces a situation now where ways of doing business have changed so that models fundamentally basing taxation upon specific physical connections over a period of time are no longer acceptable to many countries and the wider citizenry. From the multilateral perspective, the challenge is how to build a system responsive and proactive to further changes in how business is done, including, the cause of the changing expectations of consumers. We need to do this at a time of heightened urgency to mobilize resources for COVID-19 response and a sustained recovery, as well as accelerating digitalization of the economy. The OECD is sensibly looking at ways of keeping multilateral agreements up with the times. Any such mechanisms need to be fair between countries in different positions and between different stakeholders in tax systems, with accountability, at the domestic as well as international levels. They also need to be practical. Many developing countries are the places where businesses want to be. The growth opportunities are the greatest. For multilateral solutions to succeed, developing countries, including the least developed ones, need to be front and centre in the key policy and administrative decisions.

Third, any successful multilateral regime, or international taxation must have an important place for withholding taxes, which one could think of as a unilateral approach. This is because such taxes, while imperfect, have first proven to be practicability admissible. Second, they can pre-emptively combat the sometimes-elaborate structures used to disappear profits. Third, they apply it with a rolling basis to the benefit of a country's cash flow. Finally, they give some certainty to both taxpayers and administrators. Obviously, some of these benefits to governments can be negative for businesses. Once we have accepted the legitimacy and appropriateness of withholding taxes, we can work to improve them, including by better functioning and better adapted to more digitalized and contract free ways of doing business. The UN has long advocated for moderate and easily administered withholding taxes and the gains for these, discussed at a multilateral level, implemented domestically, and confirmed by treaty is stronger than ever.

[D] Point of View: Marcello Estevão – Global Director of the WB Group's Macroeconomics, Trade and Investment Global Practice (MTI)

In my view, it is important from the outset to recall the challenge of international taxation as part of a broader set of challenges facing sustainable development and inclusive growth around the world. Changes in the nature of economies, in the structure of companies, in the ways of doing business, in technology, in the composition of human societies, all contribute to an increasingly complex world. This is clear and well known; equally evident is that as globalization has made countries increasingly interdependent, as it has brought many gains, it has also had serious failings, particularly in exacerbating inequality in some places. These shortcomings have contributed to putting the global political and economic system under great stress. So effective global cooperation to solve our current challenges is the only way forward to alleviating the stress.

It is only by working together that we can revive our societies, economies, and our planet. International taxation represents one of the most important areas through which this global cooperation must be realized. If, on one hand, the scale of the challenges involved in international tax competition is arguably greater and more pressing than ever before, I believe the good news is that the scale of the challenge is matched by a much greater readiness and willingness to cooperate to solve our current issues. We have achieved some important results already, from avoiding double taxation to mutual assistance to collect taxes or recover assets, through the exchange of information and joint investigations. But the journey is long, and pressing challenges remain, including, notably, the need to find common solutions for the modernization and adaptation of the tax system to our increasingly digitalizing world.

Now, it is true that we need an efficient international tax cooperation system, there is no magic recipe for efficient cooperation. In my experience, working in both the public and the private sector, cooperation is not always smooth, progress is not always linear, nor is success always guaranteed. What we have is our key principles, our basic ingredients, that you must adhere to and encourage one another to do. This includes, first, a foundation of basic respect and appreciation of the needs and constraints that we face. Second, a common identification of the broad problems we face. Third, put in place an inclusive process that can build trust among all relevant stakeholders. Fourth, cultivating a culture of problem-solving and innovative solutions, including drawing on ideas developed within academia, IO, and civil society at large that can be put in action, of course. And fifth, bring a willingness to compromise, which means a single individual party must give due consideration to the interests and needs of the audience.

In short, cooperation is hard work, the Platform of Collaboration on Tax (PCT) is a very good example of cooperation among the four institutions. Since its inception in 2016, with the secretariat housed in my department, the PCT has consolidated the collaboration among the WB, the IMF, the OECD, and the UN in support of stronger tax systems in developing and emerging economies. This collaboration takes different forms, such as a consensus captured in toolkits and practical advice to low-capacity countries, for example, on the design and undertaking of successful negotiations on the form of knowledge sharing. The PCT website also includes an online-integrated platform with information on tax-related projects pursued by the four partners, which also contributes to better collaboration and contribution at the country level.

Now, it is not easy to ensure the international tax rules are appropriate for both developing and developed countries in the years to come. Of course, it is easy to say that you need to compromise to find simple solutions and to ensure that these solutions can be operationalized. One of the main challenges that I see currently for developing countries is the capacity to effectively implement tax rules, and here it is our responsibility (IO) to support them, to enhance their capacity in this area. On international taxation, we have already made important progress by putting together processes through which we are actively practising the key principles. For example, in the aftermath of the 2008 global financial crisis, the BEPS, the so-called BEPS initiative, has emerged and has provided tangible results. From the leadership role of the OECD and the G20 in the inception of the BEPS Project in 2013, collaboration with governments worldwide and with IO including the IMF, the UN, and the WB, has helped ensure that the inclusive framework, which initially came to fruition in Kyoto, Japan, has today over 135 countries and jurisdictions as members and fourteen active observer organizations, including the WB. In response to the enhanced priority for domestic revenue mobilization in the finance for development agenda underpinned by the 2015 Addis Ababa Action Agenda, the IMF, the UN, the WB, and other international partners have stepped up cooperation on tax matters, including the PCT. Through the inclusive framework to the PCT, through other forms of collaboration and our own capacity-building efforts, we can support developing countries, improve their capacity to effectively implement the new tax reforms that are urgently needed to address existing gaps. Through this type of collaboration support, we can help all our member countries reach a consensus on problems, such as how to tax the digital economy more effectively and fairly. Here, I'm proud to say that the WB plays its role, we have been contributing to thought leadership on international taxation. We are supporting over fifty countries in their efforts to implement international tax standards and strengthen their knowledge and capacity to deal with international tax issues. Finally, the WB partner with the four IO and others to push forward the process of compromise and cooperation. Despite the scale of challenges, I'm therefore confident that with hard work and the right processes and ingredients in place, tax coordination and collaboration will win over harmful tax competition.

Bibliography

Aubrey, Henry G. 1967. Atlantic Economic Cooperation: The Case of the OECD. New York: Praeger.

Avery Jones, John F. 1999. Are Tax Treaties Necessary? Tax Law Review 53: 1-38.

CFA. 1971. Summary Record of the 1st Session. CFA meetings 19 May 1971 (CFA/M(71)1).

Easson, Alex J. 1991. International Tax Reform and the Inter-Nation Allocation of Tax Revenue. New Zealand: Victoria University Press.

Kolm, Evelyn. 2005. The Emerging System of Double Taxation Agreements in the Late 19th and 20th Century. Development & Finance 2005(2).

McIntyre, Micheal J. 2003. Developing Countries and International Cooperation on Income Tax Matters: An Historical Review. Detroit, Michigan USA: Wayne State University Law School.

SDG. https://www1.undp.org/content/oslo-governance-centre/en/home/sustainable-development-goals/background.html.

Stewart, Miranda. Global Trajectories of Tax Reform: The Discourse of Tax Reform in Developing and Transition Countries. Harvard International Law Journal 44 (2003): 139.

Surrey, Stanley. 1978. United Nations Group of Experts and the Guidelines for Tax Treaties Between Developed and Developing Countries. Harvard International Law Journal 19(1): 1-66.

Vann, Richard. 1991. A Model Tax Treaty for the Asian-Pacific Region? (Part I). Bulletin – International Bureau of Fiscal Documentation 45: 99-111.

CHAPTER 6

Multilateralism or Unilateralism: How Should Countries Tax Multinationals?

Brian J. Arnold & Gabriella Sobodker

Digitalization, which has led to Scale without Mass, heavier reliance on intangible assets and technology, has revolutionized business models. This chapter looks at the impacts of globalization on international tax policy and provides an overview of policy responses to the tax challenges arising from the digitalization of the economy. Recent developments in international tax policy are discussed, as manifested in the form of unilateral, bilateral, and multilateral measures, to examine how these policies interact (or fail to interact) with one another. The first part of the chapter offers a brief overview of the measures proposed by the OECD, the United Nations, and governments around the globe to modernize the international tax system and adapt to current business practices. The second part examines the OECD's two-pillar proposal, focusing on the rules and parameters of Pillar Two and the main drawbacks of these proposals. The chapter concludes by drawing parallels between the different policy choices.

§6.01 INTRODUCTION[1]

The tax challenges arising from globalization and the digital economy have been at the forefront of international tax policy discussions for many years. In response to

1. As discussed by Carmel Peters, Policy Manager at Inland Revenue, New Zealand, Liselott Kana, Head of the Department of International Taxation of Internal Revenue Services, Chile, and Brian Arnold, Emeritus professor of tax law and senior adviser at the Canadian Tax Foundation in a session moderated by Anjana Haines, managing editor of the International Tax Review. The panel took place on October 15, 2020—an auspicious time, as the OECD had just released its reports on the Blueprints for Pillar One and Pillar Two and the United Nations had presented a proposal for new Article 12B only a few days before.

profit-shifting opportunities and the rapid expansion of technology, countries around the world have been re-evaluating their tax systems, which have become increasingly ineffective in taxing multinational businesses. Companies, especially those in the high-technology and digital sectors, can now use the Internet to reach international markets without having a physical presence or employees in those countries. Given the global scale of technology-based companies and the dominance of a few large companies, this new business model gave rise to international tax policy challenges for many countries, which are unable to collect tax revenues from companies that derive profits from the remote selling of digital goods and services to their citizens.

This chapter describes the ways in which globalization, by completely transforming the way businesses operate, has made current international tax legislation unfit for collecting the fair share of taxes from multinational tech companies, and discusses the difficulties in adapting to a new and ever-changing business model and ensuring fairness for all taxpayers. We provide an overview of the two different ways in which this issue is being addressed by countries and international organizations, propose new solutions, and discuss what is to come.

§6.02 DIGITALIZATION AND INTERNATIONAL TAXATION

The emergence of digitalization has revolutionized many industries through the growth of intangible assets, such as software, trademarks, and patents. Intangible assets are relied on heavily by many tech companies and often represent a significant portion of the value of their assets. Given the nature of intangible assets, it has become harder to allocate profits between countries, since intangible assets are not only difficult to value properly but are easily moved from one jurisdiction to another. The heavy reliance on technology throughout the COVID-19 pandemic has accelerated the pace of digitalization, adding an urgency to the tax policy challenges that the digital economy presents as countries around the world increase their public spending to mitigate the effects of the pandemic.

Policymakers have a broad range of measures to deal with the challenges presented by the globalized digital economy, including multilateral, bilateral, and unilateral measures. The chapter focuses on multilateral and unilateral measures because many countries, while waiting for an effective multilateral response, have adopted varying unilateral solutions.[2] The possibility of the double taxation of multinational tech companies as a result of these unilateral measures spurred the OECD to lead an ambitious effort by the international community to reach an agreement on a multilateral solution.

2. The possibility of bilateral tax treaty measures to deal with cross-border income derived from digital activities is also relevant but considered to be a second-best solution. In addition, for bilateral treaty provisions to become adopted on a widespread basis, they are typically based on the provisions of the OECD Model Convention, or, less frequently, on the United Nations Model Convention; therefore, any bilateral solution would first require changes to the OECD Model Convention and then the renegotiation of existing bilateral treaties, which would take decades, or the modification of existing treaties through a multilateral treaty similar to the Multilateral Instrument (MLI).

§6.03 POLICY PROPOSALS TO ADDRESS THE TAXATION ISSUES RAISED BY DIGITALIZATION

Both the OECD and the United Nations have proposed significant changes to what many consider to be an out-of-date international tax system in order to allow countries to collect revenues from non-resident technology-based companies. In 2015, the G20/OECD Base Erosion and Profit Shifting Project (BEPS), which "aims to create a single set of consensus-based international tax rules to address BEPS," released final reports on its 15 Action Plans. The BEPS Action 1 Final Report, "Tax Challenges Arising from Digitalisation" (OECD, 2015), led to the development in 2020 by the G20/OECD Inclusive Framework on BEPS—the group formed to facilitate the taxation of income from digital activities through a two "pillars" approach: Pillar One would change the international tax rules with respect to the distribution of taxing rights and the allocation of business profits, and Pillar Two would establish a minimum global tax on the foreign source income of multinational companies. These proposals entail fundamental changes to the international tax system and require global consensus in order to move forward. The Inclusive Framework on BEPS has agreed in principle that this two-pillar approach provides a solid foundation for a multilateral agreement on a new international tax system. On July 1, 2021, the Inclusive Framework released the Statement, a document detailing the parameters of the two-pillar solution (OECD, 2021). While the Statement diverges in some respects from the Pillar One and Pillar Two Blueprints released by the Inclusive Framework in October 2020, it also builds on the Blueprints and clarifies key elements, such as percentages and thresholds. The Statement was updated on October 8, 2021, following the endorsement of 136 out of the 140 member jurisdictions of the Inclusive Framework. Four countries—Kenya, Nigeria, Pakistan and Sri Lanka—have not yet joined the agreement (OECD, 2021).

Countries are expecting to sign a multilateral convention, through which the parameters of Pillar One will be implemented, during 2022. The convention is expected to come into effect in 2023. Pillar Two should also be brought into law in 2022, to be effective in 2023. The two-pillar solution will be delivered to the G20 Leaders Summit in Rome at the end of October 2021.

Simultaneously, the United Nations Committee of Experts has been working toward modifying the provisions of the United Nations Model Convention in order to allow countries to impose tax on cross-border income derived by non-resident companies from digital activities (United Nations, 2020). New Article 12B, which will be added to the United Nations Model Convention in 2021, will allow source countries to impose withholding tax on gross payments for "automated digital services" made by their residents (or by nonresidents carrying on business through a permanent establishment in their countries) to enterprises resident in the other contracting state providing those services.[3] The rate of withholding tax is to be agreed upon between the contracting states but is expected to be in the range of 3% to 4%. The new article also

3. New Article 12B is clearly inconsistent with Pillar One. As a result, it will likely be deleted in the next update of the United Nations Model Convention or it will not be included in any treaties.

gives service providers an election to pay tax on a net-income basis in order to avoid gross-basis taxation that may be excessive.[4] If the election is made, the non-resident service provider is taxable on its profits from automated digital services determined in accordance with a formula: 30% of the enterprise's profitability ratio applied to its revenue from digital services derived from the source country computed in accordance with its financial accounts.

While waiting for a multilateral tax agreement, several countries have decided to move ahead with their own unilateral measures in order to tax income from cross-border digital activities. These measures include expanded definitions of "permanent establishment," digital services taxes (DSTs)[5] and anti-avoidance rules, such as the UK diverted profits tax. An overview (albeit a non-exhaustive one) of the measures adopted so far follows.

In 2016, India adopted a 6% equalization levy on revenues from digital advertising in India; Israel adopted virtual permanent establishment rules; and in 2017, Hungary revived a 7.5% digital advertising tax. In 2018, DST proposals were adopted in Italy, Spain, and the United Kingdom. Shortly after, in 2019, France adopted a 3% DST, and Austria adopted a 5% DST on online advertising. In 2020, Spain adopted a 3% DST on revenues from online advertising and user data transmission, while Turkey adopted a 7.5% DST on advertising services provided through digital platforms and sales and services provided by digital platforms for digital auditory and visual content. The United Kingdom also adopted a 2% DST on revenues from search engines, social media platforms, and online marketplaces (Bunn et al., 2020). Canada has announced the implementation of a DST in 2022. As of 2021, various new digital tax proposals are under consideration around the world, and countries with existing DST provisions continue to adapt and update their legislation.

Needless to say, unilateral measures, which are rapidly multiplying worldwide and come in various forms, all have the same goal: to collect a share of tax revenues from multinational tech companies, which, until now, have paid little, if any, tax to source jurisdictions.

Faced with growing unilateral actions, Angel Gurría, the OECD Secretary-General, has warned that imbalances created by the proliferation of such unilateral measures could trigger a "global trade war" which could "reduce global GDP by more than 1 percent annually" (OECD, 2020). While some countries do seem to favor a global and consensus-based solution such as the one proposed by the OECD, other countries are growing impatient as negotiations for an international multilateral agreement drag on.

Moreover, while the unilateral digital tax measures implemented so far have generally been considered to be interim measures until a multilateral agreement is

4. The net-basis election in proposed Art. 12B(3) is unique. Although some countries provide net-basis elections in their domestic law, there is no such election in either the OECD or the United Nations Model Convention. The proposed election presents many issues of interpretation and application.
5. The October, 2021 Statement on Pillar One and Pillar Two provides that the proposals are conditional on countries eliminating their DSTs and any similar measures.

reached, it remains unclear how the interaction between the two types of measures will be dealt with. These two types of policy responses, multilateral and unilateral, have created an environment of uncertainty for both the multinational tech companies concerned and governments. As globalization continues to change business models, the international tax community is facing the challenges of the digital economy for the first time and the future remains unclear: How should governments tax the digital sector? Should multilateralism or unilateralism prevail?

§6.04 ADAPTING TO NEW BUSINESS MODELS

The root of the issue is the fact that modern business practices and digitalization allow an enterprise to be significantly involved in the economic life of a country while being subject to very little tax on its business profits in that country (Peters, 2020). This new environment creates a need to tax income from cross-border digital activities fairly while recognizing the difficulty of doing so. The difficulty can be attributed to three factors: Scale without Mass, user-value creation, and intangible assets.

First, Scale without Mass means that digitalization has allowed businesses, through Internet transactions, to locate stages of their production process across various countries while accessing a greater number of customers internationally. With digitalization, tech companies can greatly increase their market share in various countries without having any physical presence in those countries; as a result, they are able to achieve operational local scale without local mass.

Second, digital firms build up their value by expanding their user base in a country and obtaining data from those users, enabling them to develop valuable data networks. Data play a major role in the business model of digital companies, and by collecting user information, they are generally able to achieve greater market penetration in source countries.

Third, most digital companies rely heavily on intangible assets such as a strong brand and the use of software and algorithms that are essential to their platforms and key to their success. Such intangible property is not only hard to value but, given its lack of physical substance, is also highly mobile and can be shifted easily from one jurisdiction to another. Moreover, the reliance on intangible property is not limited to digital firms, which makes it all the more difficult for the international tax community to ensure that tax rules keep up with technological changes.

The COVID-19 pandemic has highlighted issues arising from digitalization, as tech companies benefit from the human need to connect while remaining physically distant. While several issues remain, the OECD's Blueprints for Pillar One and Pillar Two, along with the Statement updated on October 8, 2021, are a rich source of information to tackle the issue of Scale without Mass.

§6.05 TOWARDS AN INTERNATIONAL AGREEMENT

To understand the reasons behind the lengthy and complex negotiation process in achieving a multilateral agreement, it is important to consider the different types of economies of the countries participating in the Inclusive Framework. These countries, ranging from the United States to Swaziland, have very different needs, and reaching an agreement promises to be extremely challenging. In order to be implemented successfully, the multilateral proposal adopted should be simple and cost-effective, two characteristics that are lacking in both current proposals (Kana, 2020). Nevertheless, the essence of the proposal is revolutionary because, for the first time, the international tax community has accepted the principle of taxation at the destination (or market) instead of taxation at the origin, reflecting the need to adapt to changing business models.

With respect to the proliferation of various unilateral measures for taxing digital income, the main issue is double taxation: where the source country imposes a DST on income generated by non-resident tech companies and the residence country also taxes that income without giving credit for taxes paid in the source country, double taxation results. This double taxation is not dealt with by existing bilateral tax treaties because DSTs are not covered by the provisions of those treaties. Unless and until the Inclusive Framework produces a multilateral solution, it seems likely that countries will continue to implement unilateral measures.

[A] Pillar Two: An Overview

Pillar Two has been primarily driven by Germany and France, with the recent support of the United States (on the condition that the U.S. global minimum tax rules are grandfathered). The Pillar Two proposals are creative and comprehensive; however, they raise the two fundamental questions. First, is Pillar Two fair to developing countries? Second, is Pillar Two workable? The following section provides an overview of the Pillar Two proposals that are intended to deal with base erosion and profit-shifting issues that were not dealt with by the BEPS Project.

Pillar Two consists of two major rules aimed at ensuring that large multinationals pay their fair share of tax in countries in which they do business: a global minimum tax and an Undertaxed Payments Rule (which acts as a supporting rule to the global minimum tax). In addition, Pillar Two proposes two changes to tax treaties: a switchover rule for countries that currently use the exemption method, and a subject-to-tax rule, which would allow source countries to protect their tax base by denying treaty benefits for certain deductible intragroup payments made to group members resident in low-tax jurisdictions.

The global minimum tax will apply to the ultimate parent of a multinational group where its worldwide consolidated revenues exceeded EUR 750 million in the preceding fiscal year. A similar threshold applies for purposes of the country-by-country reporting requirements, covered by Action 13 of the BEPS Project. However, as indicated in the Inclusive Framework's Statement, countries remain free to apply the income-inclusion rule to MNEs with consolidated revenues under this threshold that are tax residents within their jurisdiction. Under Pillar Two, the ultimate parent will pay tax to its country of residence amounting to the difference between the foreign tax paid and the minimum tax on its foreign source income earned in a country either through permanent establishments or through controlled foreign corporations (CFCs) in that country. The difference between the minimum tax and the foreign tax is referred to as the "top-up tax" amount. The Statement, which, as of October 8, 2021, was endorsed by 136 out of the 140 member jurisdictions of the Inclusive Framework calls for a global minimum tax rate of 15%. To determine the minimum tax, income will be calculated in accordance with the financial accounting rules used by the ultimate parent corporation, with comprehensive adjustments for timing and permanent differences between accounting and taxable income. The foreign tax will be calculated on a country-by-country basis; however, tax paid to a residence country pursuant to CFC rules or with respect to permanent establishments in other countries must be allocated to those countries. In cases where the ultimate parent company is resident in a country that decides not to apply the minimum tax, the country in which the next-highest tier subsidiary is resident will apply the tax (assuming, of course, that it has decided to apply the tax). Thus, as long as one country in the corporate chain decides to apply the minimum tax, the foreign source income will be taxed at the minimum rate, providing an incentive for all countries in the chain to do so.

The global minimum tax will lead to significant administrative complexities for countries that choose to implement it, since the tax will be levied in addition to their regular domestic corporate income taxes, resulting in two separate corporate income taxes for the tax authorities to administer. For source countries that do not currently tax income at a rate equal to the minimum tax, any tax incentives that they provide to foreign investors will be nullified by the minimum tax, since the residence country will capture any tax foregone by the source country on the income.

A global minimum tax takes us back several years, to a time when tax-sparing provisions were commonly included in tax treaties between developing and developed countries. However, the minimum tax will have a much greater impact on a source country's tax incentives, since the tax-sparing provisions applied only in situations where companies invested in another country through a permanent establishment. In contrast, the proposed global minimum tax will apply not only to investments in a country made through permanent establishments but also to investments made through CFCs.

The Undertaxed Payments Rule is a supporting rule that is inseparable from the minimum tax. The minimum tax takes priority over the Undertaxed Payments Rule; as a result, the Undertaxed Payments Rule applies only if and to the extent that the income earned in a country is not subject to the minimum tax. However, where the minimum tax does not apply and the income earned in a country is taxed at less than the minimum rate, the countries in which payers of deductible amounts to low-taxed group members are residents can impose a tax on those payments up to the minimum rate. To eliminate the incentive for parent corporations to shift their residence to a low-tax country that does not impose the minimum tax, the Undertaxed Payments Rule will apply to any deductible intragroup payments to the parent corporation. The rules for the Undertaxed Payments Rule are extremely complex because of the need to allocate the top-up amount among the payers.

The subject-to-tax rule applies regardless of whether the minimum tax or the Undertaxed Payments Rule applies. The subject-to-tax rule is separate from the minimum tax rule and applies in priority to the Undertaxed Payments Rule. This enables source countries to charge a top-up tax on specific types of payments made to other companies in the same group where the recipient country has a nominal tax rate lower than the minimum tax rate. The minimum tax rate for the subject-to-tax rule will not be the same as the minimum rate for the global minimum tax, since the subject-to-tax rule is a tax on gross amounts, whereas the minimum tax is a tax on net income. With respect to the subject-to-tax rule, the Statement has set a minimum tax rate from of 9%. Because the subject-to-tax rule is a treaty rule, it will apply only where the contracting states agree to include it in their bilateral treaty. Further, the modification of existing treaties will require some sort of multilateral mechanism for its implementation, such as the Multilateral Instrument (MLI).

As outlined in the Statement, Pillar Two is expected to be brought into law in 2022, to be effective in 2023, with the Undertaxed Payments Rule coming into effect in 2024. The implementation plan includes the development of a multilateral instrument by the Inclusive Framework by mid-2022 to facilitate a smooth implementation of the subject-to-tax rule, in relevant bilateral treaties (OECD, 2021). An implementation framework will also be developed by the end of 2022 to facilitate the allocation of the top-up tax amount and the implementation of the Undertaxed Payments Rule.

[B] Pillar Two: Issues and Challenges

The main drawback of the Pillar Two proposals is the complexity of the rules. Developing countries with a tax rate that is lower than the global minimum tax rate will be faced with implementing a completely new tax system to ensure that they capture the appropriate revenue from multinational companies; otherwise, there is a risk of the revenue being captured by the developed countries in which those companies are resident. The complexity involved in implementing the new rules represents a significant barrier for developing countries that must be taken into account; in addition, although the work on the proposals is nearly complete, a political agreement has not yet been reached. The main challenge of the minimum tax proposals is the required balance between the needs and wants of policymakers and the technical feasibility of the proposed rules (Kana, 2020). A technical solution requires, first, a political decision, (which was reached in October 2021) but a political decision must take into account the technical feasibility of the proposals, creating a chicken-and-egg situation. To ensure that the rules work effectively, governments, policymakers, academics, tax experts, and accounting standards experts must reach a consensus. From that perspective, much work remains to be done, keeping in mind that simplicity and cost-effectiveness are keys to the successful implementation of the proposals. While 136 countries and jurisdictions have signed the Statement endorsing the two-pillar package in principle, not all Inclusive Framework members have joined the agreement, as of October 2021. Further, it is important to note that signatory countries have not agreed to adopt a minimum tax; rather, they have agreed that if they do decide to adopt a minimum tax, it will be done in a way that is "consistent with the outcomes provided for under Pillar Two" (OECD, 2021).

§6.06 BALANCING THE NEEDS OF DEVELOPING AND DEVELOPED COUNTRIES

Ensuring that tax rules are equally appropriate for both developing and developed countries is very challenging, given the different objectives and policy views held by developing and developed countries. Tax treaties are bilateral agreements, and it is important for each party to know what its most important priorities are. In Kana's view, the United Nations Model Convention is the more favorable option for developing countries and it would be worthwhile to convince developed countries that giving source countries (which are often developing countries) expanded taxing rights might be a better way to contribute to their development than relying on aid agencies (Kana, 2020).

The proposed changes to both the OECD and the United Nations Model Conventions, if implemented, will cause a significant change in the allocation of taxing rights, and it is therefore natural for countries to want to preserve their current taxing rights during negotiations. It is also important to remember that these rules may impact not only the concerned parties' taxing rights but their international tax treaty relationships as a whole, which must be kept in mind during these negotiations (Peters, 2020).

The current situation is somewhat similar to the strong opposition experienced from developed countries (especially, the United States and the United Kingdom) during the United Nations Committee's work on Article 12A of the United Nations Model Convention, which gave some extended taxing rights over fees for technical services to developing countries. The United States and U.K. members of the Committee strenuously opposed the adoption of Article 12A and insisted on the inclusion of their minority views in the Commentary. It is worth stressing that in moving towards a significantly new international tax system, it is important not to lose sight of the need of developing countries for technical assistance and capacity-building from developed countries and international organizations. Their participation in the Inclusive Framework is meaningless if they cannot obtain the required technical assistance.

§6.07 NAVIGATING MULTILATERAL AND UNILATERAL MEASURES

Countries' growing impatience for a political agreement to be reached on a global minimum tax and the various unilateral measures being implemented as a consequence, has made it unclear whether the unilateral measures imposed will remain for years to come. The main reason behind the impatience of many of these countries has been a perceived lack of fairness: tech companies have made huge profits during a pandemic that caused other sectors to suffer, but have paid very little tax on those profits, thereby eroding confidence in the international tax system (Peters, 2020). As the pandemic accelerates the pace of digitalization, many national governments have become frustrated with their limited ability to tax the profits of tech companies that do not have a physical presence in their country but are able to sell digital goods and services to a significant portion of their citizens. While, from a global perspective, a multilateral solution is preferred, national policymakers face considerable pressure to ensure fairness in their own tax systems, making unilateral measures an attractive option; moreover, moving forward with their own unilateral measures might be seen as a way to put pressure on countries and international organizations to reach an acceptable multilateral agreement.

Somewhat paradoxically, the current adoption and implementation of unilateral measures that are very similar to other countries' unilateral measures can be seen, essentially, as a move away from unilateralism and towards the convergence of unilateral measures into a harmonized international system. A country's implementation of a DST is obviously a unilateral action, but in practice, as a significant number of other countries enact similar measures, the DST may become an acceptable harmonized solution to BEPS. The question is whether a low-rate DST might be a better solution than the current Pillar Two proposals, especially on an interim basis while the international tax community works towards a better tax system. The October 2021 Statement of the Inclusive Framework clarifies that the agreement on the Pillar One and Pillar Two proposals is conditional on the elimination of all DSTs and similar measures.

§6.08 CONCLUSION

Although the international tax community has made substantial progress in addressing the taxation issues resulting from digitalization, several important challenges remain. One thing is certain: cooperation among all stakeholders—governments and policymakers, multinational organizations, tax and accounting experts, and civil society—will continue to be necessary to ensure a smooth transition towards an international tax system that is acceptable and appropriate for the taxation of business income in the new digital economy.

Bibliography

Arnold, Brian, (2020), World Tax Summit—TaxCOOP2020, Multilateralism or Unilateralism—How Should Countries Tax International Taxpayers?, Montreal (online), October 15, 2020.

Bunn, Daniel, Asen, Elke and Enache, Cristina, (2020), Tax Foundation. Digital Taxation Around the World, https://files.taxfoundation.org/20200610094652/Digital-Taxation-Around-the-World1.pdf.

Haines, Anjana, (2020), World Tax Summit—TaxCOOP2020, Multilateralism or Unilateralism—How Should Countries Tax International Taxpayers?, Montreal (online), October 15, 2020.

Kana, Liselott, (2020), World Tax Summit—TaxCOOP2020, Multilateralism or Unilateralism—How Should Countries Tax International Taxpayers?, Montreal (online), October 15, 2020.

OECD (2015), Addressing the Tax Challenges of the Digital Economy, Action 1—2015 Final Report, OECD/G20 Base Erosion and Profit Shifting Project, OECD Publishing, Paris.

OECD (2020), International community renews commitment to address tax challenges from digitalisation of the economy, October 10, 2020, https://www.oecd.org/tax/beps/international-community-renews-commitment-to-address-tax-challenges-from-digitalisation-of-the-economy.htm.

OECD (2021), Action 1 Tax Challenges Arising from Digitalisation, https://www.oecd.org/tax/beps/beps-actions/action1/.

OECD (2021), OECD/G20 Base Erosion and Profit Shifting Project. Statement on a Two-Pillar Solution to Address the Tax Challenges Arising From the Digitalisation of the Economy, July 1, 2021, https://www.oecd.org/tax/beps/statement-on-a-two-pillar-solution-to-address-the-tax-challenges-arising-from-the-digitalisation-of-the-economy-july-2021.pdf.

OECD (2021), OECD/G20 Base Erosion and Profit Shifting Project. Statement on a Two-Pillar Solution to Address the Tax Challenges Arising From the Digitalisation of the Economy, October 8, 2021, https://www.oecd.org/tax/beps/statement-on-a-two-pillar-solution-to-address-the-tax-challenges-arising-from-the-digitalisation-of-the-economy-october-2021.pdf.

Peters, Carmel, (2020), World Tax Summit—TaxCOOP2020, Multilateralism or Unilateralism—How Should Countries Tax International Taxpayers?, Montreal (online), October 15, 2020.

United Nations, (2020), Committee of Experts on International Cooperation in Tax Matters Twentieth Session. Tax Consequences of the Digitalized Economy—Issues of Relevance for Developing Countries, Co-Coordinators' Report. October 11, 2020, https://www.un.org/development/desa/financing/sites/www.un.org.development.desa.financing/files/2020-10/CITCM%2021%20CRP.41_Digitalization%2010102020%20Final%20A.pdf#page=9.

CHAPTER 7

Are Tax Havens Scapegoats?

Aimée Dushime

The tax haven phenomenon is no doubt receiving increasing attention from policymakers around the world and has become the subject of scrutiny since the global financial crisis of 2007-2008. Today, accusing fingers are being pointed at tax havens for the cause of the rising financial crisis happening in the world, as well as for the rise in corruption, money laundering and tax evasion. However, some commentators have argued that the accusations hurled against tax havens, as well as the naming and shaming of perceived tax haven countries by international organisations, such as the European Union (EU), is simply wrong and unfair. This begs the burning question: are tax havens to blame for the global financial downturn in the world today or are they merely used as convenient scapegoats to conceal the hypocrisy of governments in high tax countries? This paper addresses this issue by examining the different sides of the debate. It assesses the global positive and negative impacts of tax havens, as well as the blacklisting of tax havens by international organizations and the consequences for named and shamed countries. The Organisation for Economic Co-operation and Development (OECD) campaign and other initiatives that have been carried out by different institutions across the world to reduce the influence of tax havens are also examined.

§7.01 INTRODUCTION

The global financial system is now being defined today by issues relating to tax havens. The impacts of tax havens on the world economy have been a subject of heated discussion in recent years, with many powerful political leaders blaming tax havens for the financial instability in high tax countries and calling for their annulment (Khanna,

2021). Tax havens are often identified with tax avoidance, tax abuse and tax evasion, as it is believed that multinational corporations (MNCs) use tax havens to shift profits into low tax jurisdictions in order to avoid paying corporate income taxes in the jurisdictions where they are domiciled. Some of these organisations have proceeded to name and shame countries perceived to be tax havens by including them in a list of 'uncooperative tax jurisdictions' in order to alter the tax regimes in these jurisdictions. A forum of harmful tax practices was established by the Organisation for Economic Co-operation and Development (OECD) for the purpose of compiling a 'blacklist' of tax havens. Blacklisted countries face threats of multilateral actions in form of sanctions cloaked as 'defensive measures' including:

> Comprehensive information reporting for transactions involving listed tax havens; denial of foreign tax credits to distributions from listed tax havens; disallowance of deductions, exemptions, or credits related to transactions with listed tax havens; withholding taxes on payments to residents of listed tax havens; enhanced audit and enforcement activities regarding listed tax havens; not entering into any new comprehensive income tax conventions with listed tax havens and possible termination of existing conventions; and charges or levies on specific transactions involving listed tax havens (Sullivan, 2007).

In 2017, the European Union (EU) adopted its own blacklist of tax haven countries that erode the corporate tax revenue of its Member States. The list covers countries or jurisdictions which do not meet international standards on transparency and exchange of information and whose tax regimes are perceived to offer harmful tax practices. These jurisdictions are required to remedy their tax regimes within a stipulated time, with the attendant risk of being moved to the blacklist (Kittredge et al., 2020). Despite the supposed usefulness of the EU tax haven blacklist, the screening and selection process has been heavily criticised for lacking credibility and transparency. Smaller countries on the blacklist have complained about the discriminatory nature of the list, as it refuses to include the most important shadow financial institutions, particularly within EU member countries (KYC360, 2018). This is exemplified in the Panama Papers scandal in 2016 which revealed that many European companies, wealthy individuals, and even politicians are hiding funds in offshore jurisdictions. Oxfam's 2021 analysis report shows that five EU member countries (Cyprus, Ireland, Luxembourg, Malta and the Netherlands) continue to have economic indicators common to tax havens, such as high levels of foreign direct investments, intellectual property payments, interests and dividends, all of which significantly exceeded their economic weight (Oxfam, 2021). According to Oxfam, these indicators are strong enough to show that these five jurisdictions make use of aggressive tax practices to attract foreign flows or to act as a conduit towards other offshore centres, thereby causing a loss to countries where real profits are made. By failing to blacklist these countries due to the automatic EU exemption, it becomes unfair to named and shamed countries, particularly African countries like Botswana, which stands the risk of losing substantial foreign direct investments as a result of being listed.

In addressing the burning question of whether tax havens are being used as scapegoats by political leaders in high tax countries, an economic and moral case has been given by academic literature on the issue. Despite the criticisms levelled against tax havens, Mitchell (2006a) observed that tax havens contribute positively to the development of good policies around the world by pressuring politicians in high tax countries to reduce double taxation of saving and investment. According to him, 'many nations have lowered or eliminated death taxes and wealth taxes because the politicians have finally figured out that oppressive tax laws simply lead taxpayers to move their money to havens such as Luxembourg or Panama' (Mitchell, 2006). Since it is easier to launch attacks against scapegoats, political leaders in non-tax haven countries have found a convenient way to blame tax havens for every financial crisis occurring in the world today, having failed to admit that their own corrupt tax practices have undoubtedly fuelled the growth of these tax havens (Lynn, 2009). This chapter, therefore, analyses the concept of tax havens and the question of whether they are being used as scapegoats for government hypocrisy and incompetence. Following the introduction, the rest of this paper has the following structure. The concept and characteristics of tax havens, including the definitions offered by different international organisations such as the OECD, International Monetary Fund (IMF) and Tax Justice Network are discussed in section §7.02. The global positive and negative effects of tax havens are examined in section §7.03. The question of whether tax havens are responsible for global financial crises or are merely convenient scapegoats is addressed in section §7.04. Section §7.05 examines the issue of blacklisting of tax havens and the consequences for named and shamed countries and section §7.06 identifies the measures and initiatives that have been taken by the OECD and other international organisations to reduce the existence of tax havens. This chapter is concluded in section §7.07.

§7.02 WHAT ARE TAX HAVENS?

The historic evolution of tax havens is no doubt packed with myths and legends (Palan, 2009). Tax havens have been in existence ever since countries decided to compete globally by operating low or no tax regimes with a view of attracting businesses from high tax countries. Some historians have mentioned their existence in the form of isolated islands during the time of the ancient Greeks (Manning, 2018, 246).[1] It is believed that the oldest tax havens date back to the 1920s and 1930s and include Liechtenstein, Switzerland and Panama (Palan, 2009). The term 'tax haven' has been widely used since the 1950s, yet there is no universally accepted definition of what renders a country, territory or jurisdiction a tax haven (Palan, 2009). The term is however commonly attributed to countries or jurisdictions with low or no tax regimes which enable foreign individuals and MNCs to avoid paying higher taxes in the countries they live and operate. It is therefore used to refer to countries or jurisdictions

1. Raposo and Mourao (2013) believed that the territories offering preferential tax regimes existed back in 166BC in the Mediterranean. According to them, the island of Delos, which is currently in the territory of Greece, practised trade in such a way that was free of taxes and customs duties. The island has therefore received the attention of traders and has become a centre for trading ivory, textiles, wine and other luxurious items.

that offer ways by which foreign individuals or corporations can avoid higher income or corporate tax rates in the countries where they are domiciled. These jurisdictions provide a liberal financial environment coupled with strict confidentiality laws that attract foreign individuals and companies looking for alternative systems from high tax countries (Offshore Protection, 2021). Since tax havens offer ways to minimise taxes and to obtain financial confidentiality, they become appealing to corporate and individual investors (OECD, 1998). Although the concept of a tax haven is not in itself illegal, it has readily been confused by the illegal activities carried out by some individuals and corporations such as not declaring the income earned in such havens to their corresponding tax authorities (Hotzblatt, Jermakowicz & Epstein, 2015). Today, tax havens are used interchangeably with terms like 'offshore financial centres' (OFCs) or 'secrecy jurisdictions', as they offer financial secrecy and limit public disclosure about companies and individuals, thereby allowing them to hide their wealth and financial affairs from their home countries (TJN, 2021a; Fitzgibbon & Hallman, 2020).

§7.03 TAX HAVENS AS DEFINED BY DIFFERENT INSTITUTIONS

Several organisations have formulated different definitions and criteria in order to identify what countries or jurisdictions constitute tax havens. This section discusses the definitions offered by the OECD, IMF and Tax Justice Network and the characteristics inherent in these definitions.

The typical characteristics that have been attributed to tax havens over the years include the fact that they are small and well-governed countries, having a population below 1 million and imposing low or zero tax rates for the purpose of attracting investment and stimulating economic activity. (Altshuler & Grubert, 2004; Hines, Gumpert & Schnitzer, 2016). A study by Dharmapala and Hines (2006) shows that tax havens often display political stability, government effectiveness, accountability, rule of law, and a well-qualified bureaucracy. Since institutional quality is an important trigger for economic development, the competition among havens for capital increases their chances for growth (Narci, 2012). The higher institutional quality available in tax havens serves as an attraction to investors and MNCs, as they are offered access to good infrastructure and offshore financing activities besides tax advantages (Hines, 2004; Dharmapala and Hines, 2009). Another notable feature of a tax haven is secrecy. Tax haven countries are often called 'secrecy jurisdictions' as it is believed they offer financial secrecy and limit public disclosure about foreign individuals and companies. This characteristic feature of tax havens is often seen as creating deleterious effects on the global economy. According to Tax Justice Network, the secret nature of tax havens makes them a 'criminogenic hothouse for multiple evils including fraud, tax cheating, escape from financial regulations, embezzlement, insider dealing, bribery, money laundering, and plenty more' (TJN, 2020a).

[A] The OECD's Definition

The OECD is an international organisation established to stimulate economic progress and world trade. The organisation aims to promote policy coordination and economic freedom among developed nations while working with governments of different countries that share a commitment to improving the economy and well-being of the general population (CFI, 2021). Since the organisation was formed in 1961, the issue of tax havens has been addressed by the OECD in different ways. In the late 1990s, several efforts were made by the OECD to address the issue of harmful tax competition which it defined as an attempt made by some countries to attract foreign investment and businesses by offering generous tax incentives to investors domiciled in high tax jurisdictions. It is believed that competitions of this nature can threaten the tax bases of other OECD countries and distort the worldwide capital allocation (Jackson, 2010). The OECD recognises the difficulties in providing an objective definition of a tax haven and noted that a good way of identifying a country or territory as a tax haven is where such country or territory offers itself or is generally recognised as a tax haven (OECD, 1987). While there is no generally agreed-upon definition of a tax haven or a generally accepted list of countries that are tax havens, the OECD establishes four basic principles to employ in order to identify whether a country is a tax haven. According to the OECD, the key criteria which may be used to determine whether a country, territory or jurisdiction constitute a tax haven are: 'no or only nominal tax, lack of effective exchange of information, lack of transparency, and no substantial activities' (OECD, 1998).

The first criterion which is 'no or only nominal taxes' is the starting point in identifying a jurisdiction as a tax haven. The OECD notes that it may be sufficient to classify a country or jurisdiction as a tax haven in the event where such a country or jurisdiction offers itself or is perceived to offer itself, as a place where non-residents can avoid paying taxes in the country where they are domiciled. The second criterion which is 'lack of effective exchange of information,' involves the willingness or the ability to cooperate and share information with tax authorities of other countries or jurisdictions (Narci, 2012). The opacity of financial information is considered to be a characteristic feature of a tax haven. Since tax havens have in place a legal regime under which non-resident businesses and individuals can benefit from strict secrecy rules and other protections against scrutiny by tax authorities, they therefore prevent the effective exchange of information on these taxpayers who benefit from the low tax countries or jurisdictions (OECD, 1998).

A lack of transparency in the legislative, legal or administrative tax regime of a country or jurisdiction is also another criterion in identifying tax havens. According to the OECD, a country or jurisdiction would be considered a tax haven if it has in place non-transparent administrative practices that prevent financial institutions from providing tax authorities with information about investors. The lack of transparency and the inability or unwillingness to provide information not only allows investors to avoid their taxes in their home countries but also facilitate illegal activities, such as tax evasion and money laundering (OECD, 1998). The last criterion 'no substantial activities' implies that a country or jurisdiction may attempt to attract investment and businesses that are purely tax driven by not requiring non-resident entities to have a substantial local presence. According to the OECD, many tax havens are built in ways that enable taxpayers to generate incentives from the regime, while engaging in activities that are solely tax driven and are not substantial (OECD, 1998). The absence of substantial business activities may therefore facilitate tax evasion by foreign individuals and companies.

The OECD (1998) report also proposed the identification of 'harmful preferential tax regimes'. While tax havens are countries or jurisdictions that offer favourable tax conditions and secrecy to foreign investors, harmful preferential tax regimes refer to countries or jurisdictions that issue highly favourable tax rulings and implement preferential tax rules to attract foreign flows, thereby eroding the tax bases of other countries or jurisdictions. The report identifies four criteria for determining whether a preferential tax regime is harmful. These criteria include: 'no or low effective tax rates, ring fencing of regimes, lack of transparency and lack of effective exchange of information'. It can be seen that harmful preferential tax regimes share the same criteria as tax havens, with the only difference being 'ring fencing'. According to the OECD, there are good reasons to be concerned where regimes are partially or fully isolated from the domestic economy. This is because the fact that a country or jurisdiction has designed its regime in a way that protects its economy from the regime by 'ring fencing' provides a strong sign that such a regime has the potential of adversely impacting other countries' tax bases (OECD, 1998). Accordingly, the country or jurisdiction offering the regime may bear little or none of the financial burden of its own preferential tax rules. Taxpayers within the regime may also benefit from the infrastructure of the country providing the preferential regime without bearing the cost incurred to provide that infrastructure (OECD, 1998).

[B] The IMF

The IMF is an international organisation that aims at fostering economic growth and financial stability globally while encouraging international trade and reducing poverty (Kenton, 2020). The organisation addresses the issue of tax havens and secrecy jurisdictions differently from that taken by the OECD. The IMF avoids the term 'tax havens' but uses 'offshore financial centres' instead in creating its list, especially since the list is intended to include countries whose financial strength extends considerably beyond their own economic performance. (WorldData, 2021). Various attempts have been made to define OFCs since they started to have an impact on international financial markets in the early 1970s. There is however no generally accepted definition. In the early 1990s, some definitions were proposed by the IMF when it published data on cross-border positions of OFCs in the International Financial Statistics Yearbook. OFCs were defined by the IMF as countries where 'the banking system, acting as financial entrepot, acquires substantial external accounts beyond those associated with economic activity in the country concerned' (IMF, 1996). In 2002, in an effort to define the parameter of its data collection, the IMF Statistics Department described an OFC as a 'jurisdiction in which international investment position assets, including as resident all entities that have legal domicile in that jurisdiction, are close to or more than 50 percent of GDP and in absolute terms more than $1 billion' (IMF, 2002). It has however been noted that these definitions of OFCs do not adequately capture the intrinsic features of the OFC, neither is there a clear official list of OFC jurisdictions (Zoromé, 2007; NOU, 2009, 19). The IMF published a working paper in 2007 by Ahmed Zoromé with a view of providing an objective and quantifiable method of identifying OFCs. The paper defined an OFC as 'a country or jurisdiction that provides financial services to non-residents on a scale that is incommensurate with the size and the financing of its domestic economy' (Zoromé, 2007).

[C] The Tax Justice Network

The Tax Justice Network is an independent research and advocacy organisation which aims to address issues relating to tax avoidance, tax competition and tax havens; and also supports the engagement of citizens, civil society organisations and policymakers in order to achieve a more just tax system (Snell, 2018). The organisation pursues five major objectives:

> To raise the level of awareness about the world of offshore finance; to promote links between interested parties around the world; to stimulate and organize research and debate; to encourage and support national and international campaign activity; and to act as a vehicle for the promotion of tax justice issues at multilateral organisations such as the UN, OECD, European Union, World Bank and IMF. (Seabrooke and Wigan, 2013)

According to the Tax Justice Network, a tax haven generally refers to 'a country or jurisdiction that enables multinational corporations and individuals to escape the rule of law in the countries where they live, and to pay less tax than they should in those countries'(TJN, 2021a). In 2007, the Tax Justice Network published a list which included countries in the OECD that offer some tax haven facilities or offshore financial services, notwithstanding the fact that they do not account for a major part of the economy. These jurisdictions are regarded as 'pure tax havens' which facilitate tax avoidance through low tax rates and secrecy (Michiel, Weyzig & Murphy, 2006). The Tax Justice Network observes that countries with a broader economic base have a greater responsibility to alter their tax regime which facilitates tax avoidance and tax evasion, as not only small countries or jurisdictions should be targeted (TJN, 2007). In 2019, the organisation launched its corporate tax haven index which 'ranks the world's most important tax havens for multinational corporations, according to how aggressively and how extensively each jurisdiction contributes to helping the world's multinational enterprises escape paying tax and erodes the tax revenues of other countries around the world' (Global Alliance, 2019).

§7.04 THE GLOBAL EFFECTS OF TAX HAVENS

The global effects of tax havens may be seen from different perspectives. Under this section, both the negative and positive effects of tax havens are examined.

[A] The Negative Effects of Tax Havens

The effects of tax haven globally are considered to be very severe, as it is believed that a huge amount of money is being taken away from high tax countries to tax haven countries which would have assisted in the economic growth of the former (Syed, 2019). A report carried out by Tax Justice Network, in collaboration with Public Services International, the Global Alliance for Tax Justice and the FACT Coalition found that countries are losing over USD 427 billion in tax each year to international corporate tax abuse and private tax evasion (TJN, 2020b). According to the report:

> More tax is lost to tax havens every year due to corporate tax abuse by multinational corporations than due to private tax evasion by individuals. Multinational corporations short-change countries out of $245 billion in tax every year while people who move their wealth offshore short-change their governments out $182 billion less in tax every year. (TJN, 2020b)

It is often argued that the negative impacts of tax havens are mostly felt by developing countries than developed countries. While tax havens may have little or no impact on political institutions in rich nations, a number of indicators suggest that tax havens contribute to extremely high revenue loss in developing countries, since these countries are poor and have a weak institutional capacity which facilitates tax evasion and illicit financial flows (NOU, 2009, 19). Oxfam projects that tax havens contribute to revenue losses for developing economies of at least USD 50 billion annually. The OECD (2008) further confirms this when it observed that developing countries lose to tax havens almost three times what they get from developed countries in aid. It is therefore widely believed that the shifting of profits by MNCs to low tax jurisdictions undermines the ability of developing countries to raise tax revenues to finance development (Fuest & Riedel, 2010). Furthermore, tax havens are shown to have the potential of changing investor behaviour, thereby increasing the difference between socio-economic and private returns. Consequently, it is believed that tax havens reduce the overall value creation for high tax countries. The 'secret' nature of tax havens also has some negative effects. The secrecy associated with tax havens can be used to promote money laundering, terrorism financing and tax avoidance, thereby causing potential harmful tax competition since it hinders other countries and jurisdictions from gaining access to information about these unlawful activities.

[B] The Positive Effects of Tax Havens

Despite the growing backlash against tax havens and the arguments advanced that tax havens erode the tax bases of high tax countries through tax avoidance and tax evasion practices, several commentators have pointed out some positive effects of tax havens on the world economy, particularly for tax haven countries and non-tax haven countries. An empirical study carried out by Desai, Foley and Hines (2004) reveals that a positive complementary relationship exists between the economic activity of tax haven countries and high tax countries. They argue that although non-tax havens can lose tax revenue due to profit shifting by MNCs, tax havens can indirectly stimulate the growth of businesses in high tax countries located in the same region by reducing the cost of financing investment in those countries. Dharmapala (2008) observes that it is possible that tax havens enable high tax countries to impose lower effective tax rates on highly mobile firms while taxing immobile firms more heavily. According to him, the concerns expressed about the negative effects of tax havens may be exaggerated, especially when considering 'the robust growth of corporate tax revenues in major capital-exporting countries despite the substantial foreign direct flows to tax havens'.

A moral case has also been made by some commentators on the economic benefits of tax havens, as it is believed that tax havens shield oppressed and vulnerable groups from bad and corrupt regimes (Mitchell, 2006b). This view is derived from the notion that politicians pursue private interests which relate to high tax rates and are not solely concerned to serve the interests of voters (Brennan and Buchanan, 1980). The attacks on tax havens are therefore led by politicians who are frightened of the way low tax jurisdictions provide an alternative to their own high tax and huge spending policies in their jurisdictions (Lynn, 2009). Low tax countries and jurisdictions therefore discipline politicians in order for them not to increase taxes beyond levels desirable for the voters (NOU, 2009, 19). Modern academic literature also suggests that tax havens serve as a tool for sustainable economic growth and development due to the extensive foreign investments received by them (Hines, 2004). A study carried out by Dharmapala and Hines (2006) shows that tax haven countries often display political stability, an effective government, rule of law, good accountability measures, and control of corruption. According to a report, low taxes offered by tax haven countries do not constitute the only attraction for mobile capital, as institutional conditions which assure the safety of investments and the conduct of financial transactions may also be important in attracting foreign investors to tax haven countries or jurisdictions (NOU, 2009, 19).

[1] Are Tax Havens to Blame for Global Financial Crises or Are They Just Convenient Scapegoats?

Proponents of tax havens have provided economic justification for the continued existence of tax havens and show that havens may not indeed be blamed for the financial crisis and may just be used as a convenient scapegoat by political leaders in high tax jurisdictions.

Recent policy statements and media reports seem to emphasise that some form of connection exists between tax havens and the global financial crisis, as it is believed that the former is responsible for imposing various costs on the global capital market (NOU, 2009, 19). Prior to the COVID-19 recession, the global financial crisis of

2007-2008 has been considered by many economists as the worst economic downturn since the Great Depression of 1929. While the exact causes of the financial crisis was a matter of dispute among economists, political leaders in high tax countries blamed the low tax countries as the major source of fiscal instability that exacerbated the crisis (Christensen, 2020). The G20 leaders, for example, agreed in April 2019 that they would: 'take action against non-cooperative jurisdictions, including tax havens. We stand ready to deploy sanctions to protect our public finances and financial systems. The era of banking secrecy is over. We note that the OECD has today published a list of countries assessed by the Global Forum against the international standard for exchange of tax information' (OECD, 2019b). The OECD further reinforces this agreement when it stated thus: 'Removing practices that facilitate tax evasion is part of a broader drive to clean up one of the most controversial sides of a globalised economy' (Loomer & Maffini, 2009). The COVID-19 pandemic has no doubt brought tax havens to the limelight, with governments using state power to force businesses to de-risk their global corporate structures for tax purposes if they wish to have access to public crisis reliefs (Christensen, 2020). By working together with international bureaucrats such as the OECD, political leaders around the world have employed different bullying strategies with a view of forcing small low tax jurisdictions to change their tax regime in ways that benefit the bigger high tax countries.

Notwithstanding the growing backlash against tax havens, some commentators have argued that tax havens are not responsible for the global economic crisis and should therefore not be blamed and used as a scapegoat to cover up the incompetence and hypocrisy of governments in high tax countries and jurisdictions. According to Lynn (2009), the global financial systems are becoming more complex as governments try to squeeze extremely high amounts of tax out of the system. It therefore does not come as a surprise that foreign investors choose to move their investments to places where taxes are low and simple. In the words of Lynn, '[tax havens] provide an alternative for people who object to paying the high rates of tax that governments in most of the developed world impose ... If politicians didn't pretend they could raise more tax by plugging loopholes; they might have to start telling people how they planned to fix their deficits'. This assertion was reiterated by Mitchell (2016) in the course of discussing the crucial and valuable economic role played by tax havens in the world. Contrary to the commonly held belief that tax havens are a tool of destruction to the global financial systems, Mitchell asserts that tax havens indeed have the potential of contributing to economic growth and curtailing the greed of political leaders who tax nations into economic ruin. In this regard, Welsh (2016) present a clear case on the useful purpose of tax havens when he noted that:

> The secrecy of tax havens is a double-edged sword. Of course, it is true that secrecy allows the corrupt to shield their money from the tax authorities ... . However, tax havens also allow the honest to shelter their money from corrupt and oppressive politicians. ... one of the benefits of tax havens is that they help hold governments to account. They make it possible for businesses to avoid the worst excesses of government largesse and crazy tax systems – including the 39 percent of US corporation tax rate. They have other functions too: it is simply wrong to say that

they have no useful purpose. It is also wrong to argue that, if only corrupt governments had more tax revenue, their people would be better served.

§7.05 THE BLACKLISTING OF TAX HAVENS BY THE EUROPEAN UNION AND THE CONSEQUENCES FOR NAMED AND SHAMED COUNTRIES

International organisations such as the World Bank, the IMF, the OECD and non-governmental organisations are constantly drawing up a list of 'non-cooperative' tax havens according to their own criteria. The best known and highly controversial list in Europe is the 'blacklist' of the EU which is used by Member States to address the issue of tax abuse and harmful tax practices. In determining whether a country is a 'non-cooperative jurisdiction', the EU index measures the transparency of its tax regime, as well as whether the country's tax system allows MNCs to unfairly shift profits to low tax jurisdictions in order to escape higher taxes in other countries. The EU particularly looks into countries or jurisdictions which offer generous tax incentives such as zero corporate and income tax to foreign individuals and companies (Robertson, 2017). The EU adopted the first list on 5 December 2017 comprising of seventeen states (American Samoa, Bahrain, Barbados, Grenada, Guam, South Korea, Macao SAR, Marshall Islands, Mongolia, Namibia, Palau, Panama, Saint Lucia, Samoa, Trinidad and Tobago, Tunisia and the United Arab Emirates). After numerous objections and deletions, by the end of 2018, the list was reduced to only five countries. Presently, there are twelve countries on the blacklist of the EU and they are: American Samoa, Anguilla, Dominica, Fiji, Guam, Palau, Panama, Samoa, Trinidad and Tobago, the US Virgin Islands, Vanuatu and Seychelles. These countries have been blacklisted by the EU for facilitating international tax avoidance and financial secrecy (Prasad, 2021). The current grey list of the EU includes countries that have adopted the necessary reforms to improve transparency in their regimes along with EU partners but whose progress has not been verified and they include Australia, Barbados, Botswana, Eswatini, Jamaica, Jordan, Maldives, Thailand and Turkey (EU, 2021; Varela, 2021). The direct consequences of the EU blacklist on named and shamed countries involve the imposition of various sanctions by EU member countries, including the application of withholding taxes at a higher rate on payments received in blacklisted jurisdictions, as well as increased monitoring and audits. Banks are obliged to apply stricter due diligence to financial flows involving blacklisted countries while companies in such countries face discrimination when it comes to receiving funds and technical assistance from the EU (Sunday Standard, 2020). Named and shamed states therefore face reputational damage which may hinder them from having access to funds from international development lenders (Prasad, 2021).

Ever since the EU tax haven list was published in 2017, the list has been criticised for being too political and for failing to live up to its potential and serve its purpose. Oxfam (2021) has revealed that the EU blacklisting process is not fit for the purpose. The list continues to fail in classifying the countries which carry out harmful tax practices and allow MNCs to avoid paying taxes. According to Oxfam, the EU tax haven list exempts all EU countries by failing to evaluate their tax practices and also refuses to capture some of the world's worst tax havens, since it does not automatically blacklist zero or low tax countries or jurisdictions (Oxfam, 2021). A study carried out by Tax Justice Network reveals that EU blacklisted countries are responsible for less than 2% of global tax losses while EU member countries are responsible for 36% of global tax losses, thereby costing countries an annual tax revenue loss of over USD 154 billion (Monsour, 2020). The Tax Justice Network has over time criticised the EU's blacklist for ignoring major tax havens while focusing on jurisdictions that may be secretive but play an insignificant role in the global economy. The case of Palau and Trinidad and Tobago can be used as a very good example. Evidence shows that despite the fact that these two jurisdictions did not cooperate with international tax regulations, there were no observable tax losses created by them for other countries (Monsour, 2020). However, the same thing cannot be said for the Cayman Islands[2] which were briefly blacklisted in February 2020 but were subsequently removed from the list in October 2020 after they were deemed compliant with international tax rules. It has been shown that the Cayman Islands are responsible for 16.5% of global tax losses which equals 70 billion US dollars and amounts to the biggest share of countries' tax losses (Monsour, 2020). This fact alone is sufficient evidence to prove that the current tax haven blacklisting processes are not fit for purpose.

The EU's listing of African countries has also been considered unfair and has affected the EU-African relations with some African finance ministers pointing out that the EU has done little to crack down on its multinationals exploiting loopholes in tax treaties for the purpose of dramatically reducing their tax obligations in African states annually (Fox, 2020). It came as a shock when Botswana was grey-listed in February 2020 as a country not cooperating in the fight against tax evasion and money laundering. Botswana ministers have claimed that the listing was a 'devastating blow which had the potential of tarnishing the image and international profile of the country' (Africa Confidential, 2020). The African Caribbean and Pacific community has described the listing process as 'unilateral and discriminatory', as exemplified by the fact that third countries were not invited to participate in the drafting of the criteria for determining 'uncooperative tax havens' (Fox, 2020). Several African critics have argued that the decisions taken by the EU were made without any consultations with the jurisdictions that were placed on the blacklists (Songailaitė, 2020; Fox, 2020). As pointed out by the African Tax Administration Forum (2019), a fundamental concern for developing countries is the 'perceived geo-political, as opposed to the rational nature of the listing processes and the coerciveness of the 2017 EU list of non-cooperative tax jurisdictions'. Some scholars and economists have complained about the way smaller countries are being bullied by strong and powerful nations (Sanders,

2. The Cayman Islands are well-known to be the lairs of offshore companies. The islands were initially placed in the OECD blacklist as potentially harmful. It however came as a shock when the islands did not appear on the original list of the EU since the United Kingdom was still a member of the EU at the time the list was released in 2017. After the Brexit, the Cayman Islands were immediately on the blacklist, although just for a brief period of time. *See* the Council of the European Union (6129/20).

2002). As exemplified in the tax information exchange agreements imposed by the OECD, research shows that developed industrialised countries are not interested in concluding agreements with developing countries since the rich countries do not expect much profit for themselves from such agreements (TJN, 2010; Songailaitė, 2020). It is therefore necessary for developing countries to compete in financial markets since these countries do not have as many resources as developed countries. Notwithstanding the fact that the EU blacklists intend to name and shame countries that operate a tax regime that facilitates tax fraud and evasion, there is no doubt that the list is politically and economically bias. The blacklisting of tax havens would never achieve the intended purpose if the screening and selection process does not include major jurisdictions that facilitate illicit financial flows, including members of the EU itself (Songailaitė, 2020).

§7.06 MEASURES TAKEN BY THE OECD AND OTHER ORGANISATIONS ON TAX HAVENS

The OECD, under the direction of its Member States, has been at the forefront of fighting against tax evasion and tax abuse associated with tax havens. Since the 1990s, the organisation has spearheaded several international agreements with the aim of addressing tax avoidance by MNCs and reducing the occurrence of money laundering, corruption, and tax havens (Jackson, 2010). Initially, the OECD's campaign against tax havens was primarily focused on improving transparency and exchange of information to reduce harmful tax practices. Today, the OECD has implemented a global initiative through the Global Forum on Transparency and Exchange of Information for Tax Purposes with the aim of putting an end to bank secrecy and tax evasion through global tax co-operation (OECD, 2021). The forum, which has over 160 member countries and jurisdictions including all G20 countries and some developing countries, is dedicated to improving transparency and the exchange of information for tax purposes by ensuring the effective implementation of two internationally agreed standards on exchange of information; exchange of information on request and automatic exchange of information (OECD, 2021). The Global Forum derived its objectives from the OECD's harmful tax practices project, which was launched in 1996 at the direction of the G7.[3] As part of this initiative, the OECD has attempted to address the issue of harmful tax competition which is believed to unfairly erode the tax bases of other countries and distort the global allocation of capital (Jackson, 2010). The OECD's work on harmful tax practices came along with the Harmful Tax Competition Report of 1998 and Action 5 of the OECD/G20 BEPS Project that was adopted in 2015. According to the OECD, the 1998 Report intended to achieve the following objectives:

> Develop a better understanding of how tax havens and harmful preferential tax regimes affect the location of financial and other service activities, erode the tax

3. The Group of Seven (G7) is an intergovernmental organisation which consists of advanced economies, including: Canada, France, Germany, Italy, Japan, the United Kingdom and the United States.

> bases of other countries, distort trade and investment patterns undermine the fairness, neutrality and broad social acceptance of tax system generally. (OECD, 1998)

For the purpose of discouraging the spread of tax havens and harmful preferential tax regimes and encouraging countries that presently engage in harmful tax practices to review their existing measures, the OECD established the Forum on Harmful Tax Practices in 1998 to conduct reviews of preferential regimes in order to determine if the regimes could be harmful to the tax base of other jurisdictions (OECD 2019a). Following the 1998 report, the OECD has proceeded to publish several progress reports concerning its project on harmful tax competition. In 2000, the OECD published the first progress report on its efforts to identify and eliminate harmful tax competition which identified and listed forty-seven potentially harmful regimes within its Member States. The list of non-member tax haven countries was reduced to thirty-five from the original list of forty-seven countries. The OECD also reviewed holding company regimes but felt that further analysis of these regimes was needed. This resulted in the failure of the organisation to identify any holding company regime as potentially harmful (OECD, 2000). A second progress report was released in 2001, under which several significant alterations were made to the project. The most important alteration was the removal of the 'no or low tax rates' and 'no substantial activities' criteria which was developed by the OECD in the 1998 report for identifying tax havens. Consequently, in determining which countries or jurisdictions would be considered as 'uncooperative tax havens', the OECD would only pursue commitments from countries with respect to the principles of transparency and effective exchange of information (OECD, 2001; 2014). Another progressive report was issued in 2004 which focused primarily on the progress made with respect to eliminating harmful preferential regimes in OECD Member States. The report indicated that of the forty-seven preferential tax regime that had been identified as being potentially harmful, eighteen regimes had been abolished and fourteen were amended to remove their potential harmful features. Upon further analysis, thirteen were found not to be harmful within the meaning of the 1998 report (OECD, 2004). In 2006, the OECD published an update report on progress made in connection with the work done on potentially harmful preferential tax regimes in member countries. The OECD mentioned in the report that its initiative on harmful tax practices has fully achieved its initial aims and that the mandate given in the 1994 report had been met. It was further noted that future work on the project would focus on monitoring any new or continuing preferential tax regime identified by its member countries (OECD, 2006).

Another big initiative created by the OECD is the base erosion and profit shifting (BEPS) project which is directed towards MNCs who exploit gaps in tax rules in order to shift profits to low tax jurisdictions. The BEPS project therefore aims to 'improve the coherence of international tax rules, reinforce their focus on economic substance and ensure a more transparent tax environment' (OECD, 2013). In implementing the project, over 135 countries and jurisdictions are brought together under the OECD/G20 Inclusive Framework on BEPS. The project provides a fifteen-Action Plan that seeks to equip governments in different countries and jurisdictions with the domestic and international instruments needed to address the issue of tax avoidance. The OECD believes that with this project, countries around the world can ensure 'that profits are taxed where economic activities generating the profits are performed and where value is created' (OECD, 2019b). In 2016, a platform for collaboration of tax was launched by the IMF, OECD, UN and the World Bank with the aim of strengthening the cooperation between these organisations on tax issues. The platform 'formalises regular discussions between the four organisations on the design and implementation of standards for international tax matters, strengthens their ability to provide capacity-building support to developing countries, and helps them deliver jointly developed guidance' (OECD, 2021b). The platform's tasks are closely linked with the OECD/G20 BEPS project, as it delivers several publications designed to help developing countries implement the action plans under the project.

§7.07 CONCLUSION

The hot debate surrounding tax havens and the role they play in global financial crises have required addressing whether tax havens are the root cause of many fiscal challenges plaguing the governments of the world or whether they are merely convenient scapegoats used by powerful political leaders to conceal the hypocrisy and incompetence of governments in high tax countries.

It is safe to admit that tax havens may have some adverse effects on the global economy, particularly when abused by individuals and MNCs. However, it is also worth acknowledging that tax havens indeed play a crucial and valuable role in the economic development of non-tax haven countries and jurisdictions.

Bibliography

Africa Confidential. (2020). Listing reputations. Retrieved from https://www.africa-confidential.com/article-preview/id/13081/Listing_reputations.

African Tax Administration Forum. (2019). The place of Africa in the shift towards Global Tax Governance: Can the taxation of the digitalised economy be an opportunity for more inclusiveness? Retrieved from https://events.ataftax.org/index.php?page = documents&func = view&document_id = 35.

Altshuler, R. & Grubert, H. (2004). Taxpayer Responses to Competitive Tax Policies and Tax Policy Responses to Competitive Taxpayers: Recent Evidence. *Tax Notes International*, 34(13), 1346-1362.

Barber, H. (2007). *Tax Havens Today: The Benefits and Pitfalls of Banking and Investing Offshore.* Retrieved from https://library.law.yale.edu/research/guides/resources/tax-havens-today-benefits-and-pitfalls-banking-and-investing-offshore.

Brennan, G. & Buchanan, J. M. (1980). *The Power to Tax: Analytical Foundations of a Fiscal Constitution.* New York: Cambridge University Press.

Christensen, R. C. (2020). Covid-19 and the fight against tax havens: Opportunities and risks for developing countries. Retrieved from https://www.ictd.ac/blog/covid-19-fight-against-tax-havens-opportunities-risks-developing-countries/.

Commitment to aid flows must be combined with a crackdown on tax havens, and Britain can do more. (2008). *The Guardian.* Retrieved from https://www.theguardian.com/commentisfree/2008/nov/27/comment-aid-development-tax-havens.

Corporate Finance Institute. (2021). What is the OECD (Organization for Economic Cooperation and Development)? Retrieved from https://corporatefinanceinstitute.com/resources/knowledge/economics/oecd/.

Desai, M. A., Foley, C. F. & Hines, J. R. (2004). Economic Effects of Regional Tax Havens. *NBER Working Paper No. 10806.* Retrieved from https://papers.ssrn.com/sol3/Delivery.cfm/nber_w10806.pdf?abstractid = 601108&mirid = 1.

Dharmapala, D. (2008). What Problems and Opportunities are Created by Tax Havens? Retrieved from https://papers.ssrn.com/sol3/Delivery.cfm/SSRN_ID1279146_code231355.pdf?abstractid = 1279146&mirid = 1.

Dharmapala, D. & Hines, J. R. (2006). Which Countries Become Tax Havens? *Nber Working Paper 12802.* Retrieved from https://www.nber.org/system/files/working_papers/w12802/w12802.pdf.

Dharmapala, D. & Hines, J. R. (2009). Which countries become tax havens? *Journal of Public Economics,* 93(9-10), 1058-1068. Retrieved from https://econpapers.repec.org/article/eeepubeco/v_3a93_3ay_3a2009_3ai_3a9-10_3ap_3a1058-1068.htm.

European Union. (2021). Evolution of the EU list of tax havens. Retrieved from https://ec.europa.eu/taxation_customs/sites/taxation/files/eu_list_update_22_02_2021_en.pdf.

Fitzgibbon, W. & Hallman, B. (2020). What is a tax haven? Offshore finance, explained. Retrieved from https://www.icij.org/investigations/panama-papers/what-is-a-tax-haven-offshore-finance-explained/.

Fox, B. (2020). Countries seek removal from controversial EU 'blacklists'. Retrieved from https://www.euractiv.com/section/botswana/news/countries-seek-removal-from-controversial-eu-tax-blacklists/.

Fuest, C. & Riedel, N. (2010). Tax evasion and tax avoidance in developing countries: evidence on international profit shifting. Retrieved from https://oxfordtax.sbs.ox.ac.uk/tax-evasion-and-tax-avoidance-developing-countries-evidence-international-profit-shifting.

Global Alliance for Tax Justice. (2019). Corporate Tax Haven Index 2019. Retrieved from https://www.globaltaxjustice.org/en/latest/corporate-tax-haven-index-2019.

Hines, J. R. (2004). Do Tax Havens Flourish? *Nber Working Paper 10936.* Retrieved from https://www.nber.org/system/files/working_papers/w10936/w10936.pdf.

Hines, J. R., Gumpert, A. & Schnitzer, M. (2016). Multinational Firms and Tax Havens. *The Review of Economics and Statistics*, 98(4), 713-27.

Hotzblatt, M., Jermakowicz, E., & Epstein, B., (2015). Tax Heavens: Methods and Tactics for Corporate Profit Shifting. Retrieved from https://www.researchgate.net/publication/283047881_Tax_Heavens_Methods_and_Tactics_for_Corporate_Profit_Shifting.

International Monetary Fund. Statistics Department. (1996). *International Financial Statistics Yearbook*. Retrieved from https://www.imf.org/en/Publications/International-Financial-Statistics/Issues/2016/12/30/International-Financial-Statistics-Yearbook-1996-410.

International Monetary Fund. Statistics Department. (2002). *Statistics on Offshore Financial Centers*. Fifteenth Meeting of the IMF Committee on Balance of Payments Statistics BOPCOM-02/11. Retrieved from https://www.imf.org/external/pubs/ft/bop/2002/02-11.pdf.

Jackson, J. (2010). The OECD Initiative on Tax Havens. *Congressional Research Service*. Retrieved from https://www.everycrsreport.com/files/20100311_R40114_5eb4c3dc8bdd2a6bc8fbda0d24b763d4f8afff89.pdf.

Khanna, A. (2021). Will Tax Havens Fall Prey to Global Momentum on Anti-Abuse Tax Initiatives? Retrieved from https://news.bloombergtax.com/daily-tax-report/insight-64.

Kittredge G., Schuur, P., Volhard, P., Young, P. & Berry, T. (2020). Cayman Islands Added to EU Tax Blacklist – Consequences for Investment Funds. *Debevoise & Plimpton*. Retrieved from https://www.debevoise.com/insights/publications/2020/02/cayman-islands-added-to-eu-tax-blacklist.

KYC360. (2018). Understanding EU blacklists and tax havens. Retrieved from https://www.riskscreen.com/kyc360/article/understanding-eu-blacklists-tax-havens/.

Loomer, G. & Maffini, G. (2009). Tax Havens and The Financial Crisis. Retrieved from https://core.ac.uk/download/pdf/288286539.pdf.

Lynn, M. (2009). Tax havens are a scapegoat for government hypocrisy and incompetence. *MoneyWeek*. Retrieved from https://moneyweek.com/20114/tax-havens-are-a-scapegoat-for-government-hypocrisy-and-incompetence-46032.

Manning, J. (2018). *The Open Sea: The Economic Life of the Ancient Mediterranean World from the Iron Age to the Rise of Rome*. Princeton University Press. Retrieved from https://books.google.com.ng/books/about/The_Open_Sea.html?id=RFVGDwAAQBAJ&redir_esc=y.

Michiel, V., Weyzig, F. & Murphy, R. (2006). The Netherlands – A tax haven? Amsterdam, Centre for Research on Multinational Organisations. Retrieved from https://www.researchgate.net/publication/228129844_The_Netherlands_A_Tax_Haven.

Mitchell, D. (2006a). The Economic Case for Tax Havens. Retrieved from https://internationalman.com/articles/the-economic-case-for-tax-havens/.

Mitchell, D. (2006b). The Moral Case for Tax Havens. Retrieved from http://www.fnf.org.ph/downloadables/Moral%20Case%20for%20Tax%20Havens.pdf.

Mitchell, D. (2016). The Necessary and Valuable Economic Role of Tax Havens. Retrieved from https://www.cato.org/blog/necessary-valuable-economic-role-tax-havens.

Monsour, M. (2020). $427bn lost to tax havens every year: landmark study reveals countries' losses and worst offenders. *Tax Justice Network*. Retrieved from https://www.taxjustice.net/2020/11/20/427bn-lost-to-tax-havens-every-year-landmark-study-reveals-countries-losses-and-worst-offenders/.

Narci, H. (2012). Tax Havens & The OECD Campaign Against them. Retrieved from http://uniset.ca/microstates2/narci.pdf.

Norges Offentlige Utredninger (NOU) (2009). Tax havens and development: Status, analyses and measures. *Official Norwegian Reports 2009: 19.* Retrieved from https://www.cmi.no/publications/file/3470-tax-havens-and-development.pdf.

Offshore Protection. (2021). Advantages and Disadvantages of Tax Havens. Retrieved from https://www.offshore-protection.com/tax-havens-advantages-disadvantages.

Organisation for Economic Cooperation and Development. Committee on Fiscal Affairs. (1987). *International Tax Avoidance and Evasion Four Related Studies No. 1.* Retrieved from https://www.worldcat.org/title/international-tax-avoidance-and-evasion-four-related-studies/oclc/15749366.

Organisation for Economic Cooperation and Development. (1998). *Harmful Tax Competition: An Emerging Global Issue.* Retrieved from https://www.oecd.org/ctp/harmful/1904176.pdf.

Organisation for Economic Cooperation and Development. (2000). *Towards Global Tax Cooperation: Progress in Identifying and Eliminating Harmful Tax Practices.* Retrieved from https://www.oecd.org/ctp/harmful/2090192.pdf.

Organisation for Economic Cooperation and Development. (2001). *The OECD's Project on Harmful Tax Practices: The 2001 Progress Report.* Retrieved from https://www.oecd.org/tax/harmful/2664450.pdf.

Organisation for Economic Cooperation and Development. (2004). *The OECD's Project on Harmful Tax Practices: The 2004 Progress Report.* Retrieved from https://www.oecd.org/ctp/harmful/oecd-harmful-tax-practices-project-2004-progress-report.pdf.

Organisation for Economic Cooperation and Development. (2006). *The OECD's Project on Harmful Tax Practices: 2006 Update on Progress in Member Countries.* Retrieved from https://www.oecd.org/ctp/harmful/37446434.pdf.

Organisation for Economic Cooperation and Development. (2014). *Countering Harmful Tax Practices More Effectively, Taking into Account Transparency and Substance.* Retrieved from https://www.oecd-ilibrary.org/docserver/9789264218970-en.pdf?expires=1621771120&id=id&accname=guest&checksum=C0FB417FBB8752F756806FCAB3C24BC9.

Organisation for Economic Cooperation and Development. (2019a). Action 5 Harmful tax practices. Retrieved from https://www.oecd.org/tax/beps/beps-actions/action5/.

Organisation for Economic Cooperation and Development. (2019b). Platform for Collaboration of Tax. Retrieved from https://www.oecd.org/tax/platform-for-collaboration-on-tax.htm.

Organisation for Economic Cooperation and Development. (2021). Global Forum on Transparency and Exchange of Information for Tax Purposes. Retrieved from https://www.oecd.org/tax/transparency/who-we-are/about/.

Oxfam. (2021). EU Tax Haven Blacklist Review. Retrieved from https://oxfam.box.com/v/2021EUTaxHavensBrief.

Oxfam. Tax Havens: Releasing The Hidden Billions For Poverty Eradication. Retrieved from https://www.taxjustice.net/cms/upload/pdf/tax_havens.pdf.

Palan, R. (2009). History of tax havens. Retrieved from https://www.historyandpolicy.org/policy-papers/papers/history-of-tax-havens.

Prasad. R. (2021). Impact of the EU tax blacklist in the Pacific. Retrieved from https://devpolicy.org/impact-of-eu-tax-blacklist-in-the-pacific-20210303/.

Raposo A. & Mourao P. (2013). Tax Havens or Tax Hells? A discussion of the historical roots and present consequences of tax havens. *Financial Theory and Practice*.

Robertson, J. (2017). First tax havens blacklist published by EU. *BBC News*. Retrieved from https://www.bbc.com/news/business-42237315.

Seabrooke, L. & Wigan, D. (2013). Emergent Entrepreneurs in Transnational Advocacy Networks: Professional Mobilization in the Fight for Global Tax Justice. *GREEN Working Paper No. 41*. Retrieved from https://cris.unu.edu/sites/cris.unu.edu/files/WP%2041_GREEN_Seabrooke%20and%20Wigan.pdf.

Snell, W. (2018). The Tax Justice Network seeks two new board members. *Tax Justice Network*. Retrieved from https://www.taxjustice.net/2018/09/26/the-tax-justice-network-seeks-two-new-board-members/.

Songailaitė, M. (2020). Differences, Similarities, and Proposals for the OECD and the EU Blacklisting Measures. Retrieved from https://www.diva-portal.org/smash/get/diva2:1437899/FULLTEXT02.

Sullivan, M. A. (2007). Lessons From the Last War on Tax Havens. Retrieved from http://www.taxhistory.org/www/features.nsf/Articles/F3AA18739F0EFF008525744B0066459B?OpenDocument.

Tax Justice Network. (2007). Identifying Tax Havens and Offshore Finance Centres. Retrieved from https://www.taxjustice.net/cms/upload/pdf/Identifying_Tax_Havens_Jul_07.pdf.

Tax Justice Network. (2020a). Financial Secrecy Index. Retrieved from https://fsi.taxjustice.net/en/.

Tax Justice Network. (2021a). Tax havens and secrecy jurisdictions. Retrieved from https://www.taxjustice.net/topics/tax-havens-and-secrecy-jurisdictions/.

Welsh, T. (2016). Oxfam's 355 economists are completely wrong: Tax havens do serve a useful purpose. *City A.M.* Retrieved from https://www.cityam.com/oxfams-355-economists-are-completely-wrong-tax-havens-do-serve-a-useful-purpose/.

WorldData. (2021). The most popular tax havens worldwide. Retrieved from https://www.worlddata.info/tax-havens.php.

Zoromé, A. (2007). Concept of Offshore Financial Centers: In Search of an Operational Definition. *Working Paper 07/87*. Washington DC: International Monetary Fund. Retrieved from https://www.imf.org/external/pubs/ft/wp/2007/wp0787.pdf.

CHAPTER 8

Reforming International Taxation: Participation and Collaboration of Developing Countries

Natalia Pushkareva

The first part of the chapter summarizes key tax issues specific or especially important to developing countries, such as capacity constraints, base erosion and profit shifting (BEPS) by multinational corporations (MNE), illicit financial flows, taxation of natural resources, and blacklisting. It then discusses the challenges faced by lower-income jurisdictions when representing their interests at international tax policy fora. It highlights inclusiveness issues within international institutions working on tax policy matters, and the factors that hinder the effective participation of developing countries in international tax policy debates. The chapter also highlights the potential of regional cooperation, and the ways in which regional fora can help developing countries effectively voice their opinions. The chapter concludes that while the actual representation of developing economies in international tax policy making did increase in recent years, significant work remains to ensure developing countries are truly represented on an equal footing, and through genuine participation and collaboration.

§8.01 INTRODUCTION

As the international community embarks on an international tax reform in light of challenges to tax the digital economy, participation and collaboration of all countries in the norm-setting process become of utmost importance (Oguttu, 2020). While important progress has been made in the last few years to increase international tax cooperation, shortcomings in international proposals and negotiations remain significant in supporting the effective participation and collaboration of developing countries. Specific issues particular to the economy of lower-income countries, such as those of capacity, resources, and the proliferation of cash transactions, must be understood, acknowledged, and taken into consideration in international tax policy discussions and proposals to create a landscape that benefits all. While a shift in perspective occurred since the beginning of the Base Erosion and Profit Shifting (BEPS) project, significant effort remains to ensure all countries participate on an equal footing. This chapter discusses the challenges for the successful participation and collaboration of developing countries in the international tax reform as well as solutions to adapt current and future international tax policy to the needs of developing countries.[1]

First, the chapter aims to identify the most acute issues and concerns related to international taxation faced by developing countries and analyzes whether these are similar or different among developing jurisdictions. Second, the role international tax standard-setting bodies should play in addressing these issues and concerns is discussed. Finally, the challenges for supporting regional and international tax cooperation in developing countries are considered.

§8.02 INTERNATIONAL TAX REFORM: THE MAIN ISSUES AND CONCERNS FOR DEVELOPING COUNTRIES

The launching of the BEPS project by the Organization of Economic Cooperation and Development (OECD) marked the importance of international cooperation to face BEPS challenges that constitute a serious risk to tax revenues as well as tax sovereignty and tax fairness for all countries. In its BEPS action plan in 2013, the organization stated that in order to ensure international consensus on addressing BEPS, the perspective of developing countries would be taken into account. However, because the drafting of the initial BEPS agenda did not provide for the consultation of developing countries, many worry that the issues and ensuing solutions mainly concerned the developed world. The nature of BEPS concerns is not uniform for all countries, and BEPS schemes

1. This chapter summarizes the discussion that took place at TaxCOOP 2020 World Tax Summit, on October 14, 2020. The panel of experts moderated by Martin Hearson of the Institute of Development Studies included Annet Wanyana Oguttu, professor of tax law at the Department of Taxation and the African Tax Institute of University of Pretoria, Mary Baine, Director of Tax Programmes at the African Tax Administration Forum, LuckyStar Miyandazi, international tax specialist working on policy research and political economy analysis in Africa and Europe, Leopoldo Parada, Lecturer in Tax Law University of Leeds School of Law, Diego Quinones, partner of Quinones Cruz Abogados, Tarcisio Diniz Magalhães, Research Professor of Digitalization and Taxation at the University of Antwerp Faculty of Law and Lecturer in Tax Policy and Taxation at the McGill University Faculty of Law, Vidushi Gupta, LL.M. candidate at LSE and a 2021 Chevening scholar, Irma Mosquera Valderrama, Associate Professor and Ph.D. Dean at Leiden Law School, Joy Waruguru Ndubai, Teaching and Research Associate at the WU Institute for Austrian and International Tax Law and Doctoral Candidate at the WU Vienna University of Economics and Business, Javier Garcia-Bernardo, data scientist at the Tax Justice Network and researcher at the University of Amsterdam, Alexandra Readhead, Lead of Tax and Extractives at International Institute for Sustainable Development and myself, Natalia Pushkareva, Ph.D. candidate at the University of Urbino on October 14, 2020, as part of the World Tax Summit.

that undermine the European or American tax base often do not coincide with the BEPS concerns of developing countries.

The United Nations (UN) stressed that efforts in international tax cooperation should be universal in approach and scope and should fully take into account the different needs and capacities of all countries, in particular, least developed countries (UNCTAD, 2019), land-locked developing countries (UN Vienna Programme, 2014), small-island developing states (UN Samoa Pathway, 2014) and African economies (UNCTAD, 2020). The African Tax Administration Forum (ATAF) noted that the development of rules for global taxation should address concerns of all countries, and it should be inclusive to ensure the effective application of the international tax rules by developed, emerging, and developing economies alike.

Efforts have been taken to involve developing countries and to address some of their BEPS concerns, such as laws related to transfer pricing of commodities that were included in BEPS action measures in 2015 (OECD, 2015). The toolkits developed by the Platform for Collaboration on Tax, supported by the Development Working Group of the G20, also included specific tax concerns of developing countries, such as tax incentives and simplified methods for arriving at an arms-length price. Issues regarding capacity constraints of developing countries have also been tackled through collaborative efforts and initiatives like Tax Inspectors Without Borders. Developing countries expressed strong interest in continuing participation via the establishment of a more inclusive framework (IF). While in 2019 the OECD launched the IF formally uniting 139 jurisdictions, the extent to which the interests of the IF members are actually represented at the OECD remains unclear (Christensen, Hearson, and Randriamanalina, 2020).

In autumn 2020 the OECD released reports on BEPS Pillar 1, reallocating some profits of MNE, and Pillar 2, introducing global minimum corporate tax (OECD, 2020). Both pillars were designed to protect the tax base of every country. Whether these goals were achieved for developing countries is also subject to discussion (Lammers, 2020). In June 2021, G7 Finance Ministries "agreed on historic global tax agreement" (G7, 2021) which was also widely criticized for favoring interests of large, industrialized, developed economies (Christensen, 2021; Tax Justice Network Africa, 2021). Representation of developing countries' interests in international tax policy making remains a challenge.

[A] Capacity Constraint and Accessible Solutions

As expressed by Annet Oguttu (2020), collaboration requires that countries work together to set the norms for international taxation and that these norms are respected by all countries, and evenhandedness is applied to any country that does not comply with the norms, for example, the automatic exchange of information on tax matters. Even though many developing countries face capacity constraints in complying with the set requirements, a good number of them have enacted relevant legislation, signed the treaties, put in place confidentiality requirements, and have gone through the OECD Global Forum peer reviews, some of them being rated as "compliant" or "largely compliant." Some developing countries have benefited from this process, however, the experience of many is that there is no guarantee the information will actually be provided to them, as there is little confidence from developed countries that some developing countries will ensure confidentiality of such information or comply with the standards for data protection of sensitive business information. Thus, requests for the exchange of information or assistance in the collection of taxes are often ignored or rejected. In such cases, the OECD Global Forum does not provide any protective measures for developing countries that feel like their treaty partners are not compliant with their commitments.

Joy Waruguru Ndubai (2020) points out that compliance with norms should not be enforced upon countries with constrained capacity. Noncompliance with norms by countries due to limited capacity should not be treated in the same manner as countries that are genuinely engaging in harmful or abusive behavior. The implementation or evaluation of standards as if all countries are equal and the same, means that the system that is being implemented can never be fundamentally fair, as it fails to consider the actual challenges, i.e., the needs and the capacity of some countries. Perhaps special and preferential treatment for the implementation and the evaluation of compliance with a norm could be considered for developing countries. Also, encouraging and supporting regional organizations to assess compliance of their own countries could be a viable solution, since they probably have appropriate tools as well as a better understanding of the local context than international organizations.

Also, according to Joy Waruguru Ndubai (2020), it is relevant to assess the appropriateness of the norms and the standards for all, to question whether these are contextually relevant. Countries have different needs and different development levels, as well as information asymmetries. For example, in the case of exchange of information reports or country-by-country reports, the capacities are different in developed countries in comparison to developing economies. The information provided by these reports might be less relevant and effective for developing countries, as they might not be able to utilize it as much or if they do, the information might not produce the same returns considering the investment in these tools. This is illustrated in the recent report from the Global Forum on tax transparency in Africa (OECD Global Forum, 2020).

Finally, simplicity is extremely important, it is the most important factor. An increasingly complex system is going to create uncertainty and compliance challenges.

Ndubai (2020) highlights the importance of acknowledging the unique solutions emerging from developing countries. When discussing the digital economy, conversations tend to center around the need to find solutions for Africa, without taking into consideration or recognizing the solutions African countries have developed for themselves. While some solutions might be questionable, they should be recognized as a response, such as the over-the-top tax in Uganda. In fact, this response is quite interesting because it recognizes that some developing countries can't resort to a direct tax because it is very difficult for them to tax digital companies. As a result, they shift their focus on individuals, finding indirect solutions. Many African countries implemented excise duties, South Africa applying value-added taxes for example. The international community should evaluate what is "on the ground" before it begins to implement very complex solutions. LuckyStar Miyandazi (2020) also reiterates that the suggested policies often ignore the fact that the ATAF actually has policies. It can be easier to implement these policies rather than creating new ones at OECD/UN level.

Vidushi Gupta (2020) talks about the concern that international organizations as well as some countries don't fully acknowledge the importance of Pillar 1 for developing countries. Indeed, these rules allowing taxing rights to market jurisdictions fail to acknowledge the fact that developing countries have made an undeniable contribution to the growth of the digital economy. Some of the issues intrinsically important to developing countries have not been taken into account, such as existing inequalities at the national level and the complexity to implement Pillar 1, while there is no clarity on how much revenue developing countries will get from it.

[B] Base Erosion and Profit Shifting

According to Javier Garcia-Bernardo (2020), corporate tax avoidance harms every country, but especially so developing economies which lose an equivalent of 50% of their public expenditure on healthcare because of BEPS, whereas this is 4.5% for high-income countries. (Garcia-Bernardo and Janský, 2021). Given such dissimilar patterns, it is relevant to assess how the output produced by international organizations on this issue considers the interests of developing countries. In the specific case of the BEPS plan, many affirm there is a clear underrepresentation of developing countries. The BEPS proposal is highly complex and some question its efficiency. The OECD estimated that BEPS results in a loss of global tax revenues amounting to USD 100-USD 240 billion annually and the organization expects that Pillar 2 will result in a recovery of USD 150 billion in tax revenues and Pillar 1 with the reallocation of USD 100 million profit (OECD 2021). Pillar 2 establishes a minimal tax rate, so if an entity pays less than the minimal tax rate in a country then the parent corporation pays the tax in its jurisdiction, which are typically not developing countries. Since the minimum tax rate is likely to be around 15%, multinationals will have a huge incentive to keep shifting profits to tax havens, and the parent jurisdiction will have a huge incentive not to stop this because it benefits them. Javier Garcia-Bernardo (2020) is questioning to what extent international organizations can fix profit shifting out of developing countries unless the developing countries are not only formally involved in the process, but also empowered.

[C] Foreign Tax Investment and Harmful Tax Practice

Tarcisio Diniz Magalhães (2020) states that tax policy priorities of developed and developing countries are different, and for the latter, phenomena such as illicit financial flows, natural resources, and tax evasion are much more acute, which is something developed countries often fail to recognize.

When it comes to noncompliance with the OECD recommendations to curtail harmful tax practices, however, developed countries have the power to impose sanctions or blacklist non-complying jurisdictions. The OECD, for example, maintains a list of noncooperative tax havens (OECD, 2002), and since 2017 the European Council prepares a list of non-cooperative jurisdictions for tax purposes (European Council, 2020), which are subject to certain sanctions like reduced access to funding from European Union (EU) countries. The fact that EU blacklists criteria include countries that have not implemented the OECD Inclusive Framework Minimum Standards, even though membership to the IF is supposed to be voluntary, is a concern for many developing countries. Coercion from the EU to comply with BEPS Minimum Standards is undesirable for international collaboration and blacklisting small African countries like Namibia poses a challenge for attracting foreign direct investment (FDI) in these countries, as it affects their reputation in the eyes of other countries and potential investors. The threat to BEPS that such small countries pose simply cannot be compared to the threat posed by historical European tax havens like the Netherlands or Switzerland (Oguttu, 2020).

According to the UNCTAD report (UNCTAD 2020), one of the key tax-related issues for developing countries is inclusive growth and tax competition/race to the bottom. These countries compete for FDI and reduce their corporate tax rates, and this has been a problem for many African countries. As pointed out by Leopoldo Parada (2020) most developing countries struggle to balance attracting FDIs and complying with the international standards to avoid negative reputational consequences such as being classified as a tax haven. Developing countries can take substantially different approaches when faced with such a dilemma. Drawing a parallel with the proposition for a global minimum tax in Pillar 2, for example, the minimum effective corporate tax rate discussed in a context of ending "harmful" tax competition prompts the question if such competition is entirely undesirable for developing countries. One can ask if it makes sense for them to embrace the minimum effective corporate tax, not only from a substantive perspective but also from a formal perspective, with all its complexity and unprepared tax administrations.

A global minimum tax will have an impact in addressing the race to the bottom and tax incentives for developing countries. However, if we actually assess this measure in terms of participation and cooperation, it hardly seems fair that, while the developed countries have benefited from the current system for years, the minimum tax that is to be set will be disadvantageous to developing countries and impact their ability to use tax incentives within the guidelines of the OECD Global Forum. The OECD could provide proper guidance on how to use the incentives to promote FDI (Oguttu, 2020). For developing countries, tax incentives are now as important as ever as they start recovering from the COVID-19 pandemic. The minimum tax rate proposed by the OECD is very likely to be much lower than the statutory tax rate, meaning that for many countries it will not change anything. While this could face a lot of opposition, a potential solution to mitigate this issue could be to adapt the "Subject to Tax rule" so that it is broad in scope, covering all payments within treaties.

[D] Tax Revenues and Types of Taxation

For developing countries, the focus should be to go back to the fundamentals to determine what must be solved, before being able to tax multinationals and achieve other fiscal goals. This requires addressing both national and international levels at the same time. When it comes to the national level, the lack of resources in developing countries rather than lack of expertise can be an issue. The economic landscape in which developing countries are navigating does not necessarily mirror that of developed countries. Indeed, it can be argued that the focus on corporate income tax is misplaced when in most developing countries consumption taxation is the main source of revenues. The reality of developing countries is completely different from that of developed countries. Diego Quinones (2020) makes a similar argument about taxation of the digital economy: the international community came to a consensus that the solution to the current situation is a form of tax on revenues from digital activities, while the Value Added Tax (VAT) could in fact be a better alternative for some countries.

When analyzing issues related to developing countries, it is important to remember that we are in fact discussing diverse groups of different kinds of countries with each their own economic landscape and trends, as opposed to a single monolith group. In some developing countries, OECD statistics show a larger proportion of revenue collected from VAT. On the other hand, a report issued by ATAF (ATAF, 2020) reflecting an African perspective illustrates that some indirect taxes are not really contributing that much for some developing countries due to the low purchasing power of most taxpayers as well as the existence of a big informal sector. The report found that in many African countries, a small number of multinationals (1-4) are contributing to about 60%-80%, sometimes even 95% of the total revenues that these countries are collecting. Oguttu (2020) notes that while such revenues from just one MNE may be quite a drop in the ocean for developed economies, it is significant for small African countries, and for many of them this is all they rely on, justifying the necessity to address the corporate tax leak rather than empathizing the direct taxes in some circumstances.

[E] Allocation of Taxing Rights

Thabo Mbeki's report (Mbeki et al., 2015) on illicit financial flows estimated how much Africa loses due to illegal transactions. The main problems identified through the report were: commercial activities including abusive transfer pricing, trade mis-invoicing, unequal contracts, and criminal activities including financial fraud, organized crime, and corruption. In September 2020 UNCTAD also looked at illicit financial flows in their report (UNCTAD, 2020). They came up with a figure of USD 88.6 billion annually in capital flight, which could be invested for Sustainable Development Goals (SDG). According to Mary Baine (2020), after five years of BEPS, the consensus among African countries (at least ATAF members) is that the project will not be able to stop the illicit financial flows for a number of reasons.

Foremost, many African countries consider that it did not address one of the most fundamental concerns of African countries, which is the current imbalance in allocating taxing rights, which are unfairly weighted in favor of residence countries to the detriment of the source jurisdiction. Not only was the allocation of taxing rights not one of the BEPS original project's objectives, but the BEPS actions had a very limited impact on addressing profit shifting by MNEs for African countries, as the rules are often too complex for developing countries to benefit from them (Baine, 2020).

Since the 15-Action Plan of the BEPS project, the focus of the IF has been on dealing with the tax challenges largely connected to the digitalized economy. The efforts to reform the rules acknowledge the fact that the current policies are not designed for taxation of current business models according to which foreign enterprises can carry out business in a jurisdiction without the need to have any physical presence there.

Even if a consensus can be reached, it is not likely to address the key tax issue of the allocation of taxing rights facing Africa. At the international level, discussions must move away from the rhetoric that under taxation must first be stopped in order to tackle the allocation of taxing rights. The reality is that both issues are interconnected: the misallocation of taxing rights generates under taxation. International organizations must recognize that cooperation among all countries is what allows multinationals to create value, generate profit, and cooperative surpluses. Thus, allocating resources among all countries in a fair way is critical.

When discussing taxing rights, the precarious economic state of developing countries can't be ignored. On one hand, developing countries are stating that they cannot continue to live on international aid forever and need to raise their internally generated revenue. On the other hand, countries providing that aid are not ready to cede taxing rights to provide developing countries with more fiscal independence. How these countries are supposed to generate more revenue remains unclear (Baine, 2020).

It is important to recognize that not all jurisdictions have the same tax policy objectives or face the same administrative constraints. In addition, some developing countries are not members of the IF, so it is important to consider what will happen to those countries in case a global consensus is reached. It is likely to mean policies they do not support and are too complicated for them to implement. This might have repercussions, especially with the EU blacklisting process discussed above. Although a fair allocation of taxing rights may be an objective of the reform, the participation and collaboration throughout the negotiation process may be ill-suited to reach this goal.

§8.03 THE ROLE OF INTERNATIONAL ORGANIZATIONS IN FOSTERING PARTICIPATION AND COLLABORATION OF DEVELOPING COUNTRIES

[A] Participation: What It Means for Developing Countries

Acknowledging that globalization requires global solutions, the OECD set up an IF to foster a global dialogue on BEPS and to monitor implementation of BEPS minimal standards with all interested parties, developed and developing countries, participating on an equal footing. Many developing countries are involved in the process—currently twenty-five from Africa—including international organizations, such as the UN, and regional organizations in Africa, such as the Cercle de réflexion et d'échange des dirigeants des administrations fiscales (CREDAF) and ATAF. The question of whether developing countries have effectively participated in the IF, however, remains unanswered.

According to Oguttu (2020), although the IF seeks to ensure developing countries are engaging with developed countries on an equal footing, there are concerns that the platform does not necessarily enhance equitable participation. The experience of some developing countries is that it creates an environment allowing them to be present, but still not experiencing participation on an equal footing. Voluntary cooperation in a system is not in itself proof that the system benefits all of its participants. International platforms for cooperation and collaboration may provide for strategic interactions and agenda-setting by key actors, the prevalence of network solutions to get fast action that imposes externalities on other countries, and asymmetric relationships among countries that tilled the playing field in favor of stronger actors.

Often, when such strategic positions are being taken, many developing countries in Africa, Asia, and Latin America lack the resources to sustain the pace of the many meetings that are held, often in Europe, struggling to send officials to attend those meetings, while the representatives of developed jurisdictions easily access them. In the case of many developing countries, only a few officials work on international tax matters, and they are often seized with other domestic priorities besides attending to the international obligations. Consequently, the speed of the international negotiation process reduces the ability of developing countries to engage fully and on an equal footing with developed countries. International organizations must therefore foster an environment where the unique circumstances of developing countries are acknowledged.

For a number of reasons, it is currently very challenging for developing countries with a limited capacity to participate in international fora effectively. The complexity of global tax rules creates a barrier preventing developing economies from making their participation effective. Most of the work is really specialized, causing the limited number of high-skilled tax professionals in developing countries to spend all their time in international negotiations and discussions to the detriment of the audits back home. The whole process of participation in discussions at international bodies can be very intimidating for developing economies, and often they would rather not make any interventions due to the fear of being contradicted at best, or, in some instances, even directly attacked. People would rather give written comments as opposed to going into an open debate because it can really be daunting (Baine, 2020).

Time is another issue: the pace of global forums is very fast, the volume of the paperwork is heavy, complicating the process above the capacity of developing countries. Even when technical support is provided, it is very difficult to keep up because participants have capacity issues, technological issues, and above all, they do not have enough resources to commit to such a complex process.

The African countries can only enhance their participation and benefit from the process if they coordinate, have a collaborative attitude, and have a clear policy direction that will not only get these countries more rights but will also stop these illicit financial flows with clear and very specific laws to support the process. In the absence of this, international taxation challenges for developing countries will remain.

[B] Inclusion Versus Genuine Participation and Collaboration

As we know, merely having a seat at the table is not enough to ensure meaningful participation of developing countries in the OECD policy-making process. Decision-making power requires the opportunity to make others aware of your specific interests, and a genuine interest in mutually beneficial solutions from all parties. It is important to recognize that some countries do not even have starting positions. It is only possible to have a proper conversation when there is such initial equality, after which consideration can be given to how the rules are evening out the revenue or the consumption. Within existing differences, however, developing countries did not have a chance to benefit for years, and while the rules are being reformed, with limited participation by these countries they may suffer from this reform without necessarily getting any benefits from it. On the one hand, the OECD claims it wants to give more taxing rights to market jurisdictions. On the other, it is forcing developing countries to have minimum taxation without recognizing their reliance on that measure to attract FDI—whether it's efficient or sustainable is another debate—and designing the Global Anti-Erosion (GloBE) rules in a way that will eventually benefit the residence countries.

While Africa has twenty-five people representing the continent at the OECD Inclusive Framework meetings, Mary Baine (2020) questions how much they really get to say and how much they are listened to and get to influence actual policies. Underrepresentation is a real issue, which puts the success of the international tax reform at risk since, as long as nobody is listening to developing countries, the policies will continue to be unbalanced.

The process requires representation on fair, and not equal, footing. Treating unequals equally does not make them equal, it only increases existing inequality. There was a lot of discussion recently about Pillar 1 and how it fails to account for differences in sizes and structures of economies and the variety of roles that countries play, for example, in global supply chains of multinational companies. Actively listening to developing countries prevents paternalistic behaviors. It's crucial to consider the systemic and institutional issues of the current global negotiations and understand how actors develop the internal policies and processes within international organizations that allow for the inclusion of developing countries in active conversation. This also requires more transparency on the structure and negotiation process at the OECD.

[C] Regional Cooperation for Developing Countries

Alexandra Readhead (2020) affirms that achieving cooperation is difficult because competition is also occurring, and perhaps especially at the regional level, to attract FDI. It is therefore crucial to be realistic about what regional and international cooperation can achieve, and secondly, to be constantly ensuring regional and international cooperation is not simply reinforcing existing global norms and standards, which do not necessarily benefit developing countries. Developing countries can go their own way and pursue their own policy goals and objectives even if that is contrary to international or regional cooperation if that's the best thing for this country based on its needs. It is especially so in times of pandemic when difficult circumstances make countries prioritize taking care of themselves over international cooperation, which might result in some conflicting policy choices. Cooperation should not be pursued just for the sake of it, but rather because it is actually in the interest of the countries, particularly those vulnerable.

In supporting regional and international cooperation, some of the issues relate to prioritization. Often the priorities identified by regional or international groups are not necessarily those reflecting the issues facing developing countries' tax administration. There is a need for aligning international and regional agendas with priorities of developing countries and improving domestic revenues mobilization.

Regional bodies are important for the implementation and understanding of the international framework and for making sure the international standards are implemented meaningfully and to the benefit of the organization's members and its impact on developing countries. Regional bodies, such as ATAF, which is familiar with countries' concerns can also come up with tailor-made approaches that are fit for purpose. This example illustrates the role that regional bodies can play.

[D] The Structures of Participation: What Is the Takeaway for Developing Countries

Irma Mosquera Valderrama (2020) raises three questions about the participation of developing countries in international organizations:

(1) Why do countries participate?
(2) Who participates?
(3) Why do countries comply?

When looking at the role of international and regional organizations, one might find that in some cases, countries participate in global fora because of their incentives (assistance, projects, and so forth).

"Who participates" is also problematic: sometimes a country is represented by a person from the ministry of finance and another from the tax administration, and quite often they would have different opinions. In this case, it becomes a political over technical issue and needs coordination.

Implementation of the BEPS minimal standards is another challenge. Globaltaxgov is looking into twelve countries, some countries in Africa, Latin America, Asia, and the EU. One question it poses is why countries comply, and whether we can turn peer review, an instrument of compliance, into an instrument for learning and contextualization. Regional organizations can contribute to a change in best practices in this regard.

Lastly, we must consider the impact the pressure from the EU has on developing countries which decide to not participate in BEPS Inclusive Framework but are incentified not only to participate but also to be peer-reviewed and to receive a positive peer review.

§8.04 CONCLUSION

While decision-making processes are not only involving 37 OECD member countries, but 139 countries through the IF, this chapter demonstrates that significant work remains to ensure developing countries are truly represented on an equal footing and that this can only be achieved through genuine participation and collaboration. As opposed to trying to find ways for developing countries to implement one-size-fits-all policy standards, the specific needs of developing countries must be taken into account to adapt the standards in a way that is beneficial to them, while acknowledging the work regional bodies have already been doing on improving the tax systems of these countries.

Bibliography

African Tax Administration Forum. 2020. Impact of Value-Added Tax in Revenue Stability in Some African Countries—Policy and Compliance Gaps Using the C-efficiency. https://events.ataftax.org/index.php?page = documents&func = view&document_id = 62#.

Baine, Mary. 2020. World Tax Summit—TaxCOOP2020, Reforming International Taxation: Participation and Collaboration of Developing Countries, Montreal (online), October 14, 2020.

Christensen, Rasmus Corlin. 2021. The G7 Tax Deal: "Historic" and "Global"? / ICTD Blog https://www.ictd.ac/blog/g7-tax-deal-historic-global/.

Christensen, Rasmus Corlin, Hearson, Martin & Randriamanalina, Tovony. 2020. At the Table, Off the Menu? Assessing the Participation of Lower-Income Countries in Global Tax Negotiations. International Centre for Tax and Development. ICTD Working Paper No. 115 https://doi.org/10.19088/ICTD.2020.004.

Diniz Magalhães, Tarcisio. 2020. World Tax Summit—TaxCOOP2020, Reforming International Taxation: Participation and Collaboration of Developing Countries, Montreal (online), October 14, 2020.

European Council. 2020. Taxation: EU list of non-cooperative jurisdictions. Latest amendments made through Official Journal of the European Union on 18

February 2020. https://www.consilium.europa.eu/en/policies/eu-list-of-non-cooperative-jurisdictions/.

G7. 2021. G7 Finance Ministers Agree Historic Global Tax Agreement https://www.g7uk.org/g7-finance-ministers-agree-historic-global-tax-agreement/.

Javier, Garcia-Bernardo & Jansky, Petr. 2021. Profit Shifting of Multinational Corporations Worldwide. IES Working Papers 14/2021. IES FSV. Charles University.

Garcia-Bernardo, Javier. 2020. World Tax Summit—TaxCOOP2020, Reforming International Taxation: Participation and Collaboration of Developing Countries, Montreal (online), October 14, 2020.

Gupta, Vidushi. 2020. World Tax Summit—TaxCOOP2020, Reforming International Taxation: Participation and Collaboration of Developing Countries, Montreal (online), October 14, 2020.

Lammers, Jeroen. 2020. Can Developing Countries Do Better Than the Unified Approach? / ICTD Blog. https://www.ictd.ac/blog/developing-countries-unified-approach-digital-economy-tax/.

Mbeki, Thabo et al. 2015. Illicit Financial Flow: Report of the High-Level Panel on Illicit Financial Flows from Africa. The African Union's Economic Commission on Africa.

Miyandazi, Luckystar. 2020. World Tax Summit—TaxCOOP2020, Reforming International Taxation: Participation and Collaboration of Developing Countries, Montreal (online), October 14, 2020.

Mosquera Valderrama, Irma. 2020. World Tax Summit—TaxCOOP2020, Reforming International Taxation: Participation and Collaboration of Developing Countries, Montreal (online), October 14, 2020.

Ndubai, Joy Waruguru. 2020. World Tax Summit—TaxCOOP2020, Reforming International Taxation: Participation and Collaboration of Developing Countries, Montreal (online), October 14, 2020.

OECD. 2002. The OECD List of Uncooperative Tax Havens—A statement by the Chair of the OECD's Committee on Fiscal Affairs, Gabriel Makhlouf, Paris http://www.oecd.org/corruption/theoecdlistofunco-operativetaxhavens-astatementbythechairoftheoecdscommitteeonfiscalaffairsgabrielmakhlouf.htm.

OECD. 2015. BEPS 2015 Final Reports, OECD/G20 Base Erosion and Profit Shifting Project, OECD Publishing, Paris https://www.oecd.org/ctp/beps-2015-final-reports.htm.

OECD. 2020. OECD Global Forum on Transparency and Exchange of Information for Tax Purposes (2020), Tax Transparency in Africa 2020. Africa Initiative Progress Report: 2019 https://www.oecd.org/tax/transparency/documents/Tax-Transparency-in-Africa-2020.pdf.

OECD. 2020. Tax Challenges Arising from Digitalisation—Economic Impact Assessment: Inclusive Framework on BEPS, OECD/G20 Base Erosion and Profit Shifting Project, OECD Publishing, Paris, https://doi.org/10.1787/0e3cc2d4-en.

OECD. 2020. Tax Challenges Arising from Digitalisation—Report on Pillar Two Blueprint: Inclusive Framework on BEPS, OECD/G20 Base Erosion and Profit Shifting Project, OECD Publishing, Paris, https://doi.org/10.1787/abb4c3d1-en.

OECD/G20. 2021. Base Erosion and Profit Shifting Project Addressing the Tax Challenges Arising from the Digitalisation of the Economy, July 2021.

Oguttu, Annet Wanyana. 2020. World Tax Summit—TaxCOOP2020, Reforming International Taxation: Participation and Collaboration of Developing Countries, Montreal (online), October 14, 2020.

Parada, Leopoldo. 2020. World Tax Summit—TaxCOOP2020, Reforming International Taxation: Participation and Collaboration of Developing Countries, Montreal (online), October 14, 2020.

Pushkareva, Natalia. 2020. World Tax Summit—TaxCOOP2020, Reforming International Taxation: Participation and Collaboration of Developing Countries, Montreal (online), October 14, 2020.

Readhead, Alexandra. 2020. World Tax Summit—TaxCOOP2020, Reforming International Taxation: Participation and Collaboration of Developing Countries, Montreal (online), October 14, 2020.

UNCTAD. 2019. The Least Developed Countries Report 2019, https://unctad.org/system/files/official-document/ldcr2019overview_en.pdf.

UNCTAD. 2020. Economic Development in Africa Report 2020: Tackling Illicit Financial Flows for Sustainable Development in Africa. https://unctad.org/system/files/official-document/aldcafrica2020_en.pdf.

United Nations. 2014. UN General Assembly Resolution adopted on November 14, 2014 69/15. SIDS Accelerated Modalities of Action (SAMOA) Pathway, https://www.un.org/ga/search/view_doc.asp?symbol = A/RES/69/15&Lang = E.

United Nations. 2014. Vienna Programme of Action for Landlocked Developing Countries for the Decade 2014-2024, https://unohrlls.org/custom-content/uploads/2015/03/Vienna-Programme-of-Action.pdf.

Wier, Ludvig. 2020. International Tax Avoidance and Development. https://voxdev.org/topic/public-economics/international-tax-avoidance-and-development.

CHAPTER 9

Tax Administration in the COVID Era

Vidushi Gupta

The last decade saw significant evolution in the tax administration function across the globe. This global evolution was attributed to several factors such as access to modern technology and heightened awareness to improve cost-effectiveness. The COVID-19 pandemic, however, pivoted the priorities of tax administrations. It called for striking a delicate balance between, on the one hand, encouraging economic development and facilitating business growth in the face of adversity; while maintaining the integrity of the tax system, and collecting revenue on the other. This chapter analyses the Canadian Revenue Agency's (CRA's) response to the crisis. It first explains the approach and the priorities of the CRA prior to the pandemic. A discussion about the efforts of the CRA in dealing with the crisis and highlights the issues and challenges faced during that period follows. The chapter then provides some insights on the future of tax administration once the blow of the pandemic softens and there is an impetus on rebuilding the economy.

§9.01 INTRODUCTION

In the last decade, the tax administration function evolved considerably. This global evolution was attributed to several factors, such as access to modern technology and heightened awareness to improve cost-effectiveness. While this evolution was still underway, the world changed in an unprecedented fashion with the outbreak of the COVID-19 crisis. The pandemic led to the implementation of lockdowns in most countries, which severely impacted the volume of economic activity. This adversely impacted individual businesses, collection of revenue from taxes, and the economy at large. In parallel, government expenses on public services increased considerably.

There was therefore on one hand immense pressure to mobilize revenue, but it was also imperative to be mindful of the delicate state of the economy and the struggles of businesses at the time. The pandemic also put limitations on physical contact which required a complete overhaul of the existing infrastructure.

This chapter addresses the challenges posed by the pandemic on the tax administration function and the steps taken to address these challenges. While the chapter specifically discusses this in the context of the CRA, most of it applies equally to many other tax administrations around the world.[1]

Structurally, this chapter is divided into three broad sections. The first section discusses the perspective of the tax administration in the period up to Spring 2020, just before the COVID-19 pandemic took the world by storm. The second section focuses on the approach adopted by the tax administration in the first six months of the virus and the issues and challenges faced by them during that period. Last, the third section speculates on the future of tax administration once the blow of the pandemic softens and there is an impetus on rebuilding the economy. The discussions in each of these sections are further divided to analyse the approach of the tax administration towards one, small- and medium-sized enterprises (SMEs), and two, corporate taxpayers, such as multinational enterprises (MNEs).

§9.02 TAX ADMINISTRATION BEFORE THE COVID-19 OUTBREAK

Prior to the COVID-19 crisis, there was a notable upward trend toward improving service to taxpayers, and many tax administrations around the world were focusing on a 'people first' philosophy during this period. Treating large corporate taxpayers, such as MNEs, as clients and finding common ground with them, in an effort to consider the administration of tax as a service, was found to be an effective strategy. The CRA adopted a similar strategy as well.

Through these efforts, the CRA identified three broad areas of shared interests with large corporate taxpayers: timeliness, technical accuracy, and transparency (commonly referred to as the 'Three Ts'). Timeliness, the first of the Three Ts, broadly entailed the CRA's actions to be effective and efficient by taking the right step at the right time. Through the second T of technical accuracy, the CRA sought to grant taxpayers certainty, accuracy, and consistency, notably in its audits. Finally, the last T, transparency represented the tax authorities' commitment towards being more forthcoming with taxpayers. While such a service-based approach had its merits, it also warranted a special focus on maintaining the fairness of the tax regime.

1. This chapter summarizes the discussion that took place during the panel: Tax Administration in the COVID Era at the World Tax Summit - TaxCOOP2020 among three high-level officials from the Canadian Revenue Agency, Alexandra MacLean - Director General, International and Large Business Directorate, Compliance Programs, CRA; Harry Gill - Director General, Small and Medium Enterprises Directorate, Compliance Programs, CRA; and Ted Gallivan - Assistant Commissioner, International, Large Business and Investigations Branch, Canada Revenue Agency.

Before the COVID-19 outbreak, various specific areas were the focus of the CRA to increase the gross recovery amount notwithstanding any litigation in matters raised by the tax administrations. With regards to MNEs and international taxation, these areas included granting tax certainty through the Mutual Agreement Procedure (MAP) to genuine MNEs facing double taxation; understanding the future of taxation in the new economy in light of the OECD's Pillar 1 and Pillar 2 proposals; evaluating the use of data for preventing non-compliance; ascertaining and sharing best tax practices with other tax administrations; and engaging in effective risk management to identify aggressive taxpayers. During the relevant period, the CRA achieved a number of successes, including a significant increase in automated sharing of information. The exchange of information was likely not only to deter aggressive tax planning but also to grant the CRA access to data valuable for risk assessment and file selection. Another success story during the period was Canada's efforts in estimating the tax gap. The CRA had finished a series of reports mapping the ecosystem and identifying various tax gaps. Such reports are more critical than ever, as they are now likely to play a significant role in the post-COVID era.

With regards to SMEs, the primary objective behind the 'people first' philosophy was for the CRA to cater to their specific needs and be viewed as a trusted, fair and helpful tool to these taxpayers. The philosophy did not necessarily entail the CRA turning a blind eye to those flouting tax laws. Instead, it sought to promote voluntary compliance and ensure that all taxpayers were treated fairly.

During the period prior to the COVID-19 crisis, the CRA had implemented tangible efforts to implement its 'people first' philosophy and the Three Ts, notably with regards to SMEs. Under the ambit of timeliness, for instance, the CRA undertook to clearly communicate to taxpayers its expectations regarding timelines for processes such as audits, providing them early certainty. It also undertook to make a conscious effort to adapt its approaches to suit the circumstances of the business that it was auditing. Another tangible change prioritized under the window of timeliness was to efficiently allocate resources such that serious non-compliances would take primacy over negligible, nonconsequential. Second, under the scope of technical accuracy, several steps were taken by the CRA to develop and build technical competency within the workforce. Measures were implemented to encourage supervision and mentorship for auditors and to deliver training. A conscious step was also taken to facilitate team audits as group risk assessments were found to be more beneficial than allotting a file to a single auditor. This method not only allowed the weeding out of non-compliance but also enabled junior officers to gain experience and technical skills. Under the last T of transparency, the CRA committed to being forthcoming with taxpayers and proactively disclose information during audits. It was believed that such disclosures would contribute to a no-surprise environment for taxpayers. The underlying aim of the policy was to equip taxpayers with a sound understanding of the CRA's assessing positions so that they were able to ascertain the most suitable way forward. Another notable effort by the CRA is to align interventions if any, with the seriousness of the non-compliance and the level of risk associated with the taxpayer. The CRA adopted the strategy to merely nudge the low-risk taxpayers who intend to and have the ability to comply with their tax obligations. To this end, a liaison officer program was established, wherein dedicated tax officers would reach out to small business owners and educate them about their tax obligations. Tools such as letters and similar campaigns designed at nudging genuine taxpayers towards compliance were also used. These information campaigns aimed at educating taxpayers with regards to, notably, the best record-keeping practices, and common errors in tax returns.

With regard to the role of data in assisting the tax administration effectively target their intervention, the CRA already had access to various sources of data, including third parties, as well as foreign and provincial governments information. The CRA also made specific efforts to maintain a cooperative and productive relationship with such external parties to ensure a smooth flow of information. Other tools and avenues were also used to retrieve relevant data, including unnamed person requirements. This enabled the CRA to obtain information about unnamed third parties and utilize it to verify their tax disclosures. For instance, with respect to the construction industry, the CRA often approached building companies or real estate development companies to obtain information about third parties.

With regard to MNEs, the mandate of the CRA in this sphere was to come as close as possible to ensuring that large businesses pay corporate tax at the statutory rate applicable under laws when read reasonably. While on the one hand, the CRA aimed for maximizing tax payment, corporate taxpayers were usually bottom-line oriented. These taxpayers thus typically dedicated a significant amount of resources to pay as little tax as possible while respecting the applicable law. This contrast set the tone for the interesting dynamics between tax administrations and large businesses. It is particularly noteworthy as it sheds light on the distinction between the CRA's approach towards SMEs, as opposed to MNEs. Unlike smaller corporate taxpayers that needed to be nudged to comply with tax laws, large businesses such as MNEs were thought to be typically compliant with tax norms. However, they were observed to categorically employ their resources towards ensuring that they technically satisfied the legal requirements but often interpreted these requirements aggressively.

Despite this inherent conflict between MNEs and the CRA, the Three T approach was still implemented in this sector with certain tweaks. For instance, the second T, technical accuracy, was viewed as technical expertise in this regard. It focussed on ensuring that auditors had the requisite training to deal with complex structures. Another cornerstone of this approach was effective communication. Several auditors across the country often worked on similar structures and transactions, but the absence of a channel of communication within the CRA prevented them from gaining from each other's expertise. To rectify this situation, various standard practices and common assessing positions were issued by the CRA. Several fundamental alterations were also made on the litigation front to ensure that matters were dealt with more efficiently.

First, legal expertise was introduced into cases expected to lead to litigation at a much earlier stage than usual. This was done with an aim to ensure that lawyers who were likely to later argue the case, were familiarized with the facts at the outset. Second, there was an active effort to minimize the possibility of an objectionable tax structure being implemented by enterprises for multiple years. It was found that despite tax authorities' interventions and proposed adjustments, companies would continue to use challenged structures in subsequent taxation periods, hoping for a different outcome. To avoid the inefficiencies stemming from this practice, the CRA began to convince taxpayers to wind up the structure in question in the first instance. Third, to minimize the number of tax disputes, the tax administration for large businesses also engaged in proactively identifying legal loopholes and bringing them to the attention of the tax policy wing of the Department of Finance. A prompt correction in the law was often seen to prevent several long-drawn disputes from arising.

In conclusion, it appears that prior to the COVID-19 outbreak, the CRA, across sectors, developed a more outcome-oriented approach. During this period, it was heavily engaged in re-focusing its strategy to achieve the best outcome for the taxpayers within its jurisdiction. There were also significant and conscious differences between the approach of tax administration towards small and large taxpayers.

§9.03 TAX ADMINISTRATION DURING THE COVID-19 PANDEMIC

Several new trends developed among various tax administrations across the globe as the health crisis began to establish itself as a global pandemic. The first trend noticed specifically in the Canadian Government was embracing a faster pace in reacting to change. Several ideas were translated into legislation and then effectively administered in a much shorter period than usual. It still remains to see whether this fast pace is sustainable in the long term. The second change seen in response to the COVID-19 crisis was a greater degree of engagement and collaboration. Government bodies, private and civil society stakeholders all came together to drive the accelerated passing of meaningful reforms in these trying times. Third, the tax administration's perception of the actions of many taxpayers changed. It became apparent that several taxpayers, who would otherwise be categorized as non-compliant, were genuinely looking to correctly discharge their liability but were unable to do so due to a variety of reasons such as financial peril. On the other hand, the existence of a definitive class of taxpayers looking to take advantage of loopholes was also clearly visible. However, this class was relatively small and did not represent a majority of taxpayers. Fourth, the global community converged during these trying times and worked together towards a common goal. While activities such as sharing best practices and information about managing workforces between countries were prevalent pre-COVID-19, they moved from being theoretical concepts to actually being implemented in practice. Lastly, the concept of the tax gap gained a lot of relevance especially since governments' unplanned expenditure saw a steep rise during this time. This created an unprecedented need for the compliance function in tax administrations to amplify its efforts to bridge the compliance gap.

With respect to the administration of SMEs specifically, starting March 2020, all CRA employees were directed to stay at home and all audit programs were put on pause. However, over 3,000 CRA staff members were involved in the emergency relief program. This included the manning of phone lines for the Canadian response benefit and helping with Canada emergency wage subsidy efforts. Emergency relief was thus prioritized over audit activities. Of the tax administration programs, the Officer Liaison programme resumed in April 2020. This program however was repurposed. While it initially focused on educating taxpayers about their tax obligations, its focus was pivoted during the pandemic to educate taxpayers about government relief measures and wage subsidies.

By June 2020, audits were resumed. Initially, the intention was to focus on audits that would result in a refund to the taxpayer as the authorities did not want to hold on to taxpayers' money at a time when liquidity was low for taxpayers whose businesses were affected by the crisis. Subsequently, high-risk audits were also resumed. This category included audits that posed a significant financial risk for the Government, where the level of non-compliance was significant, or where the taxpayer had a history of being non-compliant. The authority conducting these audits were mindful of the delicate state of the economy and the struggles of businesses at the time. The primary reason for continuing the audits was to ensure the integrity of the tax system and to ensure the proper collection of tax revenue. Several challenges had to be overcome to carry on these audits. Overseeing a remote workforce, managing IT capacity, ensuring appropriate security, providing tax officials across the country with access to the requisite hardware were some of the issues that were faced. Notably, at the time the conduct of audits was also heavily reliant on in-person visits and physical presence. Physical mail correspondence was often used to communicate with taxpayers. The limitations on physical contact, as imposed by COVID-19, required the tax administration to fundamentally alter several procedures.

As far as large taxpayers are concerned, at the beginning of the crisis, there was a lack of stability and certainty in the financial market. All stakeholders had several questions and concerns about the way forward that needed to be addressed by the CRA. However, since most of the taxpayer workforce, as well as CRA employees, worked from home, there was initially a lack of clear communication channels. Similar to the administration for small businesses, IT and security systems were put in place quite quickly and the workforce was given the means necessary to function remotely. There was a conscious effort to address the financial pressures created by the slowdown of economic activity. For instance, recourse was taken to a CRA guidance to refund corporate tax instalments where the taxpayer has a legal entitlement.

While easing the financial burden on taxpayers was necessary, there was also an acute awareness that the Government would need revenues to finance public services and as well as emergency relief programs, such as the Canada Emergency Wage Subsidy program. To strike this balance, efforts were made to identify and focus audit activities on files approaching the statute-barred date.

A system was developed to salvage these files. The CRA also worked with the tax policy team to address timeline related issues which led to the passage of the Time Limits and Other Periods Act. The CRA also focused on establishing and implementing the Canada Emergency Wage Subsidy program. It was of paramount importance to strike a balance between helping employers in genuine need, while also preventing any fraud and abuse. A two-pronged test was implemented to make this determination. First, all files were out through an automated test and then some of them were manually checked. This process was generally completed within seventy-two hours. The authorities also began to run Phase 1 of wage subsidy audits shortly after. Unlike regular audits that are typically conducted at the end of the period and suffer many hurdles due to this time gap, the wage subsidy audits were conducted before the end of the year. The level of compliance and the quality of files examined in these audits were found to be very high. Training officers to conduct audits under the new and dynamic wage subsidy regime was also a considerable challenge given the unique remote working conditions. The CRA also prepared guidance to assist international and large businesses in dealing with tax matters related to international travel restrictions. There were several issues at play in this respect such as corporate tax residency, individual tax residency, cross border employment, withholding tax etc. The authorities' initial stance during the crisis was to accommodate for things that were outside individuals' or businesses' control. By the end of September however, matters were evaluated on a case-by-case basis to ensure that the guidance did not facilitate tax avoidance.

Overall, during the COVID-19 crisis, there was a conscious effort to help genuine taxpayers sail through the unprecedented circumstances while ensuring that the integrity of the tax system is maintained, and abuse is discouraged.

§9.04 TAX ADMINISTRATION IN THE POST-COVID-19 ERA

With respect to the post-pandemic world, the use of technology, digital technology, in particular, is likely to be of assistance. The use of technology in undertaking tax administration can eliminate the need for several interventions and minimize the interaction between certain taxpayers and tax authorities. This will not only improve the taxpayers' experience, but by shrinking the pool of taxpayers that need in-person interactions, it will allow the tax authority to focus their resources on aggressive tax planning.

The second trend which should be relevant in the post-COVID-19 era is the forming of collaborative alliances between stakeholders including taxpayers, tax professionals and the tax authority. There are several benefits to these alliances, such as burden reduction and simplification of the system. The COVID-19 era has shed light on the power of collective action where someone's inaction can lead to consequences for others. Using this approach to effectively communicate aggressive tax practices and consequently enforce compliance is a powerful tool that tax authorities may explore in the future. For instance, there is often a vast difference in the statutory rate of tax applicable to large enterprises and the effective rate at which they pay tax. Deriving this figure and communicating it in clear numeric terms could shine a light on aggressive tax planning practices and collectively drive tax compliance. Third, an element of tax administration that is likely to play a significant role going forward is the differential treatment for honest taxpayers who make genuine mistakes and voluntarily correct them, as opposed to aggressive tax planners looking to bring the effective rate of tax down to zero.

Specifically, in SMEs, there is an acute awareness in the tax administration that COVID-19 has severely impacted businesses. The auditors' approach also has adapted to take these changed circumstances into account. First, certain industries have been hit harder than others by the pandemic and there were questions around whether tax authorities would stop auditing such businesses. While there is an understanding of the imbalanced impact of COVID-19 and the same is being factored in choosing files for audits, the authorities have decided against ruling out auditing a sector in its entirety. Instead, they will be judging each case on the unique facts and circumstances that it presents. A similar case-by-case approach is being adopted for the audits that are already on the shelf and the impact of COVID-19 on their solvency is being factored in. Other factors that are influencing the authorities' decision to either shelf or pursue an audit file include the level of non-compliance of the file in question and the past behaviour of the taxpayer in question. The safety of the tax administration's workforce is also an issue that is of paramount importance. Periodical directives are being issued to guide auditors to resume work while still prioritizing their safety. Most audits are now being conducted remotely to the extent possible, which is a significant departure from how audits were conducted pre-COVID-19. Tax authorities are also aware of global developments and are learning from governments in other nations through organizations such as the OECD. The authorities are also closely monitoring global progress of digital compliance, specifically with the emergence of unique business models such as platforms, the gig economy, and cryptocurrencies. The CRA has created a dedicated division to explore compliance by design systems, such as e-invoicing, that make for a seamless tax administration.

In the large business segment, tax audit was brought back nearly to normalcy in June. Traditionally, these audits would be conducted by the officers working on-site from the taxpayer's office. However, due to the restrictions imposed by COVID-19, these officers had to conduct the same activities remotely from their homes. Large businesses however had the resources to quickly adapt to the changing environment. The transition was thus relatively easier.

In order to aid the recovery of the economy going forward, several steps have been undertaken to widen the Canadian tax net and minimize tax avoidance. For instance, the principal purpose test in the Multilateral Convention to Implement Tax Treaty Related Measures to Prevent Base Erosion and Profit Shifting has been enforced in Canada now. A treaty abuse prevention committee has also been established and there is proactive work on ascertaining the CRA's stance on the application of the principal purpose test. Relief measures and assistance packages have also been offered to assist the vulnerable bear the impact of the pandemic. These assistance packages however have given rise to two primary tax issues. First, to make sure that the financial support offered to assist Canadian businesses stays in Canada and is not shifted out of the country using transfer pricing and other methods. Second, the CRA is also working to ensure that assistance received by taxpayers is added to their income so their profit or loss for the period is accurately represented.

§9.05 CONCLUSION

The Canadian tax system generates over half a trillion dollars a year in revenue. Out of this, the audit function facilitates the recovery of about CAD 14 billion. It is therefore an extremely important aspect of the tax function. Given the wide variety of taxpayers it deals with, the system is also extremely complex. The outbreak of COVID-19 further underscored the complexity involved in the tax system. However, the overarching aim of the CRA remains to act as enablers for taxpayers who wish to comply with their obligations and to make it increasingly difficult for those who do not.

CHAPTER 10
Visions for the Future of Tax Administrations

Simon Morin

This chapter summarizes the perspective expressed by tax experts from around the globe on the major current and emerging trends that tax administrations must face in the 21st century. It highlights in particular the key challenges and opportunities for tax administrations in these times of technological and economic upheavals—in addition to the COVID-19 health crisis. Various challenges are discussed which, despite being broad and multifaceted, are mainly in terms of customer service and taxpayer trust toward tax administrations. The chapter then highlights the impact of emerging technologies on tax administrations, including current opportunities as well as the role that tax administrations should adopt in the race to innovation. Finally, recent creative innovations from tax administrations before addressing the impact of COVID-19 on tax administrations are presented.

§10.01 INTRODUCTION

In most industrialized countries, the financing of public services is largely supported by tax revenues. The responsibility for levying, collecting, and administering taxes is therefore central to the tax administrations' mission. By the nature of their interactions, they operate in an environment that is interdependent with that of taxpayers. Although the core mission of the tax administrations is on the whole static, the landscape in which they evolve is constantly changing, and in recent years at a pace that has accelerated.

The OECD (Organisation for Economic Co-operation and Development) recently pointed out that the exponential speed of digitalization of the economy, the emergence of new technologies and business models, and the growing availability of digital data are presenting tax administrations with unprecedented challenges.[1] Beyond these technological and economic upheavals, the consequences of the COVID-19 crisis make the tax administrations' ecosystem more complex. In addition, administrations are facing some key challenges, mainly in terms of customer service and taxpayer trust toward them.[2]

§10.02 THE CLEAR IMPACT OF THE DIGITALIZATION OF THE ECONOMY

The economic transformation has accelerated exponentially over the last decade. According to Jean Marc Niel, Secretary-General of the *Cercle de réflexion et d'échange des dirigeants des administrations fiscales (CREDAF),* this process has been particularly marked by a significant growth in e-commerce, an increase in the sale of intangible goods, and a change in the corporate business model, notably through sales on virtual platforms and the growth of the collaborative economy. The resulting dematerialization of exchanges has raised important issues regarding the taxability of these trades. For example, it is now generally more difficult to locate profits and find out who the customers are in this setting, which adds to the burden of tax administrations (Niel).

These broad trends, mainly driven by the economic digitalization and observed for already several years, have been particularly accelerated by the COVID-19 pandemic, and according to David Regan, Managing Director, Consulting—Revenue Lead at Accenture, these changes in the economy are putting even more pressure on administrations to ensure the fairness and integrity of the tax system. Like Regan, Ted Gallivan, Assistant Commissioner, International, Large Business and Investigations Branch at the Canada Revenue Agency, also points to the dramatic pace at which the digitalization of the economy is evolving. He believes that tax authorities will have to adapt and identify opportunities to better promote voluntary compliance in this context.

1. *Tax Administration 2019: Comparative Information on OECD and other Advances and Emerging Economies*, OECD (2019), online: https://read.oecd-ilibrary.org/taxation/tax-administration-2019_74d162b6-en#page1.
2. This chapter is inspired by the discussions that took place at the World Tax Summit, on October 14, 2020, among a panel of experts: Jean Marc Niel—General Secretary, CREDAF; Philippe Jacquij—General Administrator FPS Finance, Belgium; Ted Gallivan—Commissioner, International, Large Business and Investigations Branch, Canada Revenue Agency; Didier Leemans—Administrator, FPS Finance, Belgium; David Regan—Managing Director for the Revenue industry, Accenture; Iman Deschâtres—Head of Tax, Taxamo; Francis Nadeau—President, HydraLab, Canada; Katharina Gangl—Senior researcher, Institute for Advanced Studies in Vienna (IHS) and Competence Center Insight. All references to individuals in parenthesis is based on their speech at this panel.

§10.03 TAX ADMINISTRATIONS' KEY ISSUES AND CHALLENGES IN THE 21ST CENTURY

The challenges that tax administrations encounter are varied, but mostly, they are taxpayer-oriented. Moreover, while some of these issues stem from, or are at least influenced by, the digitalization of the economy and the increased development of new technologies, these same factors offer a range of opportunities to tax administrations.

[A] Reforming Taxpayers' Services

The relationship between tax authorities and taxpayers has changed significantly in recent years, and there is currently a major trend toward a customer approach. This stems mainly from the digitalization of the economy, which brings new customer service standards. Tax administrations are now facing a new challenge which is *How to meet taxpayers' expectations for real-time service?* Tax administrations must adapt quickly as we move from an era where the norm for response time was one week, to another where replies are expected almost instantly (Regan).

Since the responsibility of tax administrations to collect taxes involves a monetary contribution from taxpayers, it is important to focus on factors that will alleviate, ease and clarify the process to taxpayers. Tax administrations must first focus on the items under their control, including providing excellent, reliable, and respectful customer service. Despite the sometimes contentious nature of interactions with taxpayers, it remains essential that tax administrations pay attention to them (Gallivan).

And so, developments in automatic language processing are one way to improve customer service. In this respect, new technologies in natural language processing have the capability to automate telephone calls to tax administrations and respond efficiently to various taxpayers' requests (Regan). The taxpayers' experience with tax authorities could be further enhanced by customizing exchanges through an approach based on providing tax authorities with access to taxpayers' personal data (Regan).

Beyond the changes in technology intended to expand the services to taxpayers, the rapid evolution in tax administrations, over the last decades, suggests a transformation in the type of relationship between taxpayers and tax administrations. Thus, for Didier Leemans, Director to Personal Services at the Finance and Taxation Division—SPF, the audit role of tax administrations could be replaced by a taxpayer advisory role, while for Katharina Gangl, Senior Researcher at the Institute for Advanced Studies in Vienna (IHS) and at Competence Center Insight, taxpayers should be seen not as customers but rather as real partners with whom tax authorities work collaboratively to optimize tax collection.

However, tax administrations need to adapt their approach to non-compliant taxpayers. Accordingly, while they should promote and motivate honest taxpayers to be compliant, they should also adopt a respectful attitude toward less honest taxpayers, showing nevertheless that they have the means to enforce tax laws and regulations, and that they will not hesitate to do so if necessary (Gangl).

[B] Promoting Trust in Tax Administrations

Preserving taxpayers' confidence in the tax system's integrity is another relevant issue for tax administrations.

Beyond the compulsory character of taxes, their collection by tax administrations is based on the theory of consent to taxation, and recognition of the legitimacy of this collection power. Such legitimacy is based on the trust given by the taxpayers to the administrations. Thus, tax administrations must incorporate and develop elements promoting tax consent and inspiring trust within their organization (Leemans).

[1] Taking a Didactic Approach

Taking a didactic approach toward taxpayers is fundamental. For example, it is relevant to explain to taxpayers the purpose of tax administrations when they collect taxes to show them the relevance of their contribution to the state and thus promote tax consent (Leemans).

This may be particularly difficult nowadays, as disinformation and conspiracy theories continue to take a place in the public domain, especially through social media (Gangl).

[2] Transparency

Transparency is another factor to be addressed to strengthen consent to taxation. The recent shift from a very restricted world of information to a world where all information flows freely underlines this need in a specific way. For example, some tax administrations, including Belgian authorities, now give online access to taxpayers allowing them to see all the information the tax administration holds about them, regardless of whether it comes from internal or from foreign administrations (Leemans).

[3] Ensuring Personal Data Protection

Privacy protection must be at the heart of the tax administrations' activities. Thus, internally, every action taken on taxpayers' data must be accountable. Externally, administrations must be able to justify and objectify the reasons for a tax audit (Leemans). In terms of data security, tax authorities would benefit from limiting the information flow of taxpayers to a strict minimum, while having a security system in place to ensure personal data protection.

[4] Assisting the Taxpayers

Tax administrations can also promote tax compliance by taking on an advisory role. Advance rulings provide an example of how tax administrations can play this role.

Within this context, the administration agrees to define in advance the tax consequences of a taxpayer's intended transaction, thus reassuring him and easing the tax audit later on. The Belgian authorities also extend this advisory role to various transactions carried out by taxpayers, including individuals. Thus, the authorities use external information at their disposal. For example, it can use a bill of sale to warn the taxpayer that by selling a property that belonged to him, he may be taxed. In some cases, the authorities may even provide an estimate of the tax that will be due on a given transaction (Leemans).

[5] To Be Reactive and Proactive

By being responsive and adapting to events in taxpayers' lives, tax administrations can increase the taxpayers' compliance level. To achieve this, tax administrations may take advantage of real-time information available to them. For example, a tax administration noticing a significant decrease in a taxpayer's income could notify him in real-time that his year's tax liability will differ. By doing so, the taxpayer will feel that he is being listened to and understood; in return, he will feel more compliant with his tax liability (Niel).

Furthermore, timely communication is essential to build trust with taxpayers. As such, prompt and diligent responses to taxpayers' queries will generally motivate them to comply with tax legislation.

In a broader sense, tax administrations will usually benefit from using the tools at their disposal to maintain trust and a real-time dialogue with taxpayers. In this respect, they are advised to take a proactive approach. For example, authorities should share relevant information they hold in real-time, thereby enhancing taxpayers' compliance.

In accordance with the proactive approach, the authorities should give taxpayers access to the information at their disposal to avoid errors, i.e., they should rather maintain a positive dialogue with the taxpayers to prevent errors or spontaneously correct those (Niel).

Finally, tax administrations should adopt a dynamic attitude toward tax disputes to reduce litigation-related costs and delays. Thus, administrations should, whenever possible, favor potential compromises in cases of disputes with taxpayers, rather than engaging in long and dubious litigation processes. In some instances, such as in transfer pricing cases, where some transactions happen to recur year after year, this is likely to lead to uncertainty as a result of legal proceedings in a given year. Similar transactions, carried out by the taxpayer, will cascade as an issue into subsequent years. Administrations and taxpayers will therefore benefit from addressing these issues proactively (Niel).

[6] Keeping It Simple and Accessible

Simplicity should be central to interactions with taxpayers at all stages: registration, filing, and payment. Tax administrations can also foster a positive attitude toward tax compliance by making it simple and inexpensive to comply with tax legislation.

According to Iman Deschâtres, Head of Tax at Taxamo, tax administrations can benefit from new technologies, despite their potential complexity, as long as the interaction remains simple from the taxpayer's viewpoint. In this respect, administrations have been particularly successful in taking advantage of new technologies in recent years, especially in the area of tax compliance. For example, as a general rule, a taxpayer can nowadays file a simplified tax return online. It is worth noting that this kind of simplification is usually to the advantage of both administrations and taxpayers, as it provides an incentive to register. Thus, in the context of VAT (value-added tax) collected from non-residents, for example, administrations are satisfied with the proper tax collection, non-resident businesses are also satisfied because the registration process is simple and local businesses are equally satisfied since the distortion resulting from harmful tax competition with foreign businesses is reduced (Deschâtres).

This is particularly relevant for some taxes that may be viewed as voluntary. Thus, in some cases, external factors (e.g., customer collection) will prompt a taxpayer to register rather than making him fear the tax authorities. Accordingly, a company reporting few sales in a foreign state will first consider the ease of the registration process and the cost of compliance before deciding to register with foreign tax authorities. In some cases, a company will simply prefer to quit its sales in a given foreign jurisdiction rather than complying with a burdensome or expensive system (Deschâtres).

Tax administrations will also benefit from remaining flexible and adapting to taxpayers' needs (e.g., by accepting international payments in foreign currency), and also from being open and lenient (e.g., by accepting short payment delays). Tax authorities will also usually benefit from working with taxpayers to build trust so as to induce tax compliance (Deschâtres).

Beyond recognition of *simplicity* as a criterion, we are currently observing a growing complexity in tax legislation that must constantly be brought into line with the reality of the economic environment. In this respect, the exchanges are dematerializing across state borders. Thereupon, the impact of the international dimension must be taken into account, as this reality is now prevalent in the course of trade, not only where multinational companies are involved, but also small- and medium-sized enterprises (SMEs). Tax administrations need to have a clear grasp of what falls in their taxation domain and what does not. They need to work together to manage the risks to their tax base, even though this collaboration may be complex given the divergent interests of the states (Regan).

[7] *Supporting the Tax Systems' Integrity*

The issue regarding certain groups of taxpayers and their trust in tax administrations arises from their perception of unfairness with regard to the current tax system, and it needs to be addressed by the tax authorities since a feeling of unfairness in the tax system usually leads to a high risk of noncompliance. Thus, while legislative changes are not within tax authorities' mandate, it is important that tax administrations support the proper functioning of the tax system and advise the government to address any anomalies within this system (Regan).

[8] *Highlighting the Taxpayers' Contribution*

The changes in tax administrations in recent years have been impressive, and the contribution of taxpayers has played an important role. Tax administrations should showcase their successes and achievements while highlighting the taxpayers' contributions. By doing so, taxpayers will gain awareness of the progress made, they will better appreciate the significance of their input and, as a result, they will have more confidence in the tax system. In turn, the confidence gained will translate into a stronger compliance culture (Gangl).

[C] Navigating in an Ever-Changing Environment

While in the past, tax administrations used to interact mainly with businesses and financial institutions, they must now adapt to new players and information sources, such as real-time payment providers, as well as with software and client platforms that allow real-time interaction. Much of the interaction between these systems and the tax authorities needs to be built, and this will have to prove efficient, secure, and in real-time, which is not simple and poses a challenge to tax administrations (Regan).

The payment systems' infrastructure has evolved and payments are now generally made in real-time. Tax authorities need to take advantage of the ready availability of payment information in their audit activities. Also, digital invoicing should be considered as it reduces the burden on taxpayers further to promote tax compliance. In this regard, the Canadian tax administration is particularly interested in the approach adopted by foreign jurisdictions. It is important to integrate digital invoicing to reduce as far as possible the burden to all stakeholders by using information available in real-time (Gallivan).

On the other hand, the advent of cryptocurrencies as a currency also raises some issues to tax administrations. Beyond fearful reactions with regard to taxpayer noncompliance and a risk of facilitation to tax evasion, tax authorities should pursue their efforts to define how cryptocurrencies may ease compliance on a voluntary basis (Gallivan).

[D] Addressing the Digital Divide Effects

Despite the numerous opportunities provided by new technologies in terms of customer service, tax administrations will have to be careful to limit the digital divide that may arise from a dematerialized relationship with taxpayers. It is essential to avoid the trap of eliminating traditional communication channels, such as face-to-face or telephone services, despite the opportunities offered by online services. Indeed, while some groups of taxpayers might be open to a dematerialized relationship, some others, such as the elderly, generally prefer face-to-face interactions or telephone contacts. In addition, a number of social and economic factors (e.g., no Internet access or people with disabilities) need to be considered to ensure the continuation of a relevant service to all taxpayers, and to reduce the impact of the digital divide (Niel).

Furthermore, some taxpayers will require human contact, especially where money is at stake. Tax administrations should therefore be focusing on offering innovative services, especially online, to the interested taxpayers, without leaving behind those who prefer human interaction (Gallivan).

[E] Supporting Human Resources for a Successful Technological Transformation

For Philippe Jacquij, General Administrator at the Finance and Taxation Division—SPF in Belgium, it appears that the digital evolution is not about to fade away. In this context, it is important that tax administrations and their employees remain "agile" in order to adapt. This could be a challenge for tax administrations with an advanced age pyramid. While some employees won't be able to follow the trend, the next generations should be able to show more agility with regard to technological development (Jacquij).

New technologies and innovation in a tax administration setting are likely to require a shift with regard to needs in human resources. For example, administrations will have to address training, transition, and hiring issues. Will the tax auditors of the future become "data scientists"? (Niel).

In any case, tax administrations must remain cautious as some opportunities arising from technological advances may lead to technology adaptation issues for staff, within the organizations, as well as for taxpayers, externally (Jacquij). It is therefore essential that tax administrations consider the need to adapt to new technologies. For example, in the event of new technologies implementation projects internally, the tax administrations will need to be flexible toward their staff so that they become familiar with and adapt to the technology.

§10.04 TECHNOLOGICAL CHANGE: MANY OPPORTUNITIES TO BE SEIZED

Tax administrations should take advantage of the new growth in technologies, such as *machine learning* and *big analytics*. An interesting approach for tax administrations would be the combination of these new technologies with traditional experimental methods to ensure a steady development of the existing systems. This approach could, for example, be used on a trial-and-error basis to improve the interaction with taxpayers so as to respond appropriately to their needs. However, while these technological advances offer a significant opportunity, it will be essential to take into account the level of confidence in these, which will generally vary from state to state (Gangl).

According to Francis Nadeau, President at HydraLab, the blockchain and the advent of distributed ledger technology could transform data storage through collaborative ledgers in the coming years. While today the information is usually stored in vertical data silos, the gradual implementation of collaborative registries by tax administrations could allow multiple stakeholders to view and modify the registry, thus keeping the information in cross-sectional data silos. This collaboration between stakeholders will be feasible, to the extent that the right governance processes are defined and the cybersecurity issues are addressed.

Several issues, particularly in the area of information security, arise from the new technologies and their related opportunities. In terms of access to information, the eventual implementation of digital identity and remote services will require that tax authorities maintain measures to control user access and to confirm their identity (Nadeau).

In this respect, the main interest lies primarily in the unlimited potential provided by the new technology, a potential likely to change the habits of both citizens and civil servants and which will have an obvious impact on tax control (Leemans).

§10.05 THE ROLE OF TAX ADMINISTRATIONS IN THE RACE TO INNOVATION

In terms of innovation, some suggest that tax administrations should engage actively in the race to innovation and that they should ideally stand at the forefront, so as not to have to take steps in response. In the area of tax control, tax administrations can indeed benefit from new technologies, such as artificial intelligence. They should also focus on mass control, administrative simplification, and take advantage of *blockchain* technology to ensure the transactions are secure (Niel).

Innovation is clearly the key to the future of tax administrations. However, it is important to consider the tax administrations' limited resources that are accountable to taxpayers. Thus, administration managers must carefully analyze the technological possibilities to decide how to allocate the resources to improvements or projects which are due to emerge several years later. In this setting, while some suggest that administrations should lead the race to innovation, others argue that it would be wiser to leave the private companies and large corporations, generally known as the technology and innovation leaders, take over the role in technology development to thereafter integrate it into the tax administrations. New technologies are very expensive, and so, the role of tax administrations should be that of a facilitator, driving the technology forward without being top of the class in this area. The Canadian tax administration's approach in this regard is to develop partnerships with the private sector and to analyze the foreign tax administrations models (Gallivan).

Tax administrations will therefore have to address a major challenge by keeping up with the explosive digital evolution and identifying the innovations to be seized in the next few years (Jacquij).

§10.06 CREATIVE INNOVATIONS FROM ABROAD

Among recent innovations made by some fiscal administrations, some are clearly ingenious, an example is a Taiwanese lottery. In Taiwan, the retailers issue invoices containing a lottery number. Thus, in this setting, consumers do not hesitate to ask for an invoice to have a chance to win a prize. In doing so, consumers act as if, somehow, they were auditors.

The availability of pre-filled returns is another innovation gaining popularity. Such innovation strengthens tax compliance by improving the user experience. This actually simplifies the tax return filing process to the advantage of the taxpayer while reducing chances of error (Deschâtres). In some cases, the pre-filled return will already contain all the relevant information, and the taxpayer will only have to confirm the proposed simplified return (Jacquij).

Furthermore, the Australian government has particularly demonstrated its willingness to better link the digital distribution channel and facilitate the user experience by providing taxpayers with access to its portal via a mobile application. The application also supports the recording of digital bills and the issuance of certificates. These innovations make it possible to use the information available to the tax authorities so as to understand in real-time the impact on the annual return (Nadeau).

In terms of customer service, the Irish experience provides an important opportunity to use technology through *voicebots* to handle taxpayer queries. Indeed, the tax authority has successfully adopted a fully automated *voicebots* system capable of responding appropriately to taxpayers' queries. This technology, able to understand the taxpayers and respond to them, significantly reduces the interactions formerly managed by call centers. For example, a 30% reduction in calls handled by call centers has been observed in an American state which has implemented this technology (Regan).

§10.07 THE IMPACT OF COVID-19: NOW AND IN THE FUTURE

The COVID-19 pandemic has had a significant impact on tax administrations—and will continue to do so.

[A] Current Effects of the Crisis

Several tax administrations were already anticipating a crisis and its consequences at the internal level. Thus, many employees already had a laptop, a mobile phone, and a secure connection as they were already familiar with remote working. However, the pandemic will have accelerated a trend toward an administration where the notion of the workplace will continue to evolve, as it is still often possible to deal with a case remotely, especially through technologies that enable digital working and meetings. Managers in organizations should therefore quickly adopt a long-term vision of remote work to address key issues such as management, training, and teamwork in a telework setting. Also, an emphasis should be placed on employees' inclusion, as some of them may have a tendency to withdraw in this type of environment (Jacquij).

The COVID-19 pandemic has demonstrated the tax administrations' strong capability to adapt. For example, the Canadian tax administration has implemented, within three weeks, various taxpayer assistance programs which otherwise would have required more than a year to put in place. Thus, the crisis forced this tax administration to adopt, at short notice, an imperfect assistance program, albeit one that is constantly being improved, rather than a comprehensive and proven program over a much longer period. The approach adopted by this tax authority is a change of strategy that was necessary given the circumstances (Gallivan). Despite some significant changes, the human relationships between government officers and businesses are not to be disrupted. The creativity of tax administrations is therefore crucial (Leemans).

Many taxpayers have been or are still experiencing financial problems due to the crisis. After implementing major assistance programs to support the affected taxpayers, the tax administrations will undoubtedly have to address the tax collection issue. Their role will be to find a balance between empathy, solidarity, and tax collection, a task which, although difficult, is nevertheless necessary as the contribution of all taxpayers is required to ensure the integrity of the tax system (Regan).

In the longer term, various changes induced by the pandemic, such as the frantic pace of digitalization and the impact of the emergence of specific markets on the economy's growth, could lead to new taxes (Regan). Moreover, it appears that the crisis has led some workers to turn to the black market. This defines the context in which tax administrations must continue to promote the importance of each one's contribution to taxation (Gangl).

[B] Future-Oriented Administrations

In the coming years, the role of tax administrations will continue to evolve in line with the changes occurring in their surroundings. Among the emerging trends, it appears that technology will take a prominent place, particularly in tax service and control, while some conventional functions are likely to disappear. However, the service to taxpayers and the tax administration's "physical" character is there to remain, as tax administration will always be a public service at the disposal of citizens (Jacquij).

Indeed, in the 21st century, tax administrations are continuing to demonstrate their flexibility, agility, and evolutionary character. Administrations are more than ever oriented toward the taxpayer, who is aware that these are part of an economic chain intended to create wealth and generate tax revenues. It is with this willingness to move forward, to be focused on the taxpayer, and with this confidence in new technologies that authorities will be able to address tomorrow's problems (Niel).

While all tax administrations are particularly successful at present, they would benefit from working together and strengthening their mutual cooperation in an effort to continuously improve their practices. Administrations will generally benefit from interacting, particularly through an open cooperation platform, to share their best practices and successes, but most importantly their failures (Gangl). Although the sharing of failures is usually recognized as a key issue, it is rarely put into practice. Administrations must therefore be more open in this respect. The development process for new projects initiated by tax administrations will normally include an analysis of foreign administrations' experiences. Thus, the openness to discussions in this context will allow tax administrations to adopt good practices while avoiding the pitfalls experienced by foreign administrations (Jacquij). The progress of tax administrations through cooperation is at the heart of organizations such as CREDAF and the Network of Tax Organisations who provide an exchange platform to tax administrations (Niel).

In conclusion, the tax administration framework has been continuously evolving over the last few years. The ever-accelerating digitalization of the economy, the economic upheaval caused by the COVID-19 crisis, and the exponential growth of technological opportunities all point to a quick complexifying of the ecosystem in which tax administrations operate. It would, therefore, be difficult, in this context, to predict the issues and challenges facing tomorrow's tax administrations. However, one thing is clear: by continuing to work together on the important issues, the tax administrations will not slow down the pace. Rather, they will move much faster and even much further together (Niel).

CHAPTER 11

Emerging Technologies and Tax Administrations: At the Dawn of a Fundamental Transformation?

Jeffrey Owens & Simon Morin

The emergence of new technologies such as blockchain and artificial intelligence are rapidly changing the way in which businesses operate. Such technologies are expected to fundamentally change the environment in which tax administrations evolve as well as the manner in which tax administrations interact with taxpayers and the tax audit process. This chapter discusses blockchain and artificial intelligence technologies as well as the key opportunities for tax administrations, notably the opportunity to provide transparent and reliable information to stakeholders. This chapter also explores how such emerging technologies may provide new approaches to wealth taxation, despite historic difficulties to implement such taxes in various jurisdictions and provides certain key elements to consider in establishing how these new technologies can assist tax administrations to fulfil their objectives. This chapter finally discusses the impact of emerging technologies on tax policy, as well as the future of tax administrations.

§11.01 INTRODUCTION

Emerging technologies, such as blockchain and artificial intelligence, are changing the way that many businesses and institutions operate. Whereas some are slowly and progressively affected by these new technologies, others are radically transforming as a result of the emergence of such technologies. For instance, the emergence of blockchain in recent years has changed dramatically how certain organizations conduct their core businesses and how they interact with their customers.

Whereas businesses and other non-government organizations are generally prone to adopt emerging technologies, governments and tax administrations are generally more reluctant to integrate them, which are seen more like challenges, as opposed to opportunities. While technology-driven companies are more likely to be propelled by the catalyst effect of such technology, its impact extends well beyond innovative private companies. In fact, governments and businesses are beginning to recognize that emerging technologies, such as blockchain and artificial intelligence, can be transformational, including with regards to the way in which businesses and governments approach taxation.

The impact of emerging technologies on tax administrations, in particular on the way that they interact with taxpayers, will generally depend on tax administrations themselves; will they seek to simply adapt to the technology, or will they use this technology to transform completely the way tax systems operate?

§11.02 THE BLOCKCHAIN TECHNOLOGY

Blockchain, the technology behind Bitcoin and other digital currencies, has quickly become acknowledged as one of the most important breakthroughs with respect to global trade. In fact, blockchain and digital currencies are enabling peer-to-peer commerce on a global scale where finding, accessing, transacting, paying, and settling with counterparts worldwide has now become frictionless. Governments and major international organizations, such as the World Customs Organization, have launched various projects to study how blockchain technology can facilitate trade, notably by reducing barriers to trade.

The main advantage of blockchain technology is that it enables companies to ensure the integrity of financial transactions without the need to rely on intermediaries. Blockchain-based business models rely on computer codes that are uploaded on distributed ledgers spread across a network of servers which can be located around the globe and that work together in real-time. Blockchain technology enables its users to exchange information on payments, immediately, directly, securely, and at a low cost without having to rely on intermediaries, such as large banks. Since the distributed ledger is decentralized, firms and their customers can monitor and inspect the progress of each transaction in real-time, which provides transparency in the system. In addition to increased transparency and trust, the rapid rise of digital commerce should only increase the reliance on blockchain technology. For instance, web retailers Amazon and Alibaba alone now account for 200 billion dollars in gross sales on a yearly basis. Since the COVID-19 crisis, these companies have seen their sales turnover increased by 40% and this trend is expected to continue. The emergence of new technologies such as blockchains should not only interest multinational enterprises (MNEs) but also smaller companies. Small- and medium-sized enterprises (SMEs), which are also affected by the digitalization of the economy, should recognize and address the opportunities that such innovative technologies offer them.

[A] Blockchain-Based Technologies: Challenge or Opportunity for Tax Administrations?

In traditional markets, MNEs, financial institutions and other intermediaries play a significant role in ensuring compliance with a wide range of government regulations, including tax regulations, financial regulations, as well as investment regulations. However, with the emerging blockchain-based business models, SMEs and other entities can bypass these intermediaries and organize decentralized peer-to-peer networks rather than around a central entity. As such, the emergence of blockchain-based technology systems should continue to challenge compliance with regulations, including tax compliance.

However, while the elimination of the need to rely on intermediaries may represent a challenge to tax administrations, the very same blockchain technology is likely to bring forward new solutions and opportunities. In fact, from the perspective of governments, this technology could offer a new approach to improve tax compliance.

Since blockchain technology allows the monitoring of transactions in real-time, blockchain-based systems provide an opportunity for tax compliance to move into real-time compliance. For instance, while the tax audit process may currently extend over years after the time at which taxpayers have earned their profit and settled their tax payments, the reliance on real-time information by tax administrations is likely to reduce such delay, in addition to reducing the administrative burden and compliance costs. Furthermore, given the very nature of blockchain technology, the real-time information flowing to tax administrations should be trustworthy and transparent. Therefore, blockchain-based businesses provide a unique opportunity to rethink the nature of tax compliance, moving away from the traditional regime of periodic payments and reporting, in which audit is the main enforcement mechanism, to a real-time flow of information.

Other disruptive technologies, such as artificial intelligence provide tax administrations with an opportunity to achieve better and more effective tax compliance.

In fact, the combination of blockchain technology, which should not only provide reliable and relevant information but also provide much more information to tax administrations, and artificial intelligence should enable tax administrations to achieve significantly better risk management. Risk management is a key function to tax administrations, as it enables these organizations, which are accountable to taxpayers, to adopt an effective approach to their activities, including their audit activities. The reliance on emerging technologies by tax administrations should allow them to use their scarce resources in an effective way by directing them to high-risk areas. From an audit perspective, technology-based risk management approaches should lead to the classification of taxpayers in various risk categories, from low-risk to high-risk taxpayers. For instance, for low-risk taxpayers, interference and audit activities by tax administrations should be minimal, whereas, for high-risk taxpayers, tax administrations should adopt a focused approach to ensure that such taxpayers actually are made to comply.

As detailed information flows through tax administrations in real-time, artificial intelligence can assist in analysing large data. For instance, artificial intelligence technologies can assist tax administrations to determine potential income tax liabilities.

The possibilities of such technologies extend beyond the domestic level. For instance, at the international level, the current withholding tax system which is outdated and distortionary could benefit from these technologies to achieve stronger tax compliance. In addition, blockchain-based systems could fundamentally change the way that tax administrations manage cross-border tax disputes under the mutual agreement procedures where very limited technology is currently used. Technical platforms based on such technologies provide an opportunity to improve the dialogue between competent authorities, as well as improve the dialogue with taxpayers.

To take advantage of the opportunities offered by the blockchain and the artificial intelligence technologies, tax administrations should seek possibilities to integrate existing and emerging technologies with their vision of how they want to operate digital compliance of the future. Then, administrations should design systems in such a way that it becomes a natural part of the process by which businesses operates. Building tax systems based on the way businesses operate is a key principle in tax as this both ensures good compliance and minimizes compliance costs for taxpayers.

[B] Shifting from Informality and the Reliance on Cash: An Undisputable Opportunity

Informality and reliance on cash have been considerable impediments to tax systems which are generally based on self-assessment. Emerging technologies, such as blockchain-based technologies, are powerful catalysers to accelerate the shift from a cash-based society to a cashless society and to encourage households and companies to move from the informal sector to the formal sector. Such shifts represent a highly effective way of counteracting not only tax evasion but also money laundering, bribery and corruption. These transitions to formality and a cashless society are not only desirable but are also actually achievable because of emerging technologies. Several countries are already moving in this direction. For instance, countries as diverse as China, Kenya, India and Sweden are very much at the threshold of eliminating cash.

Tax administrations should be at the forefront of these transformational shifts as, from a tax perspective, many of the issues and challenges that tax administrations face in terms of compliance are the result of reliance on cash given the general preference of taxpayers to stay in the informal economy rather than the formal economy. In this respect, tax administrations should promote, and encourage governments and stakeholders to promote, the move from a cash-based economy to a cashless economy, and promote the move from informality to formality.

Emerging technologies should play a significant role in addressing challenges faced by tax administrations with regards to sales on virtual platforms and the growth of the collaborative economy. Tax administrations may initially view companies such as Airbnb and Uber as a risk from a tax compliance perspective. As these new businesses emerge and the business model of certain industries shifts dramatically, tax administrations are likely to be concerned with the impact on access to information, compliance with income taxes, value added taxes (VAT), social security, etc. However, beyond the challenges that virtual platforms and the collaborative economy may bring, these new technology-based companies also represent an opportunity to encourage the move from cash-based to a cashless economy. For instance, whereas cash was historically inevitable when taking a taxi ride or when lodging at a bed & breakfast, these new businesses are accelerating the shift to a cashless standard in these industries.

Tax administrations should seize the opportunity to work with technology-based companies such as virtual platforms and take advantage of the information that these companies have, as a means to increase tax compliance. Developing relationships with such businesses allows tax administrations to not only obtain a lot of information from a single central source, but such a source should also provide highly reliable information. For instance, tax administrations should consider such information when assessing whether taxi drivers or the people that rent out their accommodation are meeting their tax obligations, without the need to rely exclusively on the information provided by taxpayers.

§11.03 AN OPPORTUNITY TO ADDRESS WEALTH AND INCOME INEQUALITIES

Emerging technologies could also play a role in addressing the issue of inequalities in income and wealth which is growing among individuals throughout most countries, and also among countries. The rise in inequalities in income and wealth is not simply a moral or social issue, but it also represents an economic issue. This is supported by various work done by the IMF (International Monetary Fund) or the OECD (Organisation for Economic Co-operation and Development) which have shown that increases in inequality can lead to bad outcomes, including negative impacts on the economy. This is because inequalities in income and wealth may harm or break up social cohesion. Social cohesion is vital to the health of our economy, the bedrock of which is based on the involvement and support of citizens of all social classes. A strong social cohesion is essential to obtain support from citizens to develop and implement structural policies that will improve the long-term growth perspective. The economic arguments in favour of addressing the issue of growing inequalities complement the social arguments in its favour. Most governments, to that extent, have the will, the power and the means to reverse the growing inequality trends. These means include the education system, social benefits, a minimum wage, and also taxes, which can play a significant role in addressing wealth and income inequalities.

Historically, various approaches to wealth taxation, such as net wealth taxes, inheritance taxes or capital gains taxes, have either failed or been rejected based on their difficulty to implement. However, as emerging technologies and the work of the OECD pushes the tax transparency revolution, traditional arguments against wealth taxation may no longer be relevant. Therefore, tax administrations and governments should reassess the role that wealth taxes can play in reducing inequalities.

The main obstacle to tax transparency revolves around opaque tax vehicles and jurisdictions. For instance, such opacity encourages offshore non-compliance by allowing high net worth individuals and politically exposed persons to use offshore accounts to evade their tax responsibilities or to hide laundered money. To overcome opacity and assess tax compliance, governments and tax administrations need to have access to information regarding the ownership of tax vehicles, such as trusts, limited liability partnerships, foundations, and holding companies. In this respect, governments should consider relying on blockchain technologies to construct corporate registries, initially at a national level, which are to provide reliable and sufficient information, that are publicly accessible and that are updated in real-time. Such registries should provide a very effective way for tax administrations to identify the beneficial owners of these opaque vehicles and ensure tax compliance of the taxpayers hiding behind the veils of these vehicles. Once such registries are well established at the national level, the same technology should enable countries to launch registries at the global level.

§11.04 INTEGRATING EMERGING TECHNOLOGIES: KEY CONSIDERATIONS

As these new technologies are still just emerging, opportunities for tax administrations to fully exploit these new technologies are appear to be virtually endless. However, technology, in and of itself, is not a silver bullet and will not solve all challenges that tax administrations face. To ensure effective use of emerging technologies, tax administrations should adopt a structured approach in determining how these technologies can assist these organizations to fulfil their objectives.

First, tax administrations should have a clear understanding of the objective or the problem that the technology is expected to solve. For instance, is the purpose to increase tax compliance, or to increase customer service standards for interactions with taxpayers? Or it is both?

The second matter to consider is to recognize that the technologies themselves will solve a broken system and make it a good tax system. Tax administrations should consider carefully evaluating whether the existing system is effective prior to the integration of technology.

The third thing is that tax administrations need to review existing legislation and procedures and assess whether the rules in place are still in line with their underlying objectives. For instance, tax administrations should evaluate whether existing regulations, as well as existing compliance and reporting requirements, which were potentially developed in an analogue age, are still relevant today. Any regulation that is not relevant in the digital age should be reconsidered in order to declutter the system before introducing new technologies.

A fourth aspect to consider is the need to recognize that the success of any digitalization program is dependent on the people that carry out the transformation.

Tax administration should ensure that the individuals that push the adoption of the technology within the organization have the right profile to work in a digital age as this is key to the success of any digitalization program.

A fifth thing is the need to ensure that tax administrations have the budget to not only finance the initial investment but also to run the system over the expected period.

A sixth element is to carry public information campaigns to carry citizens in the process. Tax administrations should use such campaigns to explain the objective of the change and to reassure taxpayers that such change will lead to simplification, whether it is easing compliance or tax-paying for them.

A seventh consideration is to seek the specific engagement of the private sector, whether it is with MNEs, SMEs, technology-based or advisory companies. As such stakeholders generally stand at the forefront of the race to innovation, they can be a powerful conduit to promote change.

An eighth point to consider, which tends to be overlooked, is the compatibility and integration of the technology with other government agencies. For instance, tax administrations that develop new technical platforms should ensure that they are compatible with the platforms of the other relevant law enforcement agencies. Though this interoperability may be difficult to achieve, once it is in place, it allows for a seamless exchange of information between the different government departments, whether the financial intelligence unit, the customs units the social security unit, etc.

A ninth consideration, which may raise more difficulties, is for governments and tax administrations to explore the possibility of putting in place a unique digital identity. Even though the path to implementing a digital identity system requires overcoming numerous difficulties, the Estonian experience suggests that countries can be successful in digitalizing governments and tax administrations. In Estonia, each resident is assigned a unique digital identity upon birth which is to be used for every interaction with the government, including tax transactions.

The last key determinant is to encourage colleges and universities to develop courses that do not only train students to be good tax professionals and good tax administrators but also people that understand technology. As emerging technologies continue to transform tax administrations, tax professionals generally need three things to reach professional success in the tax field. They not only need to understand tax law, understand tax policy, but they also need to understand technology. To implement courses that combine tax and technology, different departments of universities will have to come together to develop courses that allow tax professionals and tax administrators to be comfortable with technology and the role it plays in the tax field.

§11.05 THE IMPACT OF EMERGING TECHNOLOGIES ON TAX POLICY

Emerging technologies are not only relevant to the tax administrations, but they are also opening up significant opportunities in terms of tax policy. For instance, as such technologies now render the analysis of big data possible, and as access to information continues to rise, emerging technologies allow the government to envision and model future tax reforms more easily. Therefore, the process of tax reform should change rapidly as these new technologies enable governments to measure the potential impact of such proposed reforms in an effective way. The same technologies should allow governments to review the impact of previous tax reforms and evaluate whether such reforms effectively achieved the objectives set out previously.

Emerging technologies should also open up new tax bases which did not exist before. For instance, as these technologies are based around data, data is becoming the most valuable resource that a company has. Such emerging resources represent an opportunity for governments to broaden the tax base to include data and other intangible resources emerging from these new technologies, just as traditional tangible resources are included in the tax base. Another consideration in terms of the broadening of the tax base is the taxation of robots. In view of the rapid growth and the myriad of opportunities that emerging technologies provide in the fields of automation and robotics, the ongoing debate on this matter should be pursued, notably among academics and businesses. In addition, governments should explore the activities that take place in space and the taxation of such activities. As emerging technologies continue to break down barriers, space is expected to become a major economic environment. As such, similar to the debate around the taxation of robots, the debate around the taxation of transactions in space should be put forward at this time. Governments should evaluate how emerging technologies can open up new ways of designing smarter taxes, such as smart environmental taxes as well as wealth and capital taxes.

Governments should recognize that the digitalization of their tax administration enables such administrations not only to make their country more competitive by enhancing the taxpayer's experience but also to minimize compliance costs. Therefore, governments should view digitalization as a way of competing to attract foreign direct investment as well as the digital nomads.

Despite the opportunities brought to light by these emerging technologies, the same technologies also bring challenges from a tax policy perspective, notably in respect of existing tax concepts. These challenges include the classification of workers of technology-based businesses as employed versus self-employed, for instance in the case of Uber, the difference between a corporate entity and a non-corporate entity, and the distinction between services and goods. Whereas services and goods were traditionally separate, they are generally packaged in the current digital environment and the distinction between services and goods can represent a challenge. Another challenge which is currently the subject of debates at the OECD level is the difference between the source and the residence country. As an example, the sale of printed products brings a challenge to tax administrations as the determination of the source and residency of a 3D product is far from being a simple task.

§11.06 THE FUTURE OF TAX ADMINISTRATIONS

Beyond their current impact, emerging technologies should continue to transform tax administrations in the next decade. Among such transformations, many of the traditional functions of tax administrations are likely to be outsourced to technical companies and other tax intermediaries, including, but not limited to, the collection aspect. In fact, considering the substantial capability and capacity that these new technologies offer, even the assessment process itself may be outsourced to technical companies which can rely on technology to fulfil the assessment process in a manner which may provide better results than tax administrations.

Another expected transformational change triggered by emerging technologies is the shift for tax administrations from being verifiers of outcome to being certifiers of systems. As such, tax audits are expected to focus more and more on a review of the tax control framework and tax systems. To the extent that the review of the tax control framework provides the auditor with assurance that the framework produces the right results, the need to audit outcomes may be significantly reduced. Therefore, tax audits are expected to require the production of less documents and are also expected to be more efficient for both taxpayers and tax administrations.

In addition, emerging technologies should enable tax administrations to have direct access to information relevant for tax purposes, shared by taxpayers on a daily basis. Access to such data should allow tax administrations to better apply and enforce tax laws. For instance, tax administrations could use such data to apply VAT, determine applicable payroll taxes, and determine corporate income taxes.

With respect to tax audits, the role that external auditors play with regards to the tax function may likely evolve and be extended. As tax is becoming a key consideration in terms of corporate reputation, tax strategy decisions are slowly shifting from the tax department to the careful attention of the board of directors. Considering the sensitiveness of corporate tax planning, external auditors of such companies should be more and more responsible for verifying the robustness of the tax control framework and the tax systems in place.

In addition, emerging technologies are likely to accelerate the integration between different government departments, including tax administrations.

In closing, emerging technologies should bring considerable opportunities to tax administrations of the 21st century. Tax administration should continue to envision these opportunities despite the challenges that the same new technologies may bring. Tax administrations should work closely with businesses, governments and households since all have the same interest at heart; all want our countries to grow.

CHAPTER 12

A Debate on Wealth Taxes

Foreword by Marie-Christine Esclassan

Recent discussions about rising inequalities and the impact of the pandemic bring wealth taxation as a recurring topic among activists, experts, and policy makers. The case of wealth taxation since 1982 in France, presented in the first part of this chapter, illustrates a country's experience with such policy. Then, two teams of experts debate three resolutions: first, governments should be concerned with redistributing the wealth of the wealthiest; second, wealth tax is an efficient and feasible way to combat inequality and poverty; and third, a reform of the current tax instruments can tax the wealthy more effectively. This debate allows understanding the broad arguments from two opposing views on this topic that affect the ongoing dialogue on tax reform and the taxation of the wealthiest to enhance social justice.

§12.01 FOREWORD

As a preliminary to the debate that will follow, and by way of illustration of the subject, Marie-Christine Esclassan gives some indications on the history of the wealth tax in France.

The introduction of this tax in 1982 occurred in a very specific context that I would like to recall. It is primarily an economic context of deindustrialization and of serious economic crisis, which then hit the country. However, it was above all a political context with the arrival, for the first time, of the Left in power under the Fifth Republic with the election of Mr. Mitterrand in 1981 as President. The establishment of a wealth tax was among its electoral promises. This promise will be implemented following the election and the socialist majority in the National Assembly. This tax had very strong political legitimacy in a major part of the public opinion because it was in line with the idea of social justice which had brought this party into power. This idea of social justice was embodied at the time in a slogan *Changer la vie (Change life)*, an expression of Arthur Rimbaud that the Socialist Party had taken up and made its own during the 1981 presidential campaign.

The vast majority of French public opinion strongly supported the idea of a wealth tax because they saw it as a means of achieving greater tax justice and social justice. At the same time, this tax will be strongly fought by the Right-wing opposition of the time. According to them, not only was it an uneconomical tax insofar as it taxed all forms of fortune, movable and immovable, but it was more particularly denounced as inappropriate in a context of economic deindustrialization because it has been said to deter investors and caused the relocation of the wealthiest people then leaving France. Indeed, the very wealthy then left France. The Right wing, at the time, swears that if it comes back in power, it will abolish this tax, and so they did. Following the election of the Right-wing party, this tax was abolished in 1986, five years after its inception.

In a spectacular turn of events, two years later, this tax will be reimplemented. It will be re-established following the re-election of Mr. Mitterrand to the presidency of the Republic in 1988 and the legislative elections won by the Left the same year. And so, the Left, which remains in power will, this time, try to rehabilitate the image of this tax. This wealth tax, formerly known as *Impôt sur les grandes fortunes*, will be renamed *Impôt de solidarité sur la fortune* (Solidarity Tax on Wealth) a name that is less divisive. What is sought is a new legitimacy, socially more robust and based on solidarity. At the same time, in 1988, a social minimum income was created for the poorest people and it was suggested that the proceeds of this tax be allocated to finance the solidarity income, which was done. Successive right-wing governments will maintain this wealth tax, for twenty years from the years 2000 onwards, without really modifying it, although they were hostile to it.

The Right wing became cautious with regard to this tax because it was afraid that by abolishing it, the public opinion would see there a kind of revenge of the wealthy over the less wealthy. Therefore, this tax was kept for the purpose of political caution. But the Right sought to defuse it by multiplying the capping measures, limiting the taxation amount, to the benefit of the wealthiest. And the paradox was that in the end, as the years went by, this tax weighed less on the wealthiest. But instead, new middle classes were taxed as a result of the rise in property prices. A larger part of the middle class became liable to this tax due to ownership of real estate and to taxation of the primary residence in particular.

The third notable period happens in 2018 with the abolition of the wealth tax—this solidarity tax on wealth—and its transformation into a tax on real estate wealth. With the election of Mr. Macron as President of the Republic, we have a political context that weighs deeply behind the evolution of this tax. The aim of the newly elected President of the Republic was simple: to restore France's economic attractiveness to investors, and in particular with regard to movable assets, and to ensure that movable assets and securities are no longer taxed with the wealth tax. What is the current result of deciding to restrict wealth tax to real estate assets only? It is too early to comment. We have figures from a recent report by the official organization *France Stratégie* (France Stratégie, 2020). In 2018, 130,000 individuals were subjected to the real estate wealth tax, whereas under the former Solidarity Tax on Wealth, the figure was 360,000. So, all in all, there is a substantial decrease in the number of people liable to wealth tax in France.

The justification for this reform stems from a theory, the so-called *trickle-down theory*, according to which the tax advantages granted to the wealthiest will be passed on to the less wealthy in jobs, in economic growth, because the wealthiest will not hesitate to invest, particularly in companies in France. For the time being, this *trickle-down theory* hasn't been verified. However, it has been verified that the solidarity tax on wealth raised around EUR 4 billion in revenue until 2017, which is little. In 2018, the revenue from the new wealth tax on real estate fell to 1.5 billion. Therefore, there is a significant revenue loss, with a kind of partial collapse of this tax.

§12.02 DEBATE

The purpose of the debate is to discuss the necessity, feasibility, and efficiency of taxing wealth. Two teams; one consisting of Veronique de Rugy and Dan Mitchell and the other of Erica Payne and Morris Pearl, take a position on three resolutions and finally present a closing argument. Louise Otis and Jay Rosengard chaired the debate and delivered the closing remarks.

[A] First Resolution

Be it resolved that governments should be concerned with redistributing the wealth of the wealthiest.

[1] Response to First Resolution by Veronique de Rugy and Dan Mitchell

[a] Dan Mitchell

Our position is that government should finance public goods in the least destructive manner possible. That means a tax system based on what I sometimes call the holy trinity of good tax policy, low rates on productive behavior, no double taxation of saving and investment, and no loopholes based on either the source of income or the use of it.

I think this debate is about a fundamental difference of visions. Veronique and I want to help poor people. I think our friends on the Left sometimes seem more motivated by a desire to hurt rich people. We understand that economic growth is the only sure way to improve the lives of the poor. Our friends on the Left, however, seem to think that the economy is a fixed pie and that the job of politicians is to re-slice the pie. But our contention is that the class warfare tax policies that re-slice the pie also cause the pie to shrink.

Proponents of higher taxes on the affluent often overlook behavioral adjustments due to the fact that wealthier people are more sensitive to changes in taxation. While the empirical research shows that the elasticity of taxable income is between 0.2 and 0.4 for ordinary people, for the 1 % wealthiest, the elasticity is closer to one. Now, what does all that jargon mean? It simply means that every dollar increase in the tax rate is one dollar reduction in taxable income when you're talking about high-income people. A big reason for the dramatic difference is that ordinary taxpayers will get the majority of their income, the vast majority of their income, in the form of wages and salaries. Therefore, it takes a lot of time and effort for us to change our behavior when tax rates are altered. However, rich people are not like the rest of us, or at least they are not like Veronique and me. Rich people get the vast majority of their income from business activity and investment, and that means they have a lot more control over the timing, level, and composition of their income and therefore can easily engage in tax avoidance and changes in behavior if their tax rates are increased.

[b] Veronique de Rugy

Significant increases of marginal tax rates on the affluent not only lead to changes in federal revenue but also have a broader effect on human capital accumulation and labor market efficiency. The empirical evidence in this area finds that in the long term, a more progressive tax system reduces the incentive to develop human capital. With higher taxes on the upper-income distribution, a high school student may choose not to pursue his dream of becoming an engineer or a small business owner may choose not to expand its business. There is no doubt that this sort of tax-driven inefficiency makes society worst off. Another fiscal phenomenon that is often overlooked is the adverse effect on labor income and investment that drive down labor productivity. Higher marginal taxes on profit and investment, which reduce savings, lower rate of investment and thereby reduce the stock of productive capital and hence wage growth.

So an unintended consequence of hiking taxes on high-income earners would be lower wage growth for lower-income American workers as a consequence of reduced investment in productive capital. Finally, in European countries with significant revenue collection as a share of GDP (Gross Domestic Product), taxes are generally high for everyone, not just the rich. Denmark, Sweden, and Finland have broad-based value-added taxes, 24% to 25%, and higher payroll tax. Their income taxes have a high marginal tax rate, but they apply to much more personal income than what politicians like Bernie Sanders and Alexandria Ocasio Cortez are proposing. Denmark's top marginal tax rate of 60% starts applying at 1.2 times the average income. If that were enacted here, all taxable income over about USD 56,500 would have faced a 60% tax rate.

[2] Response to First Resolution by Erica Payne and Morris Pearl

[a] Erica Payne

I have two points to make. The first one is that by using the word redistribution, the question is built into the premise that the money that we are talking about taxing actually belongs to these people in the first place. I come from the southern part of the United States (U.S.) and I have a long line of ancestors who owned slaves and exploited human beings to extract an enormous amount of wealth out of those people. So I disagree with the idea that because somebody currently owns wealth that it's the wealth that they should currently own or that should be considered theirs in any logical or ethical sense. So let's start with that number one. Number two, do governments have the right to redistribute money, so to speak. Well, I think we built into the idea of democracy that governments have the right to distribute power. We have gotten to a place where people have so much wealth that their wealth is no longer money anymore. It is power. And governments have an absolute right, in fact, they have a duty to distribute power equitably across the population.

[b] Morris Pearl

I agree with Dan that the pie is not a fixed size, and I'm also afraid of reducing the size of the pie in total. But what I'm seeing is the current system that makes inequality getting worse and worse and worse. That is what I see as contributing to the pie getting smaller. What I'm afraid of is the millions and millions of people in our country who think that they're being second-class citizens and are starting marching in the street and who don't know where they're going to get the money to pay their rent for next month. Those are the people that I'm concerned about, reducing the size of the pie because they're not able to buy the shoes and ice cream and all the other things that help business people get rich and help businesses thrive. I don't want the United States to devolve into some kind of civil unrest. I don't want to live in a country with a few rich people and lots of poor people. That's the kind of country we see in other parts of the world and it is not where people build businesses that employ people and help people get rich. We are advocating for higher taxes for the rich, not for higher taxes for people who work for a living. We believe that we need to redistribute, yes. Redistribute some of the wealth of our nation so that we avoid the phenomenon of having a few rich people and lots and lots of poor people because that doesn't work for any of us. So, yeah, we're not concerned about increasing revenue for our government in general. We are concerned about using the tax system more effectively, more progressively to reduce inequality and make it so all of our people participate in the economy. And that's what helps all the people thrive.

[B] Second Resolution

Be it resolved that wealth tax is an efficient and feasible way to combat inequality and poverty.

[1] Response to Second Resolution by Erica Payne and Morris Pearl

[a] Morris Pearl

We have a society where a few very rich people don't actually contribute very much to society as we expect all the rest of our people to do. Our current tax system is based on income. Income is what people earn and the fact of the matter is that how much money people earn has little or nothing to do with how much wealth they have. The wealthiest people in our country actually don't earn anything at all and don't pay any taxes at all because they're simply spending money that they already have. So we believe the only way to deal with the problem of gross inequality in our nation is to have policies which deal with the wealth inequality, in our nation. That is what we are most concerned about in changing the tax system somehow in order to equalize that factor.

[b] Erica Payne

Wealthy people say they can't get out of the fact that, of course, there should be a wealth tax. So now they're going to come down to whether it's feasible. Listen, we have a rover on Mars. There is zero possibility that calculating the assets of a rich person within some bound of a reasonable approximation of what they own is impossible. There is zero possibility that that is unfeasible in the United States. We have about a thousand billionaires. They have legions of people working with them right now to make sure they get out of paying anything that they theoretically should pay. Let's just reverse that and have that volume of people trying to calculate what they own. And even if you come in slightly less than what they do own and tax, you're still ahead of where you are right now.

[2] Response to Second Resolution by Veronique de Rugy and Dan Mitchell

[a] Dan Mitchell

The question is whether a wealth tax is an efficient and feasible way to combat inequality and poverty. Well, I guess I'll start by saying it is possible that a wealth tax can reduce inequality, but not in a good way. It would only reduce inequality in the sense that high-income people would suffer even greater losses than low-income people. Poverty overall would increase rather than decrease because the wealth tax would significantly reduce incentives to save and invest. All economic theories, even socialism, even Marxism, all economic theories agree that growth depends in large part on saving and investing. Now, the socialists think the government should do the investing, which is a little bit silly. But everyone agrees on this notion. The one key thing to understand economically about a wealth tax in practical terms is that it's a huge tax increase on saving and investment with the rate determined by the underlying growth of your assets. For instance, a 2% wealth tax is akin to a 40% tax on saving and investment if someone's portfolio grows by 5%. And keep in mind, that's on top of all the other existing taxes that are imposed on savings and investment. A wealth tax also is an administrative nightmare, and maybe it can be done, but we have to consider at what cost and at what damage to productive behavior.

Valuation will be very subjective. Think about things like stocks and bonds. We can look at the financial pages or financial markets online and we know the value of those assets. However, what about things like cryptocurrencies, trust, private businesses? What about non-traditional assets, jewelry, artwork, vehicles, life insurance policies, farm assets, household furnishing? So many assets don't have a ready market value.

The bottom line, from my perspective, is that a wealth tax is extremely inefficient, the administrative costs of applying a 2% wealth tax on a person with a net worth of 55 million would almost certainly surpass the USD 100,000 of revenue that the tax would raise. That doesn't make sense economically and determining which households have assets exceeding USD 50 million in and of itself, that's going to be an administrative nightmare. A survey of economic experts conducted by the University of Chicago found that 73% of economists believe that proposals for a wealth tax would be much more difficult to enforce than existing federal taxes because of issues such as valuation and underreporting.

[b] Veronique de Rugy

A wealth tax will also raise a very small amount of revenue. Not only it has very high administrative costs that will exceed how much you will raise, but also it means that when you do the net benefit, it is just probably no benefit at all for the wealth tax. Revenue raised with a wealth tax in Sweden, for instance, amounts to an average of 0.2% of GDP per year. Such was the case in Norway, Switzerland, and most other countries with a wealth tax. Replicating this in the United States would amount to less than USD 40 billion every year, and then administrative costs need to be accounted for. The ratio of revenue raised compared to compliance costs makes the tax a doubly bad idea. This explains why of the fifteen European countries that have implemented a wealth tax, all but three have abandoned it. Here are a few examples. Sweden abolished its wealth tax in 2016 because it generated a very small amount of revenue, and abolishing the tax is an attempt to boost the low level of investment, encourage entrepreneurship activity and increase employment.

I really enjoyed the presentation of the history of the French wealth tax, and what I can tell you is that since its inception in 1988, until its end in 2018, about EUR 200 billion was lost in capital flight every year. It is estimated that a tax reduces GDP growth by 0.2% per annum while shifting the tax burden, as we've heard, from wealthy taxpayers living in France to other taxpayers. So to sum up, experience from countries that have implemented wealth tax provides some key lessons. First, wealth tax lower capital stock, by encouraging the flight of capital and discourage investors from coming in. Second, high administrative costs of regular valuation can reduce net revenue so much that it barely yields more than 0.2% of GDP. And third, the macroeconomic effects of implementing the wealth tax often result in reduced economic growth rate and lower wages, which in turn lowers tax revenue even further while also lowering the welfare of many households.

[C] Third Resolution

Be it resolved that a reform of the current tax instruments can tax the wealthy more effectively.

[1] Response to Third Resolution by Veronique de Rugy and Dan Mitchell

[a] Dan Mitchell

I guess this is losing in a less bad way; tax the rich, but don't tax them with the wealth tax. But Veronique and I categorically reject the notion that tax policy should be designed to punish investors, entrepreneurs, business owners, and other high-income people. The goal should be creating opportunity for the less fortunate, not a spiteful attack on the rich, however, we define that group.

As previously discussed, a wealth tax is an especially destructive way to penalize successful taxpayers. Other alternatives that we might look at are equally misguided. Higher-income tax rates, for instance, discourage working investment and entrepreneurship. There's a lot of research showing how they encourage tax avoidance and tax evasion. Higher capital gains rates, that's another option on the table. Well, that discourages investment and innovation. Moreover, the tax is easily skirted by investors who can choose either to sit on their money or to sit on their existing investments. Higher corporate tax rates, an option that Joe Biden has proposed in the United States; that's going to impose an indirect levy on a lot of people, including ordinary workers and ordinary consumers.

And moreover, for those of you who are fixated on inequality, it's worth noting, according to a recent NBER (National Bureau of Economic Research) paper by Professor James Hines at the University of Michigan, he wrote, "Higher corporate taxes can increase income inequality even when the corporate tax burden falls entirely on capital owned disproportionately by the rich" (Hines, 2020). In other words, when you shoot at the rich, in many cases, you wind up hitting everyone out. And by the way, I also want to mention that death taxes are almost as economically foolish as wealth taxes since that levy also directly takes capital out of the economy's productive sector and transfers it to the government.

[b] *Veronique de Rugy*

Now, it doesn't mean that they are not some desirable tax reform that could collect more revenue from upper-income taxpayers. So, for instance, in the United States, politicians could get rid of the tax exemption for municipal bond interests and lower tax rates with a neutral effect on revenue. The top 1% almost certainly would pay more. In the United States, again, politicians could eliminate or curtail the charitable contribution deduction and lower the tax rate in a revenue-neutral swap. The top 1% almost certainly would pay more taxes. Obviously, with a 76,000-page tax code, it goes without saying that there are many other deductions and credits, exemptions, exclusions, and other preferences that politicians have put there, on the Right and on the Left by the way, and they benefit rich people. It could be eliminated as part of a revenue-neutral reform and bring more revenue from higher-income people. We will close with an observation that folks on the Left need to decide what they value most: is it generating revenue for redistribution or penalizing the rich.

Here's an example of how these goals can be in conflict. According to the Internal Revenue Service (IRS) Statistics of Income (SOI) Bulletin, households with more than one million of taxable income paid 4.3 billion dollars in taxes in 1980, when the top marginal tax rate for the rich was 70%. In 1988, when the top tax rate was down to 26%, households with more than a million of taxable income take 42.3 billion. Sensible people call that a win-win. But some of our friends on the Left, however, think that the Reagan tax cuts were bad. We don't.

[2] *Response to Third Resolution by Erica Payne and Morris Pearl*

[a] *Erica Payne*

I guess the first thing is; will a reform tax the wealthy more effectively than they are currently being taxed? Well, given the fact that in the United States of America today, billionaires are paying lower tax rates than any other group of people, I would say it would be difficult for us to be less efficient in taxing them, number one. Number two, many refer to these poor little rich people getting punished and being penalized and are sad for them. I mean, give me a break. Since the late 1980s, the 1% of the population has had their wealth increase 300%, while everyone else has stayed exactly the same. This did not happen overnight. If I am a wealthy heir, do nothing for all my life and take advantage of the *Internal Revenue Code* section 1031 stepped up basis, I can inherit millions, millions, and millions of dollars without ever paying a single penny in taxes. Well, anybody who actually works for a living is putting in their 37% every single day. That is absurd and it is grotesque.

[b] *Pearl Morris*

I also fundamentally disagree with some of the arguments from the other side. I'm the chairman of the Patriotic Millionaires. I think being a millionaire is great. Everyone should do that. We're not in favor of punishing anyone, especially not millionaires, but we are in favor of having rich people have higher tax rates than people who actually work for a living, not the other way around, as is currently the case here in the United States because of our recent tax laws. We also think that the idea that, taxing is removing money from the economy from the productive part of the economy, that's completely wrong.

The very wealthy people have their money in their stock portfolios, their bank accounts or whatever. That money is not being productive in the economy. The rest of the people who work for a living, people who go out every month and have to make their rent checks and pay their iPhone bills and buy ice cream and shoes. That is the productive economy. Those are the people who are actually putting their money into the productive economy.

If we change the tax system to have more of the burden on the very rich and less on people who work for a living, that will increase the amount of money in the productive economy, not decrease it. That is, in the actual long term enlightened self-interest of the very rich people is to have a more productive economy with millions of people who can afford to pay their bills every month and not have a small number of rich people and many, many poor people. I believe we are actually talking about policies that are in the best interests of both the rich and the poor.

[D] Closing Remarks

[1] Final Remarks by Erica Payne and Morris Pearl

[a] Pearl Morris

In addition to not believing in inequality being good, I also reject the idea that the experience in France is even comparable to the experience here in the United States. France had a problem because they were trying to tax millions and millions of middle-class homeowners. We are talking about wealth taxes, assigning a tax that already is being paid by middle-class people here, because here in the United States, middle-class people already pay a wealth tax on most of their wealth, which is represented by their homes. We are only asking the rich people to also pay a tax based on their wealth. We are not asking to increase taxes on millions and millions of people. We are not part of a European Union where people can be in one jurisdiction or another very easily. So I don't believe the issues from France are even comparable to the issues in the United States. I think that we need a system for the rest of the world where those people who have higher wealth and higher income pay more of their income and wealth as taxes so that we can decrease inequality.

[b] Erica Payne

The socioeconomic situation is deteriorating in several segments of our population, particularly because of the pandemic. Well, the billionaires in the first six months of the pandemic made almost a trillion dollars in the stock markets. So cry me a river with a bunch of rich people thinking they're getting punished for their success, which they basically built off the backs of hard-working people.

[2] Final Remarks by Veronique de Rugy and Dan Mitchell

[a] Dan Mitchell

I don't really cry many rivers, not even little streams for rich people. I figure they're pretty comfortable. I'd like to someday join their lifestyle, but I do cry a river, an entire ocean, if necessary, for poor people and middle-income people who depend on economic growth for their living standards and lives to improve. And when you look around the world at high tax nations, nations that have more punitive tax regimes, nations with wealth taxes, they simply don't grow as fast, create as many jobs, and as much opportunity as other countries. I think perhaps one of the big differences between what Veronique and I believe and what Morris and Erica believe is the role of capital in the economy. If you don't have capital formation, if you don't have savings and investment, you don't have economic growth. So if I was lucky enough to have picked the right parents and I basically just had one hundred million dollars handed to me just by virtue of being born into that household, I wouldn't dig a hole in the backyard and bury it there; that one hundred million dollars would be financing factories, investment startups; capital formation is key. Capital and labor are what economists call complementary goods.

I'll close with one simple point. If we wind up being like Europe with higher taxes, the point Veronique made earlier is critical. Every single European country has a less progressive tax system than the United States. You cannot finance big government without pillaging the middle class. And ultimately, I fear that while Morris and Erica may have their hearts in the right place, ultimately their agenda is going to lead to slower growth, fewer jobs, and a more burdened middle class, not a less burdened middle class.

§12.03 JUDGES' CONCLUSION

[A] Jay Rosengard

I will give you the judge's verdict; Judge Otis and I agree that the wealthy already contribute a substantial amount of total tax revenue and that unreasonable increases in their tax burden could create disincentives to invest and even lead to capital flight. However, it is less clear that the current tax payments of the very rich constitute their fair share, given the extremely unequal distribution of income and wealth pervasive today around the world. It is also unclear to us that the current inequities are politically and socially either desirable or sustainable. We are skeptical that a wealth tax can be implemented in a cost-effective manner, given the failures such attempts have encountered so far on a global scale. As the saying goes, the poor evade taxes, but the rich avoid them. The rich can always find a way to hide or move their income and wealth, and when tax loopholes are insufficient, they can engage in regulatory capture to amend tax laws to their advantage. But we do believe that current tax instruments can and should be reformed to tax the wealthy more effectively. This is both a necessity to enhance social justice and maintain social peace, as well as politically, administratively feasible, particularly reform of the personal income tax, the corporate income tax, and inheritance taxes.

This is just the beginning of an ongoing dialogue on tax reform and we look forward to continuing constructive engagement on these critical issues.

Bibliography

France Stratégie. 2020. *Comité d'évaluation des réformes de la fiscalité du capital Deuxième rapport*, Octobre 2020, available at https://www.strategie.gouv.fr/sites/strategie.gouv.fr/files/atoms/files/fs-2020-rapport-isf-octobre.pdf.

Hines, James R. Jr. 2020. *Corporate Taxation and the Distribution of Income*, BNER Working Paper 27939, October 2020, available at https://www.nber.org/papers/w27939.

CHAPTER 13

Taxation and the Society of the Future: Embracing AI and Robots

Christina Dimitropoulou & Xavier Oberson

The rise of technologies such as artificial intelligence (AI), robotics, and automation has had major impacts on the economy, business models, and the labor market. The author, Christina Dimitropoulou, examines the role of taxation in reaction to these new technologies and analyzes the concept of robot taxation. This first part of the paper offers an overview of various forms of robot taxation proposals, starting by addressing the complexities in attaching fiscal attributes to robots, such as legal personhood and the ability to pay. Taxation of robots' usage, consumption, and transaction taxes are considered. In the second part, the author addresses the international tax competition concerns that might arise from the taxation of robots and the use of AI as an integral part of business models. The chapter concludes with comments by Xavier Oberson, who provides further context on the possible solutions to mitigate the issues brought by new technologies on the labor market and against inequality and elaborates on the taxation of robots as legal fictions similar to the taxation of enterprises.

§13.01 INTRODUCTION[1]

The advancements in new disruptive technologies, such as robots and AI are gradually transforming the nature of work and signal a shift in how value is created. Automation

1. This chapter is reflecting on the discussions that took place on October 14, 2020, in the context of the World Tax Summit—TaxCOOP2020, between Yoshua Bengio and Xavier Oberson regarding the future of taxation in light of the technological developments in Artificial Intelligence (AI) and robotics. The arguments of both experts are presented and are further enriched with some clarifications and comments by the author.

anxiety is not new, but there are arguments that this time is different and actions should be taken.[2] Concerns around the future of employment have been coupled with the relevant concerns on increasing global economic inequality and unequal distribution of wealth (Piketty, 2015), together with the sustainability of tax systems and their ability to adapt to the challenges of the 4th industrial revolution (Brynjolfsson & McAfee, 2012, 2014; Ford, 2015). Robot taxes and automation taxes have been discussed so far as a way to address the above challenges either with a short-term or long-term view.[3] Currently, there is no detailed legislative proposal about how a robot tax could or should be actually designed but several suggestions have been nevertheless made by scholars at the tax policy level. Apart from the technical difficulties of introducing a robot tax, it is also argued that this type of tax is likely to have adverse effects in terms of promoting innovation and in light of the tax policy goals that it aims to address (Englisch, 2018).[4] In addition, a coordinated approach shall be opted for in case a robot tax or a tax on AI is about to become reality. The importance of the stakes at hand justifies the discussion among different stakeholders already now, even if the negative effects of AI automation are not imminent. The discussion on robot taxation is framed between the optimistic view and the pessimistic view regarding the effects of robots on employment. The optimists adopt a Schumpeterian approach of a so-called creative distraction according to which AI is connected to the 4th industrial revolution and (as it has happened also in the previous industrial revolutions) even though many jobs are going to be replaced by AI, other new jobs will be created in their place (Frey & Osborne, 2013). Under this approach, there may be no need for taxation of robots. However, there is also a second pessimistic scenario under which robots and AI are going to replace more jobs than those that will be created, and that will happen at a pace and scale that the economy will not be able to adapt adequately in order to sustain social and economic cohesion. This is based on the argument that this time it is different from the previous industrial revolutions and more importantly, on what AI seems to represent.[5] In case the second pessimistic scenario becomes a reality, at least in the future, the States will have an immense fiscal issue. The fiscal issue is

2. The argument that this time is different focuses especially on the potential of AI which is radically transforming the balance between labor and capital, as more and more tasks that previously used to be done by workers are taken over by robots and AI. Within the OECD, 14% of jobs are highly automatable while 32% are at risk of facing substantial change in the way they are performed. The combination of the scale and pace of AI automation is the reason that both the labor market and the tax systems may prove unable to follow the economic and technological development (OECD, 2018).
3. For instance, short-term measures focus on reskilling the current workforce in order to adapt to the changes in the labor market while longer-term measures require more radical changes in the states' educational systems. Taxes for regulation of the economy are also a short-term solution that could slow down the pace of automation in order for the human workforce to be reskilled and at the same time help the internalization of the social costs of robotics and artificial intelligence.
4. Since one of the main goals of the "robot tax" is founded on the principle of neutrality, there is a risk that the tax may create more distortions than the ones it aims to solve.
5. In fact AI tends to assimilate more and more human thinking and this is the reason of an augmented anxiety of the future of employment in case not only routine jobs but also non routine jobs are taken over by AI. Some even speak about a general disruption and disappearance of work as we know it today (remunerated work or work with no supervisor and under a certain framework).

concentrated in the loss of the labor tax base, which in many countries,[6] represent the largest tax base financing States' needs. In face of these two opposite scenarios, it is difficult to take one position or the other, especially where no reliable empirical evidence currently supports either scenario and therefore cannot instruct the receipt of certain measures. There are though certain economic studies measuring the effect of AI and other similar technologies in the labor market and the division of labor, but those studies do not share the same results and the data used cannot prescribe for a generalized solution (Guerreiro, Rebelo & Teles, 2020; Acemoglu & Restrepo, 2017). Moreover, most of the studies take as an assumption that robots qualify as "industrial robots." This is the only available definition of a robot and is also measurable. However, AI systems may or may not fall under this definition which makes the results of the relevant studies a bit uncertain. In view of the above uncertainty, we could only adopt a precautionary approach to robot taxation. As Oberson suggests, we should discuss robot taxes as if the negative outcome from the use of AI is likely to come and prepare a fiscal plan in face of that risk.

§13.02 TAXATION AS AN INSTRUMENT TO ADDRESS THE SOCIAL AND ECONOMIC EFFECTS OF AI

Governments are indeed faced with major challenges resulting from the negative social and economic effects of AI and should take measures in order to reform their social services respectively. However, more and more scholars are skeptical as to whether taxation is the right way to address those issues. First and foremost because it is very difficult to define what a robot is. This is a fundamental technical and practical problem since in the science of informatics almost everything could qualify as a robot. There are, for example, many intermediary systems that attribute to robots the characteristic of "autonomy" and all these autonomous systems interact with each other. Therefore, it is practically impossible to define what exactly should constitute a robot. The second reason for skepticism around robot taxation refers to the impact of the tax on the social and beneficial effects of technology in society. Specifically, imposing a tax on robots and AI for the purpose of compensating the loss of work and labor's substitution might have adverse effects because AI automation is going to apply also to new services that will have an enormous social benefit for the general public (namely, in the field of education, healthcare and the general humanitarian sector). For these reasons, the real question we need to ask ourselves is not what is a robot for the purpose of imposing a tax on technologies that qualify as robots but rather what is or is likely to be the impact of the activities of the enterprises using robots and other advanced technologies in society and the common good.[7] In view of the above, the role of taxation should

6. Especially in the United States and Europe.
7. This question disconnects the robot definition from finding an appropriate solution and focuses on the outcome of the use of robots, namely, the social and economic effect of the excess use and concentration of technology by few. Excess concentration of technology seems to assimilate, according to Bengio, to excess concentration of wealth that creates disparities among society and has to be addressed. We would say that this view is not far from the one currently being proposed

concentrate on how to align the activities of the private sector with social justice assuming that the former are exploiting their power and are responsible for the increase of inequalities. Besides, States have the right, under certain conditions, to intervene in the economy through taxes so as to regulate certain economic behavior in a way that will serve the social values of our society. In that direction, taxation has indeed proven quite effective (IMF, 2019).[8]

§13.03 ROBOT TAXATION PROPOSALS IN A NUTSHELL

[A] Robots and Legal Personhood

One of the interesting questions that has been raised regarding the taxation of robots is whether robots qualify as "persons" for tax law purposes and whether we could attribute legal personality to robots in the same way as we do for companies. The tax community is divided in that respect. For example, some argue that this could entail further unintended consequences regarding the responsibility that rests on the company using robots or AI since AI is not currently a "person" but rather systems implemented by people for a certain cause. It is still people who are held legally responsible for robots' actions, who make judgments, who plan and apply AI systems. If, however, we consider AI as a separate legal person this might be further dangerous for the social equilibrium in our society. In addition, scholars from the computer science field acknowledge that we are still far away from dealing with AI systems that exhibit levels of autonomy justifying the attribution of responsibility to them and thus, legal personhood.

On the other hand, reasons to reject the argument on attributing robots' legal personality can be equally found in the theory of social contract. That is, if we recall the reasons why legal entities are considered as separate legal persons than individuals taking part in them, it is because the law decided to attribute to the entities themselves the legal responsibility of the actions of the entity in order to align their activity with the "social contract." It is hence important that this social contract continues to apply among people that live in the society, therefore, between people that use and program the robots and people that are negatively affected by them.

For other scholars, including Oberson, who first talked about the possibility of attributing robots legal personality in the future, taxation of robots as separate legal persons is one of the various paths that robot taxation can take. The option of attributing robots' legal personality was initially found in a proposal put forward by the

on the need for a global excess profits tax. *See*, i.e., Christians A. & Magalhaes T. D., 2020. "It's Time for Pillar 3: A Global Excess Profits Tax for COVID-19 and Beyond," TaxNotes Int'l 507.

8. Bengio seems to be in favor of a sort of Pigouvian tax regulating the negative externalities of automation considering that taxes based on this logic, such as, among others, alcohol taxes, tobacco taxes, carbon taxes, prove to be effective in both changing behavior and revenue collection. Several economic studies on carbon tax and other taxes on harmful economic behavior based on the "polluter pays principle" prove that these taxes provide strong incentives to the "polluters" to efficiently reduce the harmful economic activity while shifting to more socially desirable behavior.

European Parliament. The Report of 2017 of the European Union (EU) Committee on Legal Affairs (EU Committee on Legal Affairs, 2016) addressed, among other issues, the potential responsibility of robots from a civil law perspective and less from a tax law perspective. Such a proposal would meet many obstacles in its implementation that have mainly to do with the lack of an objective definition of robots. However, it has been argued that such a revolutionary approach could possibly apply as a second phase of robot taxation, in the more distant future. To answer whether robots could qualify as "persons" for tax law purposes, it is necessary to resort to the justifications of attributing tax personality to legal entities. Among the reasons for which States decided to tax legal entities as such is mainly the separate entity approach and the alleged separate tax ability of the entity itself. Therefore, legal personality for robots would have to be premised on the idea that robots have their own tax capacity or ability to pay. In further, such a tax on robots might need to have a constitutional foundation, assuming that in many countries the principle of ability to pay is founded in their constitution (stemming in most of the cases from the general constitutional principle of equality). The problem that seems to arise is that robots do not have their own money or financial resources and for this reason, they might not be able to pay the tax if any. It is usually a human that eventually exerts dominion and control over the robot's resources that makes the application of traditional tax principles to robots hard to apply (Hoffer, 2020). In view of the above, if tax law considers that treating robots as persons might serve specific needs and that legal and constitutional issues as those described above could be overcome, then taxing robots as such could be considered as another tax law fiction, similar to taxation of corporations.

[B] Taxation of Robots' Usage

Following the criticism of attributing legal personality to robots for tax purposes, the majority of tax scholars seem to approach robot taxation as a way to reform the taxation of businesses. In particular, instead of questioning how robots should be taxed, we should rather question how to reform the taxation of enterprises in view of the expansive use of AI and robots and the need to direct AI towards its beneficial use for society. This could take for example the form of a tax similar to the carbon tax that aims to address the negative externalities of carbon usage by certain enterprises or the form of tax incentives towards innovative but also socially beneficial investments. Other options of taxing robots' usage include the introduction of a deemed salary income tax on the employer displacing workers with robots or of a turnover tax based on the ratio of the replacement or usage of robots versus workers etc. The latter approach however reveals the huge tasks of both companies and tax administrations to distinguish between robots displacing and robots enhancing human workers and is immediately linked to the effects of automation on employment which is already hard to measure (Dimitropoulou, 2020). In this regard, although robots and AI create some imbalances for the labor market and the fiscal state, such imbalances go beyond robots as such. Especially since science produces knowledge and enterprises create technologies based on the above knowledge. The technologies in turn are exploited for the purpose of making more profits and therefore, taxation should be discussed on the basis of how it could assist in re-establishing the social and economic equilibrium in society.

For example, Bengio argues that if there is loss of work due to the use of robots and AI—and this is just the beginning of an envisaged disruption brought about by AI—States could think of ways of compensating the workers that lose their jobs by levying taxes on the turnover of companies using these disruptive technologies. This turnover tax can be further based on a ratio between robots and labor occupied by a company or a ratio of labor substituted by robots (Abbott R. & Bogenschneider B., 2018). This form of taxation in principle intends to reduce the benefits/advantages that these companies receive by using such technologies. However, the justification and logic of imposing a tax on companies that use advanced technologies for the purpose of curtailing the excessive benefits that these companies receive from the use of AI should go beyond robots as such and the loss of work. It should rather focus on reducing inequalities and internalizing the negative externalities of robots' usage in society. Therefore, the robot tax justification should come closer to the justification of a carbon type tax, meaning a tax that would attempt to address the negative externalities created by the users of highly advanced technologies for the rest of society. This type of tax is the best illustration of how taxation can penalize certain economic behavior and also effectively change such behavior for the common good.

It is more and more accepted that the use of technology is a factor that exacerbates economic inequalities in society as it allows enterprises that are rich to become richer, deepening therefore the discrimination gap among different individuals and stakeholders. However, states do not only have to deal with unemployment and economic inequalities but also with the loss of a significant taxable base, including social security and unemployment levies that are currently imposed on workers. This tax base has to be substituted for the sustainability of the tax system and also for the assistance of the current and future workforce. In this regard, robot taxes could indeed function as eco-type taxes. Namely, as similarly to eco-taxes, the company that pollutes the environment is obliged to internalize the cost it creates for the environment through the imposition of Co2 taxes, the employer of robots could also pay a fee to the state for the costs that his/her choice creates for the labor market.[9] This form of taxes departs from the theory of reinstitution of work—assuming that this is the primary reason to impose a robot tax—and concentrates on tax incentives that States might want to offer in order to encourage human employment. It is hence, another confirmation that any robot tax inspired by any tax design would have to be evaluated by reference to the general principles of tax policy and to the tax system as a whole.

9. The proposal is centered on the general justification of such tax design and does not take into account difficulties of implementation that are present to both carbon taxes and any potential robot taxes.

[C] Consumption and Transaction Tax Options

Consumption taxes are going to be equally affected by AI and robots as people that become unemployed lose part of their ability to consume if they have no other income than income from employment. Therefore, a possible solution could be to reconstruct the consumption tax base by a consumption tax for robots. However, robots or the work performed by robots is already currently taxed under the value added tax (VAT) systems of many countries. This means, for instance, that a car manufactured by a robot or a juridical service rendered by an automated system are both subject to VAT that is paid by the person receiving the good or the service. However, in the context of taxing robots, Oberson argues that it is not unthinkable to consider a robot being a VAT subject itself[10] for the purpose of imposing and collecting the VAT from the customer. This is probably feasible from a technological standpoint. It is further argued that if the robot itself will collect from the client the consideration for the good it produced or the services it rendered, it would be easy to establish its taxpaying capacity reflected in the amount received directly from the customer.[11] The VAT or consumption type taxation for robots is also based on the idea that there is added value from the use of robots that is not currently being taxed.[12]

A transaction type tax on data used by robots is also an option that is being discussed lately especially in the global digital tax debate. Therefore, a possible tax on the use of AI is based on the collection of enormous amounts of data and the question that arises is whether we can tax those data that are considered as the raw material of AI. This is a proposal that is currently being debated at the Organisation for Economic Co-operation and Development (OECD) level in the context of taxation of the digital economy and more recently in Pillar 1 and 2. It also draws upon the value of the users whose data are actually collected and monetized by large digital companies and the promotion of taxation according to value creation. A tax on data is mainly a tax on the transactions of data which however comes with a lot of problems in its implementation. In fact, taxing data is in the same line as taxing robots. This means that the collection of personal data can be used for both good and bad purposes and is difficult to draw a line if we want to dis-incentivize only the harmful use of data. For instance, the use of data in data analytics is highly beneficial for society if used for predictions in the field of healthcare that can prevent or cure diseases. On the other hand, the use of data and data analytics for controlling democratic processes and influencing public opinion in a biased way can have a serious impact on the democratic process itself (i.e., if used for manipulating elections). It is difficult for someone to be convinced that taxing data is the appropriate way to tackle the negative consequences of the use of AI.

10. Clarifying that this could be an option, even though attributing a legal personality to robots may not be currently necessary.
11. The author considers that this is rather an argument in favor of the liquidity of this sort of tax on robots' resources, rather than an argument proving that the robot has legally a taxpaying capacity. The latter is connected to the possibility of considering a robot as a person for either income or VAT purposes and is not automatically fulfilled by the fact that robots may possess for some time the consideration received for the sale of their goods or services.
12. *See also* Abbott R. & Bogenschneider B. (2018).

There are, however, several other issues that probably States have to address relevant to the subject matter such as the proprietary rights on personal data, how individuals can actually negotiate the contract terms when they agree to allow companies to use their data, etc. But these issues depart from the rationale of taxing data or AI for the purposes already mentioned.

[D] Robot Taxes for Redistribution

Taxation of robots can be more easily comprehended from the economic impact that robots have on the production process. For example, if there is added value produced by robots following the replacement of a significant number of workers in different tasks and occupations, this value should be distributed among society for the benefit of those that become worse off. It might be either for the protection of those that become unemployed or for the whole society in accordance with the principle of equity. Re-instituting equity among society by reason of unequal distribution of wealth is not only something that we might think of but is rather necessary to be done. Technology can benefit societies a lot. Either through the facilitation of production of new goods or through the increase of efficiency in the production of goods. However, it can also cause harm, that is, for instance, by reducing employment opportunities.

The issue of wealth concentration is a thorny issue that concerns both national states and the international community and for this reason, international cooperation is again very important. The question of redistribution does not only relate to the taxing side of the government's function but also to the spending side. It is questioned how governments will make better use of the revenues collected in the event of a robot tax. Robot taxes can be designed to have, as their purpose, wealth distribution and in this case, they would be in line with their object and purpose if the revenues collected are used for redistribution purposes. On the one hand, assuming that robot taxes are used for allowing the labor market to adapt to the new technological challenges there is a period of transition and during this period robot taxes are going to aid those that have to be reskilled and reenter the labor market. On the other hand, maybe in the more distant future, the question of redistribution touches upon what most economists have for a long time advocated for, namely the institution of a universal basic income (UBI) for all. In sum, the question of how to tax robots and how the proceeds of these taxes are going to be used are two separate questions. If robot taxes are going to be earmarked[13] for funding an unconditional minimum income is something that should not be confused with how a robot tax can be designed or whether a robot tax should be implemented, to begin with. This is because the UBI can very well be implemented without taxing robots as such.

13. *See* i.e. Chand V., Kostic V. & Reis A. (2020).

§13.04 INTERNATIONAL TAX COOPERATION

[A] International Tax Cooperation and Coordination

International cooperation in the field of robot taxation is equally crucial as in any other tax affecting international trade. As we can see from the case of carbon taxation, in the absence of international cooperation companies will more likely relocate to other countries where the price of using robots might be less or nonexistent and that will disturb the global equilibrium but also the purpose of imposing the tax at a national level. The question of international cooperation comes second and requires that we have previously identified whether taxing robots is the right way to go and how this can happen. Therefore, how the international tax framework would apply is a matter of how robots would be treated for tax purposes[14]

Taxation of robots will signal a fiscal revolution and the international community should indeed take measures to address excess global competition. It is already observed at the level of the OECD as far as the taxation of the digital economy is concerned. Moreover, the difficulty of the OECD member states to reach a consensus on this matter emphasizes the complexity of the issues addressed but also the fact that delays in reaching consensus exacerbate the negative effects of tax competition. This is one of the additional reasons why taxation of robots should be discussed already now in order to be able to have reached a global consensus within a reasonable time.

[B] International (Tax) Framework for Regulating the Use of AI

Despite the international tax competition concerns and how AI and robots can be taxed, there are other issues caused by the use of AI that depart from their taxation as such but are equally relevant for tax purposes. These issues relate to the procedural guarantees of taxpayers and the rule of law when AI is used in decision making. There are currently a few international organizations that monitor the use of AI and provide global guidelines that help in reducing biases and discrimination in decisions issued by AI systems or ensuring that these decisions will conform with human rights and the procedural guarantees of an administrative process. The question that arose based on the above is whether we should allocate to international fora and organizations the responsibility of framing the use of AI and whether these organizations will pay the necessary attention to the stakes presented by different national states. Some countries have already instituted an international partnership (i.e., France, Canada, Germany, the US, India, Italy, the EU, etc.), called "*Global Partnership on AI*,"[15] focusing on guiding the use of AI in accordance with human rights and respecting inclusion, diversity, innovation and economic growth. It is a scientific global forum dealing with

14. *See*, i.e., Chand V., Kostic V. & Reis A. (2020), proposing a global education tax that should be earmarked and Carvalho L.L. (2019), proposing to include robots in the personal scope of tax treaties.
15. *See* le lancement du partenariat mondial pour l'intelligence artificielle (16/06/2020), available at https://www.economie.gouv.fr/lancement-partenariat-mondial-intelligence-artificielle.

standardization and coordination of the use of AI that would be in line with social needs. It is formed by a group of experts that shall propose certain actions on governments, although governments must embark themselves and take the appropriate actions irrespective of the said initiative.

In the field of taxation, we could also think of other networks and organizations that could possibly put forward the idea of promoting an international framework and assist in the coordination of the use of AI, such as the International Fiscal Association (IFA). IFA organizes an annual congress where tax professionals, academics, and policy makers can take part and exchange ideas. On the other hand, experts may help in consulting the governments on the appropriate way to handle the use of AI but eventually, it is the political will that will determine which action shall be taken. Therefore, experts should insist on finding a political consensus on the subject matter. What is key in all possible actions to be undertaken in the near future is that firstly, AI is not something to be afraid of and secondly, taxation may be one of the policy instruments to use for addressing labor market's disruption and/or tackling social and economic inequalities.

§13.05 THE NEED FOR A GLOBAL FRAMEWORK ON THE USE OF AI

The limits of the use of AI is another dimension of the policy on AI and touches upon the substance of the whole robot tax debate. Is it for example possible to curtail the use of AI for the purpose of balancing the inequities in the labor market and society? In fact, there is no general answer to the above. It is more than evident that instead of limiting horizontally the use of AI and inhibiting innovation, we would rather set up a framework. Besides, large digital companies agree on some sort of regulation; however, it is important to pay attention to the details. There are several stakes at risk when we use AI, among which are: (a) the quality of data that feeds the system that may result in making the system take discriminatory decisions; (b) the explainability requirement, referring to how the system reached its decision, etc. There are also other AI applications that can be dangerous, for example, in the military. The point is not to totally ban the use of AI in these situations but rather to regulate its use and agree on a framework that will take into account multi-disciplinary factors, such as psychology, morality, and ethics. The ability of current computers is still far from understanding abstract concepts and therefore, they cannot literally replicate the ability of humans to think. As a result, a framework is a necessity but its design must be made intelligently.

Framing the use of AI extends also to the field of taxation as it is related to how the design of robot taxes would not impede innovation; a constant critique of those opposed to robot taxes in general. Nevertheless, innovation is a parameter with which many taxes had to deal with patents, copyrights, and IP rights and, although we may have decided to tax all the above, innovation was not penalized.[16] However, the question which policy makers are currently struggling to answer is how to adapt the

16. At least to an extent that these taxes did not have to be suspended or abolished if the effects on innovation were severe.

decisions of AI to the rules applying for human beings. This is, for example, the case where a judge is using an automated system to reach a decision that is going to affect the lives of human beings and for this reason, it is imperative that the reasoning of that decision is comprehensible. This is even more so since, in case of any error, we cannot hold the robot responsible for it. There are studies showing that AI algorithms can often be biased, not intentionally but because the programmer unconsciously when training the algorithm transposes these biases into the system. These issues are putting pressure on the States and their institutions as they challenge the rule of law and the judiciary process and have to be evaluated with caution. One solution that has been proposed in such cases in order to mitigate the biases of the AI system is to introduce an intermediary between the judge and the AI[17] that will explain the way by which AI reached the decision. All possible solutions come with many challenges confirming that it is more than necessary to regulate the use of AI that affects many aspects of human life and set the framework of how the preparation for the future should be made.

§13.06 TAXING ROBOTS OR THEIR USE: ADDITIONAL COMMENTS BY XAVIER OBERSON

We had a very interesting debate with Yoshua Bengio, during the World Tax Summit—TaxCOOP2020, on October 14, 2020, regarding the potential taxation of robots. As a follow-up to the contribution of Christina Dimitropoulou, I take the opportunity to add a few additional comments about this proposal.

[A] Introduction

The fear of human workers losing their jobs as a result of the development of machines is a very old preoccupation. However, with the 4th industrial revolution and the corresponding use of AI, including robotics, this issue has raised worldwide attention. Indeed, the impact of such development is highly controversial. Recently, some studies have added to this lively debate between the pessimists and the optimists an intermediate position, by arguing that, at least in the short run, most routine workers would be affected by the development of robots.[18] In our view, there are reasonable arguments in favor of all the various thesis on the economic impact of AI.

It appears at this stage very difficult to have a clear view on the future impact which also depends on the development of the technology, the behavior of workers, and the global use of AI. It seems however that many human workers will be affected and replaced by autonomous machines. In order to develop such a new system of taxation like taxation of robots, we all agree that we need an international consensus

17. Because even the judge herself may be biased by the decision of AI even if she has the last word and reviews the AI decision.
18. *See* Guerreiro J., Rebelo S. & Teles P., Robots Should Be Taxed, for a While, CEPR Policy Research, 20, August 2020; Thuemmel U., Optimal Taxation of Robots, CESifo Working Paper No. 7317, October 2018.

and that, to reach such an agreement will take a considerable time. As the discussions about the taxation of digital economy have shown, notably in the context of the BEPS Initiative, the Inclusive Framework at the OECD level and within the UN, any major changes of the tax system requiring a global framework should aim at a balanced and fair solution. Therefore, not only do we believe that taxation of robots could be a solution to address the issue of development of AI in the labor market and against inequality, but we are convinced that the essential elements of this model should be discussed right now.[19]

[B] Robot Taxation Proposals in a Nutshell

Since the early debate about robot taxes, which really started to emerge as of 2016, this concept has been discussed extensively and has also raised many critical comments.[20] As part of this lively discussion, at the outset, some clarifications appear necessary. First, in order to justify any adequate model of taxation of robots, the characterization and purpose of all the potential categories of robot taxes need to be analyzed. There are different proposals to tax robots, each based on specific policy justifications. The analysis of these projects is thus quite different depending on their purposes and structure. Second, among different models of robot taxes, a crucial distinction has to be made between taxing the use of robots, on the one hand, and taxing robots as such, on the other hand. This reason for this subdivision is based on the constitutional principle of ability to pay. At this stage, robots are not legal persons, they are not capable of having any ability to pay taxes. So far, robots are used as production factors of enterprises or persons using them.

Third, even within the various categories of taxes on the use of robots, there are also different policy perspectives. For example, while the author has advocated for a tax based on the so-called *imputed salary* of enterprises using robots, other focus more on robots as production factors of enterprise and favor a so-called *automation* tax.[21] Finally, there is also another perspective, which is to use robot tax as Pigouvian taxes, namely designed as a policy instrument to internalize the social costs resulting from unemployment. This tax is more viewed as a transitory mechanism, which could help

19. Oberson X., Taxing Robots, Helping the Economy to Adapt to the Use of Artificial Intelligence, Elgar Publishing, Cheltenham, UK, Northampton MA, USA, 2019, pp. 9 ff.; Oberson X., Taxing Robots? From the Emergence of an Electronic Ability to Pay to a Tax on Robots or the Use of Robots, 9 World Tax Journal 2017, pp. 247 ss, 251.
20. For recent contributions about robot taxes, *see* notably, among others, Chand V., Kostic S & Reis A, Taxing Artificial Intelligence and Robots: Critical Assessment of Potential Policy Solutions and Recommendation for Alternative Approaches, 12 World Tax Journal 4, 2020, pp. 1 ff.; Kovalcev R., A Taxing Dilemma: Robot Taxes and the Challenges of Effective Taxation of AI, Automation and Robotics in the Fourth Industrial Revolution, The Ohio State Technology Law Journal 2020, p. 182 ff, p. 182 ff; Dimitropoulou Ch., 2019. Robot Taxes: Where Do We Stand? In: CFE 60th Anniversary, Liber Amicorum, IBFD, 55 ff.; English J., Digitalization and the Future of National Tax Systems: Taxing Robots?, in: Haslehner W., Kofler G., Pantazatou K., & Rust A. (ed.), Tax and the Digital Economy, Wolters Kluwer, The Netherlands 2019, p. 261 ff; Mazur O., Taxing the Robots, 46 Pepperdine Law Review 2018, p. 1.
21. Abbott R. & Bogenschneider B., Should Robots Pay Taxes? Tax Policy in the Age of Automation, 12 Harvard Law & Policy Review 2018, p. 1.

workers to adapt to the new economy. This solution should, in our view, be analyzed in adequation with its special policy purpose and would require a design adequate with the objective of this measure, in accordance with the principle of proportionality. This model would require more flexibility in the legal design, notably with a possibility to adapt the scope of the tax, the applicable rates, following the evolution of technology and its impact on the labor market.

[C] Taxation of Robots as Such

At the beginning of the discussion about taxing robots, the author has proposed, not only to tax the use of robots by enterprises, with on a so-called imputed salary but taxing robots *as such*. This solution, which appears as of today the most controversial, could be adopted in a second stage, once we have implemented a legal solution to introduce an ability to pay of robots. We should clarify here that what we are talking about is not a subjective ability to pay similar to the ability to pay of humans. Indeed, robots have no personal needs; they don't need to eat and have no kids to raise. What we are considering here is a so-called *objective* ability to pay which is similar to the ability to pay off corporations in the form of capacity of payment based on the principle of separation.[22]

The profit tax on corporations is also based on the limited liability of the enterprise and is mostly designed as an integrated system, which combines an advanced payment of the tax on profits until the funds are distributed as dividends to the shareholders. The design of the corporation tax on profits, including rules in order to alleviate double economic taxation, took a considerable time to be implemented by the legislator. We do not see why we could not consider today to introduce a tax capacity to robots, under some specific criteria designed by the legislator, integrated into the global tax system. The legislator should be in a position to adopt a flexible solution, which encompasses the evolution of AI. Recent technologies already allow for the separation of funds. A tax could be designed on some forms of smart robots, i.e. autonomous AI, that have the capacity to retain funds, decide how to invest them, and, therefore, would have an objective ability to pay, compared to the ability to pay of corporations.

The EU Parliament also has considered in the past the possibility to create a new legal personality for smart robots, defined under a series of criteria. During the works of the EU Parliament, the Commission on legal affairs has discussed the possibility to tax robots, notably in a draft report of 2016, which reads as follows:

> Bearing in mind the effects that the development and deployment of robotics and AI might have on employment and, consequently, on the viability of the social security systems of the Member States, consideration should be given to the possible need to introduce corporate reporting requirements on the extent and proportion of the contribution of robotics and AI to the economic results of a company for the purpose of taxation and social security contributions; takes the

22. Same opinion, Dimitropoulou, *supra* note 20, p. 65.

> view that in the light of the possible effects on the labor market of robotics and AI a general basic income should be seriously considered, and invites all Member States to do so.[23]

On February 16, 2017, the EU Parliament finally rejected the idea of introducing a system of taxation of robots.[24] In the 2016 proposal, the EU Parliament looked at a robot tax more as a tax on the *use* of robots, taking into consideration the contribution of robotics to the economic results of a company, thus focusing on robots as production factors. Our proposal would go beyond that approach and recommend taxation on robots *as such*, as defined by the legislator, which would become a new legal person with a tax capacity.[25] As discussed previously, in order to become subject to tax, the granting of the legal personality is not even necessary. Following that model, robots could become subject to some types of profit tax, in a comparable way as corporations, and also as persons subject to VAT. In this respect, we could even imagine that robots could be programmed not only to charge the output VAT on their taxable supplies but credit the input VAT on supplies received. Robots as such would in fact be regarded as tax collectors for the State.

In addition, there are new interesting developments, which would, in our view, not only advocate but even require in the long run the introduction of robots as a new taxpayer.[26] With the development of AI, robots would gain autonomy and be more and more capable to act independently, enter into contractual relationships, receive funds, and decide how to use them. This evolution could create new opportunities for tax avoidance and even tax fraud. We should therefore also consider granting a tax capacity to robots, as a new form of (electronic) person, in order to safeguard the integrity of the tax system.[27] Therefore, a system of control by humans should be put in place, in order to ensure that the tax requirements are met. A tax on robots as such would include an official registration of robots and of the beneficial owners of these algorithms.

[D] Definition of Robots

Many critics, including Bengio during the discussion, focus on the difficulty to define a robot for tax purposes. Admittedly, this is a fundamental and delicate issue. Based on the principle of legality and equality of treatment, a practical and appropriate definition of robots as a taxpayer is required. In our view, this is however not an impossible task.

23. European Parliament, Committee on Legal Affairs, Draft Report with recommendations to the Commission on Civil Law Rules on Robotics (2015/2103(INL)) 2016, p. 10.
24. European Parliament resolution of 16 February 2017 with recommendations to the Commission on Civil Law rules on Robotics (2015/2102/INL).
25. Oberson, *supra* note 19 (2017), 3.2. and (2019), pp. 131 ff.
26. *See*, Oberson X., Taxing Robots—The Rise of a New Taxpayer, Bulletin of International Taxation 2021, volume 75, p. 370.
27. *See also* De Lima Carvalho L., Spiritus Ex Machina: Addressing the Unique BEPS Issues of Autonomous Artificial Intelligence by Using “Personality” and “Residence”, 47 Intertax 2019, pp. 425 ff., 430 f (who considers the need to introduce a tax on robots also for the purpose of the international attribution of profits).

First, we need to clarify which category of robot taxes we are talking about, namely, either a tax on the use of robots (tax on imputed income, automation tax, Pigouvian tax) or a tax on robots as such. Each category of robotax would require a specific and adapted definition which should be in accordance with the purpose of the tax. In general, we favor a flexible definition which considers the autonomy of AI and should be form neutral. We should focus on autonomous AI, which has the possibility to enter into contracts worldwide with users and consumers. We are not talking about taxation of vacuum cleaners or dishwashers, as some critics have pointed out, but at a major disruption in the economy with potential important losses in human labor income and, at the same time, creation of value triggered by the use of AI.

[E] Other Alternatives

During the conference, alternative options than taxing robots were discussed. The current works at the OECD level, in the Inclusive Framework, on the design of Pillar 1 and 2, represent an indirect way of addressing the taxation of AI. Multinational companies in the digital economy have access to customers and users worldwide and may benefit from the data obtained, classified, and processed by the use of algorithms. These works however do not specifically address the issue of taxing the value created by the use of robots instead of workers. It focuses on new rules of profit attributions for large multinational entities (nexus rules), beyond routine profits, which should follow a formulaic approach. Pillar 2 would apply a minimum effective profit rate of tax to large multinational entities. This system focuses on the profit tax on corporations and would rely on consolidated books of account. A tax on robots would represent a major change, which would go beyond these proposals and address the profits and consumptions arising from the use of AI from a global perspective. Another alternative is the taxation of data. This idea would require further analysis and notably include the difficult task of distinguishing between positive data, that foster growth and welfare, and negative information (spam, fake news, etc.).

Bibliography

Abbott, Ryan & Bogenschneider, Bret. 2018. "Should Robots Pay Taxes? Tax Policy in the Age of Automation". Harvard Law & Policy Review. 12.

Abbott, Ryan & Bogenschneider, Bret. 2018. "Should Robots Pay Taxes? Tax Policy in the Age of Automation". Harvard Law and Policy Review. 12. available at https://robotic.legal/wp-content/uploads/2018/06/Should-Robots-Pay-Taxes.pdf (Accessed: March 10, 2021).

Acemoglu, Daron. & Restrepo Pascual. 2017. "Robots and Jobs: Evidence from US Labor Markets". NBER Working Paper No. 23285. available at https://www.nber.org/papers/w23285.pdf (Accessed: March 10, 2021).

Bengio, Joshua. 2020. World Tax Summit—TaxCOOP2020. Taxation and the Society of the Future. Embracing AI and Robots. Montreal (online). October 13, 2020.

Brynjolfsson, Erik & McAfee, Andrew. 2012. Race Against the Machine: How the Digital Revolution Is Accelerating Innovation. Driving Productivity. and Irreversibly Transforming Employment and the Economy. 5th ed. Digital Frontier Press. U.S.

Brynjolfsson, Erik & McAfee, Andrew. 2014. The Second Machine Age: Work. Progress and Prosperity in a Time of Brilliant Technologies. W.W. Norton & Company. U.S.

Carvalho, Lucas de Lima. 2019. "Spiritus Ex Machina: Addressing the Unique BEPS Issues of Autonomous Artificial Intelligence by Using 'Personality' and 'Residence'". Intertax. 47(5).

Chand, Vikram & Kostic, Svetislav & Reis, Ariene. 2020. "Taxing Artificial Intelligence and Robots: Critical Assessment of Potential Policy Solutions and Recommendation for Alternative Approaches". WTJ. 12(4).

Christians, Allison & Magalhaes, Tarcisio, Diniz. 2020. "It's Time for Pillar 3: A Global Excess Profits Tax for COVID-19 and Beyond". TaxNotes Int'l 507.

Committee on Legal Affairs (2016). Draft Report with Recommendations to the Commission on Civil Law Rules on Robotics (2015/2103(INL)). Available at http://www.europarl.europa.eu/sides/getDoc.do?pubRef = //EP//NONSGML%2BCOMPAL%2BPE- 582.443%2B01%2BDOC%2BPDF%2BV0//EN (Accessed: March 10, 2021).

DeLaney Thomas, Kathleen. 2018. "Automation and the Income Tax". Columbia Journal of Tax Law. 10(1). available at https://scholarship.law.unc.edu/cgi/viewcontent.cgi?article = 1448&context = faculty_publications (Accessed: March 10, 2021).

Dimitropoulou, Christina. 2019. "Robot Taxes: Where Do We Stand?" in: Van Thiel. Valente and Raventos-Calvo (2019): CFE Tax advisers Europe—60th Anniversary Liber Amicorum. IBFD Amsterdam.

Dimitropoulou, Christina. 2020. "Scaling Back Tax Preferences on Artificial Intelligence—Driven Automation: Back to Neutral?". WTJ. 12(2).

Englisch, Joachim. 2018. "Digitalization and the Future of National Tax Systems: Taxing Robots?". available at SSRN: https://ssrn.com/abstract = 3244670 (Accessed: March 10, 2021).

Ford M. 2015. Rise of the Robots: Technology and the Threat of a Jobless Future. Basic Books. London.

Frey, Carl Benedikt & Osborne, Michael A. 2013. "The Future of Employment: How Susceptible Are Jobs to Computerization?". available at https://www.oxfordmartin.ox.ac.uk/downloads/academic/The_Future_of_Employment.pdf?link = mktw (Accessed: March 10, 2021).

Guerreiro J. Rebelo S. & Teles P. (2020). "Should Robots Be Taxed?". available at https://www.kellogg.northwestern.edu/faculty/rebelo/htm/robots.pdf (Accessed: March 10, 2021).

Hoffer, Stephanie R. 2020. "Tax Theory & Feral AI. Public Law and Legal Theory Working Paper Series." No. 524. [online]. available at http://ssrn.com/abstract = 3520608 (Accessed: March 10, 2021).

IMF. 2019. "Fiscal Policies for Paris Climate Strategies—From Principle to Practice". IMF Policy Paper 19/010.

Mazur, Orly. 2019. "Taxing the Robots". Pepperdine Law Review 46. available at: https://digitalcommons.pepperdine.edu/plr/vol46/iss2/2 (Accessed: March 10, 2021).

Oberson, Xavier. 2019. Taxing Robots—Helping the Economy to Adapt to the Use of Artificial Intelligence. Edward Elgar Publishing. London.

Oberson, Xavier. 2020. World Tax Summit—TaxCOOP2020. Taxation and the Society of the Future. Embracing AI and Robots. Montreal (online). October 13, 2020.

OECD. 2018. Policy Brief on the Future of Work: Putting Faces to the Jobs at Risk of Automation. available at https://www.oecd.org/employment/Automation-policy-brief-2018.pdf (accessed: March 10, 2021).

Piketty, Thomas. 2015. "Capital and Wealth Taxation in the 21st Century." National Tax Journal. 68(2).

Soled, Jay A. & DeLaney, Kathleen Thomas. 2019. "Automation and the Income Tax". Columbia Journal of Tax Law. 10(1). available at SSRN: https://ssrn.com/abstract=3316388 (Accessed: March 10, 2021).

CHAPTER 14

Towards a Green Economic Recovery

Elena Belletti[*]

There is broad consensus in the international community that a green economic recovery would be crucial to rebuild after the COVID-19 pandemic. However, in practice, few governments are making significant expenditures to stimulate the green economy: fiscal stimulus in advanced economies averaged around 20% of GDP and less than 2% of GDP in low- and middle-income countries. The delay in climate action is costing trillions of dollars each year, and the world risks losing a great opportunity to make a transition towards a fairer and more sustainable economic model.

Based on a conversation with twelve experts, the chapter explores how tax policy can support a green economic recovery and provides a framework for thought and action by governments and the international community. The framework includes examples of both tax policy and expenditure strategies and a discussion on how a multilayered approach can reinforce national action with international cooperation. The chapter also analyzes how the green transition can help create fairer, more inclusive societies—for example, investing in low-emissions sectors can improve gender equality, and scaling up communication on environmental taxation can improve transparency and ultimately strengthen trust in governments.

§14.01 INTRODUCTION

The COVID-19 crisis had deep impacts on public finances, as economies slowed down, public expenses rose and tax revenues fell. In addition, the crisis has been slowing

* The views expressed in this chapter are those of the author only and do not necessarily represent those of the United Nations.

down the efforts of some countries to pursue initiatives towards sustainable development, and in some cases, environmental legislation has been rolled back (Conservation International, n.d.).

During the financial crisis of 2008-2009, just like now, there were calls for a global green new deal and sustainable recovery. As is clear now, the world missed an important opportunity to shift to a more sustainable economic model in 2009; we must be careful not to replicate the same mistakes.

This chapter explores how tax policy can support a green economic recovery to provide food for thought for governments and the international community, in their efforts to recover from COVID-19 and build a more resilient and sustainable economy. The content is inspired by the discussions among twelve experts.[1]

§14.02 A FRAMEWORK FOR PROMOTING A GREEN ECONOMIC RECOVERY

A green framing of relief and recovery stimulus measures is imperative to build system resilience, support public health efforts, lower the probability of future pandemics and reduce the risk and impact of environmental degradation and climate change. Green fiscal spending is also one of the best investment options available: every million USD spent on green infrastructure can create over 7.5 jobs, compared to around 2.7 jobs for the same amount invested traditionally (Coalition of Finance Ministers for Climate Action, 2020); every dollar spent on nature restoration gives a nine-time return on investment (Nature4Climate, 2020).

As Paul Lanoie notes, there are some success stories about green economic instruments being extremely effective at changing behaviors, create a greener and more responsible economy, and raising revenues to multiply their effect, such as:

- British Columbia, Canada: Between 2008 and 2013, a carbon tax resulted in a 7% reduction in the use of gasoline per capita (Antweiler and Gulati, 2016).
- France: A "bonus-malus" system for the purchase of new vehicles has been in place since 2008, which encourages the choice of a low-carbon vehicle and penalizes the purchase of more polluting models with a tax (varying between

1. This discussion took place at the World Tax Summit on October 15, 2020, among Tasnim Alan, Deputy Commissioner of Taxes (Deputy Director), Central Intelligence Cell, National Board of Revenue, Bangladesh; Elena Belletti, Economist, Financing for Sustainable Development Office, United Nations; Ali Benryane, Cofounder and Chairman, Board of Directors, CAP Développement Durable; Jacqueline Cottrell, Senior Associate at Green Budget Germany and a member of the international programme committee of the Global Conference on Environmental Taxation; Grant Ervin, Chief Resilience Officer and Assistant Director for the Department of City Planning Pittsburgh; Antoine Genest-Grégoire, Ph.D. Student in public politics at Carleton University and Associate Researcher, Research Chair in Taxation and Public Finance, Sherbrooke University; Yvette Lind, Assistant professor in tax law, Copenhagen Business School; Santiago Lorenzo, Head of Sustainable Finance, Climate Action Network International; Himanshu Sharma, Manager, UNEP Green Fiscal Policy Network; Quentin Parrinello, Tax Justice and Inequality Advocacy Officer, Oxfam France; Marta Villar Ezcurra, Professor of financial and tax law at the CEU San Pablo University (USP-CEU, Madrid); Paul Lanois, Commissioner for Sustainable Development of Quebec.

EUR 35 and EUR 20,000). The system had a positive effect in lowering average CO_2 emissions from new vehicles (Dauteuil, Hanafi, and Jousseaume, 2020).
- Singapore: Between 2000 and 2018, through a water tariff, Singapore reduced per capita water consumption by around 15% (Singapore's National Water Agency, n.d.). Low-income families benefitted from a tax refund, aimed at countering potential negative impacts of the measure.

So far, announced stimulus packages are expected to negatively affect the environment in 16 of the G20 countries; additionally, out of the total quantified green stimulus, only 2.8% is aimed at improving biodiversity or preserving ecosystems (Vivid Economics, 2020). The world needs a green recovery because over half of global GDP is dependent on high-functioning biodiversity and ecosystem services (World Economic Forum, 2020). By 2100, climate change could be five times as deadly as COVID-19; the economic damage will likely compare to a COVID-size pandemic every ten years and will continue to multiply unless necessary action is taken (Gates, 2020).

Green fiscal policy reform is an important element in governments' toolkits for COVID-19 relief and recovery. These reforms can rationalize inefficient expenditures to create valuable fiscal space, as well as to enable better management and reallocation of scarce public resources to priority sectors. For Himanshu Sharma, green fiscal reform elements could include reforming environmental harmful and inequitable subsidies, internalizing climate and pollution externalities, and introducing tax shifts.

Phasing out fossil fuel subsidies, which currently amount to over 425 billion dollars per year at the global level (UNEP, OECD and IISD, 2019), could free up resources to invest in a green recovery while incentivizing more sustainable consumption and production models. Equity concerns could be addressed by replacing the subsidies with direct payments that support the incomes of vulnerable workers or communities.

Internalizing climate and pollution externalities could include health, climate, and pollution costs into the price of goods and services. Pricing carbon is one way to do this; currently, seventy-seven countries, states, and cities are applying a price on carbon, covering around 20% of global emissions (World Bank, 2020). In cases where a carbon price is not feasible due to specific national circumstances, a carbon fee system offers a possible alternative. These approaches can help countries step up their climate ambitions while raising public revenues; appropriate design can ensure the protection of low-income and vulnerable households.

[A] Broadening the Outlook: From Fiscal Reform to an Ecologically and Socially Fair Transition

The COVID-19 pandemic can represent an unprecedented opportunity to challenge business as usual. It has brought to light the fact that the world is experiencing multiple crises—of the economic system, of societies, of current modes of consumption and production, as well as of climate and the environment. Governments at the national and subnational level had been experiencing the twin challenges of climate change and rising inequality since before the pandemic; however, shocks like COVID-19 are force multipliers on these stressors, causing a shift in the tectonic plates of urbanization, globalization, and climate change.

In the past decades, the prevailing economic model has caused public finance to shrink, with a major impact on the ability to raise revenues and spend them towards creating fairer societies. In fact, inequality has been on the rise (United Nations, 2020a), health systems have been chronically underfunded, and projects to fight against climate change and pollution have not been appropriately leveraged with public money.

There is a consensus in the international community that a "green and just" recovery is necessary; however, consistent decision-making in this direction is still lacking. In this context, it is imperative to consider how decision makers are shaping narratives and how they are translating them into concrete actions for economic recovery within an ecologically and socially fair transition.

There is a perceived tension in post-COVID recovery, between building back quickly and building back better. One important point to consider is that this dichotomy is often incorrect; as the world has been learning, there are many policies (e.g., in the areas of energy efficiency, building retrofitting, etc.) which can be implemented quite quickly while yielding green dividends. However, the main question is whether these short-term policies would be able to decarbonize the global economy in the long term. In fact, the world has also been learning from the past recession that these "low-hanging fruits" can deliver green benefits quickly, but not at the necessary scale and not for a sustained period of time.

Another point to consider is that building back better is an insurance for the future. Revenues that are spent now for climate change adaptation and mitigation are helping save money in the long run by lowering the likelihood and reducing the impact of disasters, preserving nature, and allowing economies and societies to flourish.

Therefore, green economic recovery measures should be evaluated taking into account their future potential cost savings: for example, a recent study estimate that each year of delayed action to reach the 1.5 degrees stabilization target could cost the world USD 5 trillion and could erode 18% of the world GDP by 2080 (Sanderson and O'Neill, 2020). Just considering reductions in the impact of disasters, reconstruction savings amount to USD 15 for every dollar invested in risk reduction and prevention, and USD 4 for every dollar invested in disaster-resilient infrastructure (United Nations, n.d.).

At the local level, a relatively small city like Pittsburgh (Pennsylvania, United States) experienced twice the normal amount of precipitation for two years in a row and had to invest 15% of their capital budget to remediate landslides and floods—with major impacts on the availability of revenues for other uses (Ervin, 2020).

Environmental protection and the fight against climate change are intimately intertwined with the management of public finance, and therefore with the fiscal dimension.

Governments should consider new and alternative approaches to mobilize domestic revenues to spend towards environmental protection and green financing in general. Additionally, economic instruments such as carbon pricing are the most cost-effective way to decarbonize, achieve behavioral change and raise revenues—as they allow polluters to choose the cheapest way to lower their emissions. That means that revenues can be used much more efficiently for other uses; during an economic recession, that is particularly important.

There is also plenty of private capital looking for returns, but green projects that are sufficiently bankable or that guarantee a high enough yield are lacking. For example, building a clean energy infrastructure can attract investment from data centers that are hungry for electricity while also trying to meet low-carbon pledges.

The barriers to investments in green projects are definitely in their governance and in the accessibility of funds, rather than in the availability of financing. Capacity building in this area could make a huge difference for project owners, looking for a better understanding of how to structure projects, how to de-risk them, how to make them bankable, and how to leverage them by raising public funds. From the government side, implementing a green reform, and communicating clearly about it, can help create a stable investment climate and improve the attractiveness of projects. Attracting capital to the right projects means not only job creation but also a snowballing effect to leverage transition within specific industries, especially those that pollute the most.

Fiscal aspects are crucial in this transition, and they should not be limited to a stand-alone tax reform, but rather a complete rethinking of the current model of socially and economically focused public management, to include environmental and climate aspects in the fabric of planning public policies. These policies need to be carefully planned and considered: a poor fiscal reform can result in an inadequate stream of revenues, that affects the availability of public funds for action in the social and environmental space. Additional potential unintended consequences are the inability to change behaviors towards more responsible ones, and other missed opportunities at the macroeconomic levels, such as difficulties in creating green jobs. For developing countries, the challenge is made more difficult by issues related to sovereign debt and the prevalence of tax incentives, with a push to a race to the bottom to compete against tax havens.

In a high-income country such as France, with ample fiscal space, a tool to ensure that companies shift to more sustainable models has been to include green conditionality to bailouts for large corporations, for example in the case of Air France (Bannon, 2020).

Costa Rica represents a success story of an ecologically responsible transition (Green Fiscal Policy Network, 2019). A global leader in biodiversity and environmental policies, in 1997 Costa Rica introduced a pioneering model of Payments for Environmental Services (PES) (World Bank, n.d.), a scheme that managed to protect over one million hectares of forest (Barton, 2013) by paying landowners for the ecosystem services that the forest provides—such as storing carbon and protecting biodiversity. Additionally, the country has been successfully reforming harmful fossil fuel subsidies. It also introduced a range of measures to incentivize the development of clean energy infrastructure (including a voluntary carbon market and the promotion of the efficient use of energy and electric vehicles). This transition shifted its trade balances and its entire economic model to achieve carbon neutrality by 2050 (Green Fiscal Policy Network, 2019).

Another interesting example is Bangladesh, the second-largest RMG (ready-made garment products) exporter in the world (WTO, 2020). An emerging economy prior to the COVID-19 crisis (International Monetary Fund (IMF), 2020), Bangladesh has been focused on attracting investment to stimulate job creation and lift the population out of poverty; incidentally, the majority of workers in the RMG industry are women, and the sector has been responsible for a large share of the inclusion of women in the formal economy (IMF, 2020a). Like other South-East Asian countries, Bangladesh has been granting tax incentives to foreign investors, particularly in the form of a reduced corporate tax rate. However, shifting towards a green economy model has been at the forefront of the efforts of Bangladesh, and so they decided to introduce a further reduced corporate tax rate (by 2.5%) to RMG factories with green building certification (KPMG, 2019). As a result, Bangladesh has the highest number of Leadership in Energy and Environmental Design (LEED)-certified factories in the world (Textile Today, 2019). While this contributes to environmental protection and climate change mitigation in Bangladesh, it has also been strategic in attracting interest from European buyers and investors, and in supporting a female-driven sector.

However, many developing countries have been unable to implement similar measures. This inability has been due, in part, to two interlinked challenges: the low public acceptability of fiscal measures in general, and green taxation in particular; and the pressure to operate a "race to the bottom" to attract foreign companies, which has reduced the fiscal space.

[B] Increasing Public Acceptance of Environmental Taxation to Support a Green Economic Recovery

For countries at all levels of development, moving towards a green economic recovery is often hindered by low public acceptance of taxation, and environmental taxation in particular. This can be a problem both in raising additional revenues for environmental action and in changing behaviors through measures such as carbon taxation. In developing countries, low public acceptance of taxation is sometimes linked to a general mistrust in public policies and administration; this can be caused, for example, by widespread corruption and tax evasion, or by unfair tax systems that grant very flexible and generous tax benefits to attract foreign corporations. As a result, a green fiscal reform might not be well accepted—as perception might be that average citizens would be unduly burdened, while companies would most likely receive some exemption or evade taxes altogether.

To tackle these challenges, there are a number of possible approaches. First of all, it is important to restore a positive public perception of taxation, and frame it not as a punitive approach but rather in a positive light—and the good reasons to implement a particular tax should be explained carefully. Ultimately, tax is the price to pay for a civilized society and a fundamental element in the social contract.

Governments should think about how to show accountability and communicate their efforts to improve the fairness of the fiscal system; for instance, using tax revenues as promised can demonstrate transparency and quickly build trust. For example, France chose to build trust by communicating broadly and transparently on their green budgeting. The 2021 budget bill classifies expenditures according to the contribution that they would make towards a green transition, and carbon-intensive investments are openly shown (Fetet & Postic, 2020).

When embarking on a green fiscal reform, governments should similarly focus their communication on the value of a clean environment and the benefits of sustainability for society, rather than portraying environmental taxation as a punishment for pollution or emissions. This is particularly important as the ultimate goal of environmental taxes is to shift behavior towards more sustainable choices; for this reason, final consumers usually bear the burden of the tax and should understand the full reasoning behind the increase in prices as an incentive towards greener choices.

A specific strategy that is often used to generate public acceptability when introducing environmental taxation (and pioneered by Sweden) is to start environmental taxes at a low rate, and then slowly increase it. This also helps to ensure the stability of revenues generated by the tax over time, as the polluting behavior is reduced.

[C] Preserving and Expanding the Fiscal Space to Finance a Green Transition

Developed and developing countries face different issues with their fiscal space. While developed countries typically have ample fiscal space (with the issue often being strategies for revenue use), low- and middle-income countries often don't reach that 15% tax-to-GDP threshold which is traditionally considered as the minimum for development (Gaspar, Jaramillo and Wingender, 2016). Furthermore, recent evidence suggests that tax-to-GDP ratios closer to 20% would more realistically finance sustainable development (Long and Miller, 2017).

In fact, since the financial crisis, there has been a substantial (and widening) gap in the availability of fiscal space between developed and developing economies (Kose et al., 2017). UNEP will launch the Global Recovery Observatory project, which is tracking the fifty largest economies and assessing the environmental impact of stimulus spending. One of the major findings was that fiscal stimulus in advanced economies averaged around 20% of GDP, whereas in low- and middle-income countries it averaged less than 2% of GDP (O'Callaghan et al., 2020).

As developed economies release massive stimulus packages, they have to choose what share of these packages will be devoted to promoting a green economy, and what share, on the contrary, will continue to support high-emission industries, such as fossil fuels. So far, advanced economies have not been directing their stimulus packages towards the promotion of green activities—at least, not at the scale that would be needed, which ultimately will determine what the impact will be (Vivid Economics, 2020).

At the local level, cities have been experiencing a shrinking of their fiscal space as well. For example, a relatively small city such as Pittsburgh (Pennsylvania, United States) had a projected gap of USD 100 million in its budget because of the pandemic (Davidson, 2020). Given the lower revenues, and the little support received from State, provincial and municipal partners, the city would have to face potential layoffs and personnel moves, as well as lower investment in infrastructure and services offered to the population.

At the municipal level, a green economic recovery would require agility and acceleration in the implementation of the climate and justice strategies developed locally, as well as better control over those policies; these strategies are fundamental to create force multipliers and stimulate a positive social and ecological transition. In the case of Pittsburgh, local officials have been advocating for giving the municipality more control over some forms of taxation and management of assets. For example, the city could use part of its USD 700 million operating and capital budget to leverage ESG opportunities on the ground, that could be sponsored by pension funds. This way, the savings of Pittsburgh residents could be safely invested in projects on the ground that improve the quality of the electric grid, clean the water systems, make roads and bridges safer, and build more affordable housing—rather than in equity funds on the other side of the globe.

Environmental taxation, including carbon pricing, represents an important opportunity both at the national and subnational levels, as these tools can expand the fiscal space, especially for low- and middle-income countries. According to OECD estimates, a carbon price of EUR 30 per ton would generate a global increase in revenues of 1.3% (Marten and Van Dender, 2019). While the impact of environmental taxation would be different depending on the country's situation, the increase can represent a huge opportunity to expand the fiscal space of countries which do not currently raise sufficient revenues. On the other hand, according to the IMF, a carbon price of EUR 75 per ton would enable the world to reach the commitments of the Paris agreement by 2030 (IMF, 2019); the question is whether such a high price would be feasible in the majority of countries. Nevertheless, increasing the fiscal space is a very important component of this type of measure, and advanced economies have an excellent opportunity to lead the way.

Moreover, environmental taxation can provide opportunities for better, more coordinated governance. As these measures are often managed or designed jointly by different governmental entities (e.g., Ministries of Finance and of Environment), they can break down barriers and streamline administration.

In addition to "traditional" tools such as carbon pricing, the Climate Action Network and other nongovernmental organizations have been advocating for broader and more aggressive environmental taxation measures (CAN Europe, 2016a and 2016b), such as a financial transaction tax and a climate damages tax.

Countries should also take into consideration the problem of falling revenue from environmental taxes: as these measures are introduced and scaled up, the incentive for polluters is to decarbonize and move towards less polluting activities. While this outcome is desirable from an environmental point of view, it would result in a reduction of revenues, and consequently in a contraction of the fiscal space created by those instruments. However, the issue of falling revenues can be addressed quite well with tax design: a gradually increasing tax rate can compensate for falling revenue from environmental taxes. In fact, this is the approach used by several countries (e.g., Sweden, as mentioned above). While raising rates is not necessarily a solution to compensate for revenues in the longer term, and governments should not shift the majority of the tax burden on environmental taxes anyway, this is definitely something to keep in mind at least in the medium term. Overall, falling revenues from environmental taxes should not be seen as a big concern, and governments can find new sources of taxation in the longer term.

[D] Promoting Green Economic Recovery as a Tool for Improving Gender Equity

Another important dimension of a green economic recovery is the potential co-benefit of gender equality.

Climate change does affect women in particular, mainly because women represent 70% of the world's poor, but also because natural disasters multiply the risk for unsafe situations, where women are at concrete danger of violence—for example, lack of shelter (Osman-Elasha, n.d.).

The economic recession caused by the COVID-19 pandemic is quite unusual. In previous recessions, such as the 2009 financial crisis, the most impacted sectors were those where a majority of men were employed, such as the industrial sector; as a result, it was mostly men that lost their jobs. On the other hand, the current recession, caused by lockdowns, has created a different pattern. Jobs in sectors where most women are employed (such as services, hospitality, and education) have been impacted more heavily, while women have also faced additional burdens due to an increase in informality and additional demands in unpaid care work, such as taking care of children and the elderly.

This is one more reason why the response to this crisis should not be based on lessons learned from previous economic recessions, but rather be tailored to the specific circumstances. Often, in previous recessions, stimulus packages would be directed towards infrastructure and promoting industrial sectors; this seems now like an inadequate response as it doesn't address the climate crisis, but also it does not restore the jobs lost by women.

In COVID-19 recovery plans, governments should consider stimulating sectors that are not traditionally considered, such as education, childcare, elderly care, public health, culture, and science. These are not only high-return investments from a social point of view, but also have a much smaller environmental impact than traditional industrial and construction sectors.

Having more resources devoted to culture, science, education, and health would not only help societies thrive but also decouple growth and well-being from heavy reliance on natural resources. As more women are employed in these sectors than in construction or industry, a green recovery can also help enhance gender equity.

[E] Reinforcing National Action with International Cooperation

There is often a perceived juxtaposition between multilateral and unilateral approaches in the fiscal area as if countries had to decide whether to privilege international agreements or resort to domestic legislation to improve their tax systems. Reality is much more nuanced, and the most effective solutions often consist of multilayered approaches, with international cooperation informing national action.

While the transition towards a socially and ecologically responsible economy needs to be supported by strong political will at the national level, international agreements and treaties are a crucial tool for countries to cooperate and reach global and shared solutions. Climate change and zoonotic disease are global problems that do not recognize national sovereignty and do not stop at borders—and each country has a role in prevention, mitigation, and adaptation.

Although a multilateral coordination instrument for green taxation has not been established yet, international tax cooperation is allowing countries to coordinate their efforts, with a view to fight the drain of resources and even expand their domestic fiscal space. For example, anti-avoidance provisions were introduced in tax treaties among signatories of the Multilateral Convention to Implement Tax Treaty Related Measures to Prevent Base Erosion and Profit Shifting (OECD, n.d.).

However, international agreements do not have the power to establish new taxing rights—and tax treaties only have the power to protect taxing rights that exist in the domestic law. Sovereignty over tax matters is, and will likely continue to be, a national prerogative.

Harmonization is one potential solution to recognize both national sovereignty and the need for coordination. In the green fiscal space, this would translate, for example, in a group of countries agreeing to introduce a carbon pricing system in their domestic legislation, in accordance with some agreed-upon parameters; or to revise their existing instruments towards a common model. Agreeing on a minimum carbon price in G20 countries (or a subgroup of the G20) could be a step in this direction.

While the idea is certainly appealing, implementing harmonization in practice is often challenging. For example, the European Union has been trying for over ten years to revise the 2003 Energy Taxation Directive, which contains minimum criteria to harmonize energy taxes in Europe. After extensive public consultation, a next step is planned for mid-2021, within the framework of the European Green Deal; however, it is still uncertain whether consensus on further harmonization will be reached.

Harmonization can get progressively more challenging as the pool of countries expands. Besides the legal aspects, global harmonization efforts would have to take into account differences in society and demographics, socioeconomic conditions, and education—including tax literacy. Additionally, governmental capacities in the fiscal arena vary, and the fiscal space of many low- and middle-income countries has shrunk in a race to the bottom to attract investments or is limited by the drain of resources that are lost to illicit financial flows and tax evasion.

This heterogeneity in conditions—and therefore in responsibility for climate action—is recognized by the principle of common but differentiated responsibilities.

This principle should also be applied in the context of green fiscal reform and guide the world towards a green economic recovery. Multilateral cooperation can provide a platform to get to a common understanding of what are the issues at stake, and how to solve them fairly and inclusively.

However, governments should also be supported in building a solid domestic foundation in the policy and fiscal spaces, which also takes into account the needs of the subnational levels—where a lot of climate action happens but is often forgotten in the international conversation. A global supporting effort is fundamentally needed (with the backing of the United Nations as an organization with universal membership) to promote the development of broader fiscal spaces within countries, and their use for an ecological transition. While international conventions are sometimes criticized for their low ambition, other forms of international coordination (such as cooperation among a group of countries, technical assistance, etc.) can be very effective in supporting developing countries to reach their green economic objectives.

§14.03 CONCLUSIONS

Governments and the international community should consider the disruption created by COVID-19 as an opportunity for economies and society to transition towards ecologically and socially fair models. The world has already lost an opportunity for a green economic recovery in 2009 when governments did not "walk the talk" and chose to continue investing in traditional, dirty industries. The delay in climate action is costing trillions of dollars annually at the global level—investing in green infrastructure is not only financially sound but results in significant savings in the long run by mitigating the impact of further pandemics, climate change, and natural disasters.

When implementing stimulus packages, governments should also consider the potential co-benefits; for example, investing in care, public health, education, and culture (low-carbon emission sectors)—rather than in traditional infrastructure—would help bring women back to the workforce, following the massive job loss suffered during the pandemic.

Governments should not only attribute significant shares of recovery packages to climate and environmental investment but also work to make existing projects more bankable and attract (or leverage) private investment. Taking a more comprehensive approach, governments should also use economic instruments to shift public behaviors towards a more responsible and sustainable model (e.g., through environmental taxation) and improve communication to generate public acceptance of green measures and support a green economic recovery. To reinforce the social contract with citizens, governments can implement a series of measures, for example, increase the transparency of public budgeting, show that revenues are used in a responsible way, and give more autonomy to local governments to collect revenues to be invested in sensitive projects on the ground.

The role of international cooperation is also fundamental to support governments of developing countries in expanding their fiscal space and introducing green measures, depending on their national circumstances. The most effective solutions often consist of multilayered approaches, with international cooperation informing national action; the needs and potential at the subnational levels—where a lot of climate action happens, but are often forgotten in the international conversation—should also be taken into account more prominently in the conversation.

Bibliography

Antweiler, W., & Gulati, S. (2016). Frugal Cars or Frugal Drivers? How Carbon and Fuel Taxes Influence the Choice and Use of Cars (SSRN Scholarly Paper ID 2778868). Social Science Research Network. https://doi.org/10.2139/ssrn.2778868.

Bannon, E. (2020, June 3). Air France's Bailout "Climate Conditions" Explained. Transport & Environment. https://www.transportenvironment.org/publications/air-frances-bailout-climate-conditions-explained.

Barton, D. N. (2013, November 29). Payments for Ecosystem Services: Costa Rica's Recipe. International Institute for Environment and Development. https://www.iied.org/payments-for-ecosystem-services-costa-rica-s-recipe.

Climate Action Network, CAN Europe (2016a, March). Financial Instruments to Address Loss and Damage Associated with the Adverse Effects of Climate Change. Submission to the Executive Committee of the Warsaw International Mechanism on Loss and Damage. https://unfccc.int/files/adaptation/groups_committees/loss_and_damage_executive_committee/application/pdf/can_submission_to_the_excom_of_the_wim_on_loss_and_damage_finance.pdf.

Climate Action Network, CAN Europe (2016b, April 26). Financial Transaction Tax: A Tool to Fund Our Future. CAN Europe. https://caneurope.org/financial-transaction-tax-a-tool-to-fund-our-future/.

Conservation International (n.d.) Global Conservation Rollbacks Tracker. https://www.conservation.org/projects/global-conservation-rollbacks-tracker.

Dauteuil, M.L., Hanafi, O., & Jousseaume, M. (2020). Environmental Taxation in France. Greening the French Culture of Taxation. CepInput Studies n. 12/2020. https://www.cep.eu/fileadmin/user_upload/cep.eu/Studien/cepInput_Umweltsteuern_in_Frankreich/cepInput_Environmental_Taxation_France.pdf.

Davidson, T. (2020, September 2). City Treasurer: Pittsburgh Faces $100 Million Less Revenue Because of Pandemic. TribLIVE.com. https://triblive.com/local/new-treasurer-pittsburgh-faces-100-million-less-revenue-because-of-pandemic/.

Coalition of Finance Ministers for Climate Action (2020). Better Recovery, Better World: Resetting Climate Action in the Aftermath of the COVID-19 Pandemic. Group of Experts Report. https://www.financeministersforclimate.org/sites/cape/files/inline-files/Better%20Recovery%2C%20Better%20World%20FINAL.pdf.

Fetet, M. & Postic, S. (2020, October 8). France's Green Budget: What's Next?. Institute for Climate Economics. https://www.i4ce.org/france-green-budget-climate/.

Gaspar, V., Jaramillo, L., & Wingender, P. (2016). Tax Capacity and Growth: Is There a Tipping Point? IMF Working Paper WP/16/234 https://www.imf.org/external/pubs/ft/wp/2016/wp16234.pdf.

Gates, B. (2020, August 4). COVID-19 Is Awful. Climate Change Could Be Worse. Gates Notes. https://www.gatesnotes.com/Energy/Climate-and-COVID-19.

Gopinath, Gita (2020, April 14). The Great Lockdown: Worst Economic Downturn Since the Great Depression. IMF Blog. https://blogs.imf.org/2020/04/14/the-great-lockdown-worst-economic-downturn-since-the-great-depression/.

Green Fiscal Policy Network (2019). Costa Rica—Country profile. https://greenfiscalpolicy.org/policy_briefs/costa-rica-country-profile/.

International Monetary Fund, IMF (2019, October). Fiscal Monitor: How to Mitigate Climate Change. IMF Fiscal Monitor Reports. https://www.imf.org/en/Publications/FM/Issues/2019/09/12/fiscal-monitor-october-2019.

IMF (2020a). Helping Bangladesh Recover from COVID-19. IMF Country Focus. https://www.imf.org/en/News/Articles/2020/06/11/na-06122020-helping-bangladesh-recover-from-covid-19.

IMF (2020b). Fiscal Monitor, October 2020. Policies for the Recovery. IMF World economic and financial surveys. https://www.imf.org/en/Publications/FM/Issues/2020/09/30/october-2020-fiscal-monitor.

IPBES, Intergovernmental Science-Policy Platform on Biodiversity and Ecosystem Services (2019). Global Assessment Report on Biodiversity and Ecosystem Services. IBPES Secretariat, Brondizio, E.S. Settele, J., Díaz, S. & Ngo, H.T. (editors). https://ipbes.net/global-assessment.

Kose, M.A., Kurlat, S., Ohnsorge, F. & Sugawara, N. (2017, August). A Cross-Country Database of Fiscal Space. World Bank Policy Research Working Paper 8157. http://documents1.worldbank.org/curated/en/601211501678994591/pdf/WPS8157.pdf.

KPMG (2019). Taxation Handbook of Bangladesh. https://assets.kpmg/content/dam/kpmg/bd/pdf/Taxation-Handbook-2019.pdf.

Long, C., & Miller, M. (2017). Taxation and the Sustainable Development Goals. Do Good Things Come to Those Who Tax More? Overseas Development Institute Briefing Note. https://www.odi.org/sites/odi.org.uk/files/resource-documents/11536.pdf.

Marten, M. & Van Dender, K. (2019). The Use of Revenues from Carbon Pricing. OECD Taxation Working Papers, No. 43. https://doi.org/10.1787/3cb265e4-en.

Nature4Climate (2020). Nature-Positive Recovery for People, Economy and Climate. Nature4Climate (N4C) Coalition Report. https://nature4climate.org/nature-positive-recovery/.

O'Callaghan, B., et al. (2020). Global Recovery Observatory. Oxford University Economic Recovery Project. https://recovery.smithschool.ox.ac.uk/tracking/.

Organisation for Economic Co-operation and Development, OECD (n.d.). Multilateral Convention to Implement Tax Treaty Related Measures to Prevent BEPS. https://www.oecd.org/tax/treaties/multilateral-convention-to-implement-tax-treaty-related-measures-to-prevent-beps.htm.

Osman-Elasha, E. (n.d.). Women in The Shadow of Climate Change. United Nations. https://www.un.org/en/chronicle/article/womenin-shadow-climate-change.

Sanderson, B.M., & O'Neill, B.C. (2020). Assessing the Costs of Historical Inaction on Climate Change. Scientific Reports, 10(1), 9173. https://doi.org/10.1038/s41598-020-66275-4.

Singapore's National Water Agency, PUB (n.d.). Singapore Water Story. https://www.pub.gov.sg/watersupply/singaporewaterstory.

Textile Today (2019, September 19). Bangladesh Has Highest Number of LEED Platinum-Rated Garment Factories. Textile Today Desk Report. https://www.textiletoday.com.bd/bangladesh-highest-number-leed-platinum-rated-garment-factories/.

UNEP, OECD and IISD (2019). Measuring Fossil Fuel Subsidies in the Context of the Sustainable Development Goals. UN Environment, Nairobi, Kenya. https://wedocs.unep.org/bitstream/handle/20.500.11822/28111/FossilFuel.pdf?sequence=1&isAllowed=y.

United Nations (n.d.) Our Impact. United Nations Office for Disaster Risk Reduction http://www.undrr.org/about-undrr/our-impact.

United Nations (2019, November). Emissions Gap Report 2019. UNEP—UN Environment Programme. http://www.unep.org/resources/emissions-gap-report-2019.

United Nations (2020a). World Social Report 2020: Inequality in a Rapidly Changing World. United Nations Department of Economic and Social Affairs https://www.un.org/development/desa/dspd/world-social-report/2020-2.html/.

United Nations (2020b). Preventing the next pandemic—Zoonotic diseases and how to break the chain of transmission. UNEP—UN Environment Programme. https://www.unep.org/resources/report/preventing-future-zoonotic-disease-outbreaks-protecting-environment-animals-and?_ga=2.104064448.1123779306.1615241919-1861719779.1614727156

Vivid Economics (2020) Greenness of Stimulus Index (Second Edition). Finance for Biodiversity Initiative. https://www.f4b-initiative.net/publications-1/second-edition-green-stimulus-index.

World Bank (n.d.). Costa Rica Overview. https://www.worldbank.org/en/country/costarica/overview.

World Bank (2020). State and Trends of Carbon Pricing 2020. World Bank. https://openknowledge.worldbank.org/handle/10986/33809.

World Economic Forum (2020). Nature Risk Rising: Why the Crisis Engulfing Nature Matters for Business and the Economy. New Nature Economy Series. https://www.weforum.org/reports/nature-risk-rising-why-the-crisis-engulfing-nature-matters-for-business-and-the-economy.

World Trade Organization, WTO (2020). World Trade Statistical Review 2020. https://www.wto.org/english/res_e/statis_e/wts2020_e/wts20_toc_e.htm.

CHAPTER 15

Supporting the Economy and SMEs in Times of Crisis

Félix-Antoine Ste-Marie

Small- and medium-sized enterprises (SMEs) across the world share many of the same challenges, including those related to liquidity, financing, and a general lack of resources. The pandemic increased pressure on those aspects. In fact, for most SMEs, the pandemic resulted in a decrease in revenues and yet required new investments to adapt and digitalize their businesses. The intervention of the government became key to their survival. Even before the pandemic, many governments thought it necessary to offer preferential treatment for SMEs in their tax system. The effectiveness of these incentives may be questioned as studies have shown that it is becoming less and less likely for SMEs to close the gap and become large companies. Moreover, some of the incentives would instead act as a deterrent. The help provided through pandemic measures was to ensure the survival of the SMEs during the crisis and a minimal cash flow for businesses. Although necessary, these new measures did not address the pre-existing issues, for which a comprehensive tax reform may be the only solution. Implementing a tax reform is a difficult, almost impossible task. However, the pandemic may have just brought us the perfect opportunity to launch a reform based on principles, such as simplicity, flexibility, innovation, and durability.

§15.01 INTRODUCTION

SMEs play an important part in our economies. They face challenges that are specific to their size and realities that differ from those experienced by large enterprises. Many measures were put in place in order to help them. As our society evolved, those measures needed to evolve also to the point where we have reached such a high level of complexity that our tax systems are becoming an obstacle for SMEs' growth rather than a tool. The pandemic crisis has done nothing to ameliorate the situation of SMEs and have rather brought us to the crossroad. This chapter will provide an overview of challenges experienced by SMEs as well as tax incentives offered by governments before and during the pandemic. This analysis brings us to question the effectiveness of our tax systems and of measures put in place, and discuss the possibility of a tax reform.[1]

§15.02 CHALLENGES FOR THE SMES

[A] Usual Challenges

The concept of SMEs is usually defined in relation to the number of people they employ, their annual turnover, or their balance sheets. Different countries or organizations will use different thresholds to categorize an enterprise.[2] Even with those differences in classification, the impact SMEs have on our economy is similar in most countries. For example, they usually represent more than 99% of all businesses and account for an important portion of the jobs and employment growth.[3] Also, they generate an important portion of the taxable business income[4] (OECD (2015a). Beyond the impact on our economy, SMEs across the world also share some of the same challenges. Among those, the question of liquidity and financing, as well as the lack of resources, are issues frequently raised when discussing SMEs.

The *OECD SME and Entrepreneurship Outlook* 2019, (hereinafter, the "*Outlook*") outlines the importance for SMEs to have access to financing in order to evolve but also the difficulty for SMEs to obtain financing:

> Typically, SMEs face structural barriers in accessing finance. Internal barriers include a lack of collateral to be provided to funders and investors as guarantees, insufficient financial skills of small business owners and managers and a lack of knowledge and awareness about funding options and alternatives. Market barriers

1. During the conference *Taxation in times of Crisis: Supporting the Economy and SMEs* (hereinafter "Conference"), held on October 13, 2020, the panelists Geneviève Mottard, President, CEO and Secretary, Ordre des CPA du Québec, Emilio B. Imbriglio, President and CEO, Raymond Chabot Grant Thornton, Nicolas Duvernois, entrepreneur and founder of Pur Vodka, the Hon. Perrin Beatty, President and CEO, Canadian Chamber of commerce and Gerhard Huemer, Director, Economic & Fiscal Policy, SMEs united under moderator Rochard Rubin, Journalist at the "Wall Street Journal" have discussed many of the issues regarding SMEs in our tax system before and during the pandemic as well solutions to those issues. Some of these insights are included in this chapter.
2. For example, some will consider an enterprise to be an SME if there are less than 500 employees while other if less than 250 (OECD (2015), *Taxation of SMEs in OECD and G20 Countries*).
3. In Canada, SMEs represent 99.8% of all businesses. In 2019, 88.5% of employed individuals in the private sectors were employed by SMEs. Even more, since 2014, almost 75% of employment growth is attributable to SMEs (Government of Canada, *Key Small Business Statistic—2020*). In the United States, almost two-thirds of new jobs come from small businesses (Office of the United States Trade Representative, *Small business*). Finally, on average in the OECD, start-ups account for half of the jobs created (OECD (2021), *Business dynamism during the Covid-19 pandemic: which policies for an inclusive recovery?*)
4. OECD surveys showed that on average SMEs are responsible for 63% of the taxable business income. This percentage remains the same whether the classification is made based on employee or turnover (OECD (2015), *Taxation of SMEs in OECD and G20 Countries*).

> include information asymmetries between financial institutions and the SME management, and relatively higher transaction and borrowing costs for funding institutions to serve SMEs (OECD, 2019).

The International Monetary Fund surveys also demonstrate the inequities SMEs may face, especially in emerging countries. For example, in the Middle East and Central Asia, SMEs only receive approximately 7% of total lending, although they represent over 96% of the businesses and employ around 50% of the private workforce (IMF, 2019).

The question of cash on hand or liquidity is also a major issue for many SMEs as it put them more at risk in case of an unexpected event (such as a worldwide pandemic) (OECD, 2021). A JP Morgan study conducted in the United States with approximately 597,000 SMEs showed that 25% operate with less than thirteen days of cash buffer and half with less than a month (twenty-seven days). Those numbers do not account for the effect of the pandemic (JP Morgan, 2016).

SMEs also experience a general lack of resources that can take many forms. First of all, they usually experience difficulties with hiring skilled workers as pointed out by the OECD in its Outlook:

> However, SMEs typically have greater difficulty in attracting and retaining skilled employees than large firms because they tend to lack the capacity and networks needed to identify and accessing talent. More importantly, they tend to offer less attractive remuneration and working conditions compared to larger firms (Eurofound, 2016) and therefore have difficulty competing for highly skilled workers. Recent results from the OECD/Facebook/World Bank Future Business Survey show that as many as one-third of SMEs report that recruiting and retaining skilled employees is the most pressing challenges for their business (Facebook/OECD/World Bank, 2018).

On this matter, the European Commission's survey shows that finding experienced workers was the main concern of SMEs in Europe in 2019 (European Commission, 2019). This prevents SMEs from being competitive and tends to increase the gap between SMEs and larger corporations (OECD, 2019). This lack of skill may result in SMEs being less innovative and being less able to adapt to new changes (OECD, 2021).

Another consequence of limited resources is that even before the pandemic, many SMEs were lagging behind when it comes to the use of new technology and the digitalization of the economy. This could be the result of a lack of resources such as infrastructure and skills (OECD, 2020).

[B] Impact of the Pandemic for SMEs

The SMEs were seriously affected by the pandemic because it directly impacted the liquidity but also because it required a drastic change in their business model that many did not have the resources to address. In other words, the pandemic increased the pressure on the already challenging aspect of the SMEs. Many reasons may explain the impacts felt by the SMEs, including:

(1) An overrepresentation of SMEs in the most impacted sector of the economies, such as wholesale and retail trade, accommodation and food services, professional services, and other personal services. In those sectors, SMEs are responsible for approximately 75% of the employment in comparison with 50% when all sectors are considered (OECD, 2020).
(2) Some countries have imposed a total lockdown on non-essential businesses. (BBC News, 2021).
(3) Most SMEs have experienced a disruption in the supply and demand chain. (OECD, 2021).

As a result, most SMEs experienced a decrease in revenue. The OECD surveyed SMEs across thirty-two countries to evaluate the impacts of the pandemic. The results showed that between 70% and 80% of the SMEs have had a drop in their revenue or sale since the beginning of the crisis. According to the surveys, the drop averaged between 30% and 50%. Those drops in revenue resulted in accrued pressure with regard to liquidity putting SMEs at a bigger risk (OECD, 2021).

At the same time, SMEs were forced to adapt, digitalize their business and review their safety procedure. The intervention of the government became essential to the survival of many enterprises (OECD, 2020).

§15.03 SUPPORT FOR THE SMEs

[A] Pre-Pandemic Intervention

Many countries have included preferential treatment for SMEs in their tax system. These preferences are usually justified by the importance of SMEs in the economy, for example by creating jobs, or simply as a means to compensate the market failures that affect the SMEs. These preferences may take many forms, including reduced corporate tax rate, tax deductions, tax credits, and tax exemptions (OECD, 2015):

- Reduced tax rate: This one is straightforward. Many tax regimes incorporate lower corporate tax rates for SMEs.
- Tax deductions: In some countries, SMEs will benefit from the increased deduction since it reduces their taxable income and allows for reinvestment of the amount that would otherwise be payable. The deductions can take the form of accelerated depreciation on some investment or flexibility on loss carry-over.
- Tax credits: The objective of tax credit is to reduce the cost of the investment by SMEs. Investment tax credits for example offer support for the purchase of new equipment or for research and development expenses. When it comes to R&D, SMEs will usually benefit from a higher percentage of credit and/or a higher rate of the refundable portion. This is not an exhaustive list of the tax credit destined to SMEs and many countries have designed other credits such as those concerning employment that are popular.

- Tax exemption: Some countries' taxation systems also include tax exemption for SMEs. For example, in the Netherlands, unincorporated SMEs are exempt from tax on 14% of their profit.

Many other measures exist to support SMEs. The tax incentives' objective is to incite the SMEs to grow but also to help them address cashflow issues. But are these policies effective? Some research has shown that tax preference for SMEs does not always have the expected results. On the contrary, some policies would rather act as a disincentive for growth and suboptimal uses of resources. For example, an IMF study concluded that an incentive may act as a deterrent since SMEs will limit their growth to avoid losing the incentive. It may also cause resources to be affected to certain businesses and may help businesses that are not viable. (IMF, 2017)

Moreover, Gerard Huemer questions the actual effectiveness of the "lower tax rate" by pointing out that the actual effective tax rate of bigger companies is often lower than SMEs' "incentive" tax rate. Indeed, even though small corporations benefit in many countries from lower tax rates and better tax incentives, they do not necessarily pay lesser taxes in proportion to the revenue generated than large ones.[5] The digitalization of our economy and globalization have allowed larger corporations to put in place complex tax structures that reduce their effective tax rate below those "preferred" tax rates. This situation has been a concern for the OECD for many years now. (OECD, 2015).

As voiced by Nicolas Duvernois, the growing complexity of our tax systems is also a concern for SMEs. It creates a feeling of unfairness since a high level of skills is required in order to comply and that usually comes at an expensive price. In fact, an analysis from the OECD noted that the cost of compliance for SMEs can be higher in proportion than larger corporations (OECD, 2015).

Finally, the effectiveness of the tax incentives could be questioned in light of Professor Vivaj Govindarajan and their collaborators' findings (Govindarajan and al., 2019). They analyzed the gap between large and small companies and their evolution over the recent years and concluded that the possibility for companies to change categories (i.e., small becoming medium and large and large becoming small) is growing thinner. Approximately 15% to 20% of small corporations became medium or large corporations every year before the early 2000s. That number has been cut in half since and the trend seems to indicate that the decrease will continue. To explain those results, they make the following observations:

- Contrary to what we may think, small enterprises are not necessarily more innovative than large ones. In fact, large corporations are making more and more investments in R&D. The small business simply cannot follow the rhythm and it is harder for them to remain competitive.
- The number of small businesses that cannot cover their expenses is highly superior to large ones.

5. For example, some of the biggest US corporation did not pay federal tax in 2020, including FedEx and Nike. (Ingraham, 2021)

They conclude that without substantial investment in intangible and fewer loss small businesses were fated to remain small (Govindarajan, 2019).

[B] Intervention During the Pandemic

In order to prevent the economy from crashing, governments came up with an array of measures and aids, including some directly targeting SMEs. In these troubled times, governments were creative using new methods, some of which were tested for the first time (OECD, 2020). The importance of governments' interventions has already been demonstrated in many surveys and analyses. For example, surveys with regard to liquidity shortage tend to demonstrate that without the government's intervention, the failure rate among SMEs would have increased from 4.5% to 12.1% (OECD (2021).

Measures can be divided into two categories: health measures and economic measures. Throughout the crisis and as of today, one of the purposes of the intervention is one regarding health and the prevention of the COVID-19 outburst. Lockdown or other similar policies have taken many forms depending on the country. In its most extreme form, it consists of a complete lockdown, with all businesses being closed except for a few essential ones, such as grocery stores and pharmacies. Some have imposed curfews starting as early as 6 pm. Some decided to close specific businesses, such as restaurants, cinemas, and gyms. Schools and universities have been closed. The direct impact of all these measures on SMEs is easy to see: businesses were closed. Not all SMEs were able to adapt, either because of the lack of resources or because of the nature of their businesses. In a similar way, many borders were closed, limiting expansion opportunities and in-person contact with manufacturers or clients (BBC News 2021a, *COVID: How are European countries tackling the pandemic?*).

Under these conditions, SMEs had to reinvent themselves. What was asked of them was to do so when their resources were at their lowest. Aware of the necessity to support the businesses, the governments came up with multiple economic measures to provide relief and assistance during the crisis (Enache and Al., 2020):

- *Salary-related measures*: Salary subvention can take one of two forms. First, some governments, such as Canada, offered subventions for salaries in order to incite corporations to retain or rehired their workers.[6] Second, many countries, such as Switzerland or Mexico, deferred the social security tax payments to a (certain degree), payments to be made by employers.
- *Corporate tax measures*: With the same idea in mind one of the most popular relief was to delay the statutory date of production for tax returns and of income tax payments. Romania even offered a 5% rebate for corporations that paid on time. Other countries, such as Norway, introduced loss carryback rules.

6. One of the objectives of such measure was to have the work force mobilized and ready when the economy would restart.

- Refund: Many measures were put into place in order to accelerate the treatment of reimbursements for corporations. New Zealand, for example, put in place an early claiming of R&D credit procedure to help taxpayers get the funds, as fast as possible.

These are only a few examples of the measures used and there are many more, such as those related to rent subventions, consumption taxes, and loans. All these measures have one common objective: ensure a minimum level of liquidity or cash flow for businesses. As explained, this was essential for SMEs' survival, and we can see how governments understood it and acted accordingly (OECD (2021a)).

Even with the importance of government assistance, the SMEs' awareness of the multiple programs remained an issue. In their study, John Eric Humphries and his colleagues analyzed the impact of the CARES Act in the United States. They concluded, "small businesses had the least awareness of government assistance, and the slowest growth in awareness after the passage of the CARES Act" (Humphries and Al., 2020). In their opinion, this could lead to believe that some of the SMEs missed out on early relief. This tends to show again that many SMEs lack the resource or expertise to benefit from tax incentives put in place for them. (Humphries and Al., 2020)

Finally, the help received during the pandemic although beneficial does not address the pre-existing inadequacies of our tax system with regard to SMEs.

§15.04 WHAT NOW?

The question that might be raised at this point is: why weren't the government's tax incentive (pre-pandemic) effective and instead resulted in a more and more complex system?

The Hon. Perrin Beatty brought forward one approach that could explain the situation, an interesting theory with regard to how tax laws were built over the recent years. He qualified the approach taken by governments as "tinkering" with the law. According to the Oxford Dictionaries to tinker means:

> *Tinker (with something)* to make small changes to something in order to repair or improve it, especially in a way that may not be helpful (Oxford Dictionaries online[7]).

And it is exactly what governments have been doing. They have kept making small modifications, small fixes resulting in only small adjustments, inadequate to the changing business environment. The tinker approach does have some advantages. It is easy to use in the sense that it does not require modifying the law as a whole. Each subsequent government may add a little provision here and there, depending on the interest they want to promote. Also, this approach allows maintaining the status quo which may be politically advantageous. Reforming a tax code will indubitably require revising the situation or advantage received by a certain group of people. You may end

7. Link to definition: [https://www.oxfordlearnersdictionaries.com/us/definition/english/tinker_2]

up alienating a larger portion of the population than intended. In a sense, people have become used to the inadequacies of the actual system. The status quo allows the government to give some small advantage to one group or another and make political gain without alienating the rest of the population.

In the ever-changing environment we live in, the notion of status quo is an illusion. The tinkering has far reached its limit and experts agree that the actual system is inefficient, outdated, complex, and unfair. Indeed, complexity is by far the first consequence of the tinker approach. It occurs because you need more and more modifications in order to maintain the system. It results in a tax law being so complicated that only a handful of professionals can grasp all implications. The second consequence is an outdated law. Trying to fix the legal set of rules, to fit the reality has its limits. At some point, the "fixing" might even become part of the problem. When the frame of the law is simply not adapted to the new reality, even new provisions will miss the point. The third consequence, inefficiency, is the result of a complex outdated law. Inefficiency occurs when compliance requires much effort and costs with unintended results. Finally, all this will ultimately lead to unfairness or a sentiment of unfairness as clearly expressed by Nicolas Duvernois.

[A] Need for a Reform and Why Has It Not Been Done?

We have reached a point where the only way to address the changes and eliminate the complexity is by undergoing a tax reform. What does it mean to have a reform? As mentioned by Geneviève Mottard, a holistic approach is needed for a tax reform in order to adapt the system to new business realities. For example, CPA Canada identifies four key questions to guide a reform in Canada.

> CPA Canada believes it's time to consider all aspects of our tax system and answer four key questions:
>
> - Does Canada's tax system align with international trends and promote global competitiveness?
> - Does Canada's tax system help businesses grow and innovate?
> - Do Canada's tax expenditures achieve their goals at the right cost?
> - Does Canada's personal tax system promote compliance and deliver social benefits efficiently and effectively? (CPA Canada).

Even though it seems like the logical approach, why has it not been done yet? From a Canadian point of view, why has no government tried it since 1967? Many reasons could explain the unwillingness to proceed.

The process of lawmaking is, in itself, the first obstacle to a successful tax reform. Most modern democracies are built around the principle of separation of powers between the Executive, Legislative, and Judicial branches. Therefore, for a reform to be successful from a lawmaking point of view, you will need the Executive and Legislative to be aligned. It is easier said than done.

The proximity between members of the executive branch and the legislative branch will vary between countries and can be an obstacle. Time, in elected democracy, is another obstacle to implementing a major reform.

Let assume there is an alignment between the government and the Legislative (on all levels required); the implementation of a reform will nevertheless require time. As explained by Mrs. Mottard, the design of a tax reform should involve different actors.[8] An independent commission should probably be put in place with the objective to assess the current system and come up with the diagnostic and recommendations. The second step would be to act on this report. A team of legislators should be put in place to draft the new body of legislation. Again, different actors will present their comments and recommendations on the draft. And finally, once the project has taken an acceptable form, it will be adopted. All these steps must be completed before an election could change the governmental orientations. In most countries, governments are elected for terms between four to six years. If a newly elected government takes a year to familiarize itself with the issues and fully assume its role and takes the last year to work toward its reelection, it becomes almost impossible to accomplish a tax reform through one term. At this point, rather than being *why has it not been done?* The question should really be: *can it be done?*[9]

For these reasons, it is a lot easier for a government to tinker with the law than to go through a reform. A reform also implies relinquishing the power to tinker. The Hon. Perrin Beatty explained that one of the reasons why no reform has been made is because the government wants to retain control over the law and the possibility to make tinkering. Indeed, the reform will aim for a comprehensive set of rules, limiting tinkering opportunities. A reform also means that you might be required to let independent people tell you how it should be run. Hence, wanting a reform requires courage. It requires the courage to face issues. It requires to be confident that the favorable political conditions will remain for two or three mandates. Especially when the reform, although beneficial, may not result in short-term benefits.

Finally, the Hon. Perrin Beatty also warned about diverging interests. More than an obstacle, it is a trap. When you have the political conditions and the time, the question is how you should compose with diverging interests. It is understandable that all actors will want to benefit from the new legislation. Be it oil companies, insurance companies, financial industries, technology sector, health sector, social organism,

8. Those could include CPA, Bar associations, consumers associations, lobbies, etc.
9. Laura Blessing in her article (Why tax reform is hard?) explained how difficult it would be implementing a reform in the United States. She mentioned:

> Tax reform is rare because it is hard. It tends to take years of substantive work to produce: the 1986 Tax Reform Act took about two years, and former Ways and Means Chair Dave Camp took three years to put together his 2014 proposal (which still failed). It involves concentrated costs (often to vocal interests) and diffuse benefits; special political circumstances are generally seen as being needed to insulate the process from these strong, moneyed headwinds. Traditionally, strong Presidential support, firm congressional leadership, effective messaging, and political insulation are seen as important. (*See* CRS scholar Gravelle's piece, beginning on page 457.) Meanwhile, the increasing salience of electoral cycles on legislation, and the steep decline of regular order, make the kind of sustained focus necessary even harder still.

agriculture, etc. Once a process is undergoing, the government must resist the temptation to give in to the multiple interests that could lead to an unsuccessful reform. Going back to Canadian history will provide a good example on this matter. In 1966, the Royal Commission on taxation came to the conclusion that the existing system was inefficient, complicated, and lacked fairness. Due to opposition from all these divergent interests, the result was that the reform included only a few of the recommendations. Sixty years later, we are still discussing the same issues of fairness, inefficiency, and complexity.

[B] Opportunities Brought by the Pandemic

Emilio Imbriglio reflected on the opportunity brought by the pandemic and expressed the idea that the crisis brought an alignment of conditions that together may give us the perfect momentum to reform our tax laws. There are many reasons why the pandemic could be considered an opportunity to make the reform:

- *Necessity:* The first opportunity is one of necessity. Tremendous amounts have been invested to protect the economy. These will need to be reimbursed, but how? While most businesses are still fragile, we cannot expect governments to simply increase taxes. Nor should the solution reside in letting future generations deal with this debt. Under these conditions, a tax reform may be the solution to readapt our system to new realities and address the problem.
- *Cooperation:* The second opportunity is one of cooperation. The pandemic has reminded us of what can be accomplished when we work together. We have seen opposed politicians working together, local initiatives put in place to help the community, and overall, a lot of sacrifices made for the common good—not only economic but also with regard to the exportation of vaccines. The willingness to cooperate varies among countries, but there is clearly a momentum that could be exploited.[10]
- *Awareness:* The third opportunity is one of awareness. The pandemic accelerated many changes that were already taking place. It also gave us a glimpse of what the future could hold. For example, conciliation between family and work takes another perspective when you suddenly start working from home.

With these conditions aligned, we are now better positioned to have a successful reform than we have never been in the last years. At the international level, we have recently seen countries agree on the principle of a minimal tax rate for corporations something that seemed impossible to reach (BBC News, 2021b).

If such an agreement now seems feasible, we can think that a reform of domestic laws for SMEs could be possible.

10. The question is how long will this momentum last? Probably not so long. For example, at the international level we have started to see a resurgence of protectionism, not only economic but also with regard to the exportation of vaccines.

[C] Tax Reform

[1] Principles to Build On Our Tax Reform

In addressing the Digital Economy, the OECD reiterated the following principles that should guide the design of a tax system: Neutrality, Efficiency, Certainty and Simplicity, Effectiveness and Fairness, and Flexibility (OECD, 2014).

From an SME's perspective, the first one that comes to mind is usually simplicity. Simplicity means having an understandable rule that allows for better compliance, but also for making the right decision or better decisions. Usually with simplicity comes certainty, and efficiency in compliance and application. Ultimately, a simple rule, easy to understand, will increase the perceived fairness. SMEs usually do not have the internal expertise nor the time to understand or comply with complex rules, nor the resources to hire the professionals to do so. This results in a sentiment of unfairness (OECD, 2014).

We also need our tax code to be effective. We want the policies adopted to have the expected results. Finally, we need flexibility. The OECD specified that:

> Taxation systems should be flexible and dynamic enough to ensure they keep the pace with technological and commercial developments. It is important that a tax system is dynamic and flexible enough to meet the current revenue needs of governments while adapting to changing needs on an ongoing basis. This means that the structural features of the system should be durable in a changing policy context, yet flexible and dynamic enough to allow governments to respond as required, to keep the pace with technological and commercial developments, taking into account that future developments will often be difficult to predict. (OECD, 2014)

A tax reform should be built in a way to ensure innovation and durability. To do so it needs the flexibility to evolve with the changes that the societies go through.

[2] Danger of Equality

As you may have noted, equality is not part of the principles. Emilio Imbriglio warns that equality is an inadequate measure of the success of a policy. Equality must be distinguished from equity or fairness. Equality only means "the same." Trying to achieve the same treatment for taxpayers should never be an objective for taxation. As Imbriglio said: "One solution fits all is more than often one solution fits none."

He explained that a tax system must be discriminatory. It must be prejudiced. It must favor emerging businesses, innovative businesses as well as green initiatives. We must not be afraid of having different treatments between different sectors or between regions. For example, remote regions might have different needs, or the impacts on employment might differ.

The difference between SMEs justifies a difference in treatment.

[3] How Should It Change

The way a reform is put in place and the values prioritize will vary depending on each country. During the conference, many ideas and principles to build on were discussed from an SME's perspective. First of all, the reform should emphasize innovation and its multiple aspects. It means that a taxation system should favor innovating businesses. We should encourage existing businesses to develop new products, new procedures. It goes beyond providing help to adapt. Our policies should be not only to maintain but to create. This could require, among other things, specific incentives for start-ups. A second aspect that should be prioritized is the creation of employment. This will be obtained partially with innovation and the creation of new sectors or start-ups, but it can also mean helping actual workers to adapt to new jobs. Finally, a reform should be based on sustainability and responsibility. Societies have evolved, and we need a tax reform to reflect these changes. Sustainability can mean sustainability not only regarding the environment but also regarding new social standards. We need the reform to put the environment in front and hence any tax incentives or other forms of support should come with conditions regarding it. As Imbriglio stated, we need to stop giving money without expecting the highest level of morals and standards.

Finally, although these values may vary, any tax reform should be in accordance with the principles discussed in the previous section, while keeping in mind the danger of falling back to the tinker approach.

§15.05 CONCLUSION

The importance of SMEs is not to be neglected. In most countries, they provide for more than 99% of businesses, they hire more than two-thirds of privately employed people, and they also have great importance in new jobs creation. They also share the same challenges regarding resources, liquidity, and financing. With this in mind, many governments have put in place tax preferences for SMEs. However, the effectiveness of these measures can be questioned. The pandemic directly impacted those challenges and has had many negative effects on SMEs often forcing them to change their business model. Fortunately, governments have intervened with an array of measures to provide some relief, especially ensuring that they would keep a minimum level of liquidity. The pandemic has exposed many flaws in our systems and accelerated some of the changes that were gradually taking place. It also provided us with the opportunity to take a good look at our tax system and implement a reform. Indeed, our actual system has become too complex to the point where it becomes an obstacle for many SMEs. That leads to a sentiment of unfairness. We have reached a point where minor modification will not do the trick anymore and the implementation of a tax reform seems to be needed. The implementation of a reform is no simple task and requires favorable political conditions that last long enough to adopt and implement the reform. Maybe the pandemic brought the opportunity we needed to move forward with a reform. If a large number of countries can agree on a minimal corporate tax rate, why wouldn't we be able to agree at the national level on a reform of the tax system?

Bibliography

BBC News (2021a), *COVID: How Are European Countries Tackling the Pandemic?*, February 3, 2021.

BBC News (2021b), *G7: Rich Nations Back Deal to Tax Multinationals*, June 5, 2021.

Laura Blessing, *Why Tax Reform Is Hard*, online, The Government Affair Institute, Georgetown University, https//gai.Georgetown.edu/why-tax-reform-is-hard/.

CPA Canada, *Canada's Tax System: What's So Wrong and Why it Matters?*, online https://www.cpacanada.ca/en/the-cpa-profession/about-cpa-canada/key-actibvities/public-policy-advocacy/cpa-canada-tax-review-initiative/canadas-tax-system.

Enache, Elke Asen, Daniel Bunn & Justin DeHart (2020), *Tracking Economic Relief Plans Around the World During the Coronavirus Outbreak*, Last updated May 6, 2020, https://taxfoundation.org/coronavirus-country-by-country-responses/.

European Commission (2019), *Survey on the access to finance of enterprises*, Analytical Report 2019.

Government of Canada, *Key Small Business Statistic—2020*, https://www.ic.gc.ca/eic/site/061.nsf/eng/h_032126.html.

Govindarajan Vijay, Baruch Lev, Anup Srivastava & Luminita Enache (2019), *The Gap Between Large and Small Companies Is Growing Why?, Harvard Business Review*, August 16.

Humphries, John Eric, Christopher Neilson & Gabriel Ulyssa (2020), "The Evolving Impact of Covid-19 on Small Businesses Since the CARES Act," *Cowles Foundation Discussion Paper* No. 2230, Cowles Foundation For Research in Economics, Yale University, April 2020.

IMF (2019), *Financial Inclusion of Small and Medium-Sized Enterprises in the Middle East and Central Asia*, IMF staff team led by Nicolas Blancher, No. 19/02.

IMF (2017), *The Right Kind of Help? Tax Incentives for Staying Small*, IMF Working Paper prepared by Dora Benedek and al.

Christopher Ingraham (2021), "Dozens of America's Biggest Businesses Paid No Federal Income Tax-Again," *Washington Post*, April 5, 2021.

Diana Farrell and Chris Wheat (2016), *Cash Is King: Flows, Balances, and Buffer Days, Evidence from 600,000 Small Business*, JP Morgan and Chase Co. institute 2016.

OECD (2014), *Addressing the Tax Challenges of the Digital Economy*, OECD/G20 Base Erosion and Profit Shifting Project, OECD Publishing, Paris.

OECD (2015a), *Preventing the Granting of Treaty Benefits in Inappropriate Circumstances, Action 6—2015 Final Report*, OECD/G20 Base Erosion and Profit Shifting Project, OECD Publishing, Paris.

OECD (2015b), *Taxation of SMEs in OECD and G20 Countries*, OECD Tax Policy Studies, No. 23, OECD Publishing, Paris.

OECD (2019), *OECD SME and Entrepreneurship Outlook 2019*, OECD Publishing, Paris.

OECD (2020), *Coronavirus (Covid-19): SME Policy Response, OECD Policy Response to Coronavirus*, OECD Publishing, Paris.

OECD (2021), "Business Dynamism During the COVID-19 Pandemic: Which Policies for an Inclusive Recovery?", *OECD Policy Responses to Coronavirus (COVID-19)*, OECD Publishing, Paris.

OECD (2021), *One Year of SME and Entrepreneurship Policy Responses to COVID-19: Lessons Learned to "Build Back Better,"* OECD Policy Response to Coronavirus, OECD Publishing, Paris.

OECD (2021), "An In-Depth Analysis of One Year of SME and Entrepreneurship Policy Responses to COVID-19: Lessons Learned for the Path to Recovery," *OECD SME and Entrepreneurship Papers*, n° 25, OECD Publishing, Paris.

Office of the United States Trade Representative, *Small Business*, https://ustr.gov/issue-areas/small-business.

Oxford Dictionaries, online: https://www.oxfordlearnersdictionaries.com/us/definition/english.

CHAPTER 16

Tax Ethics and Inclusiveness

Richard Murphy

Tax ethics has always suffered from a problem with perspective. It would seem that any tax ethic ever promoted has always suffered from a bias towards the viewpoint of its promoter. This is as true for the tax professions as it has been for tax authorities and those who have wished to promote the idea that there is no such thing as tax ethics, and that there are merely issues of legal compliance. In this chapter, a different approach is taken. It is assumed, following the tradition of philosopher John Rawls, that a tax ethic is only valid if it is equally acceptable to whoever might be promoting it. This in itself delivers a new measure of equality. The inherent conflicts in existing positions are resolved by suggesting a new code of conduct for tax ethics where the principle is that all parties within tax have reciprocal obligations to each other and that these are fulfilled when all act openly and transparently with the objective of ensuring that tax compliance is achieved where that is defined as paying the right amount of tax (but no more) in the right place at the right time where right means that the economic substance of the transactions undertaken coincides with the place and form in which they are reported for taxation purposes.

§16.01 INTRODUCTION

Writing about professional ethics is hard. Even deciding from which viewpoint to approach that issue is difficult. The perspectives of the practising accountant, the tax academic, the tax campaigner, tax authorities, the taxpayer, and others all differ. Each role suggests its own, distinct, perspective on this issue. Finding a way to reconcile those potential approaches is problematic, which demonstrates the problem inherent in any approach to the professional ethics of tax. The issue is much discussed, but the discussion all too often ends up reflecting a particular perspective. It would seem as if the answer to any question on the professional ethics of taxation might be prefaced with the question 'who is asking?'[1]

The argument in this chapter is that this is inappropriate. Drawing on a Rawlsian perspective[2] the suggestion is that any approach to the ethics of taxation should be universal. It is suggested that the answer to the question 'who is asking?' should be 'It does not matter: when it comes to ethics perspective should not influence the answer. There is a universal approach we should be seeking.' That is the goal.

That said, it is important to note the protagonists in this field and to suggest what their commonplace views might be. The taxpayer all too often has one of two perspectives. The first is that if it is legal they will happily do it.[3] The second is that if it is illegal they will do it so long as the chance that they will get away with it is high.[4]

The tax professional, on the other hand, has a different perspective. Their goal is very often to do whatever they can to earn a living in a way that does not lead them into professional dispute and disrepute, whether with their client, tax authority or disciplinary authority. The dimension of 'getting away with it' has an obvious role to play in their thinking, again.

In contrast, the tax authority has the task of collecting the tax that they believe to be due under the prevailing law of the tax jurisdiction in which they work. On occasion, this can lead to absurd outcomes. In 1869 Lord Cairns said in the UK's House of Lords, which was then its Supreme Court[5]:

> If the person sought to be taxed comes within the letter of the law he must be taxed, however great the hardship may appear to the judicial mind to be. On the other hand, if the Crown, seeking to recover the tax, cannot bring the subject within the letter of the law, the subject is free, however apparently within the spirit of the law the case might otherwise appear to be. In other words, if there be admissible, in any statute what is called an equitable construction, certainly such a construction is not admissible in a taxing statute.

Few now would think this an appropriate interpretation of the law for use in the 21st century. Oxford tax professor Judith Freedman has, for example, argued in favour of general anti-avoidance principles (Freedman 2006). The legal concept of equitable interpretation of law has come into play in the meantime, and is to a greater and lesser extent implicit in the numerous general and targeted anti-avoidance provisions that are

1. The debate here builds on comments made in a discussion at the TaxCOOP2020 World Tax Summit where I joined a panel to discuss ethics, inclusiveness and other issues. Many thanks to my fellow panellists Åsa Gunnarsson, Nina Olson and Philippe Van Parijs: their contributions to debate were much appreciated and my thanks to the editors of this book for this opportunity to follow up on and broaden what I had the chance to say.
2. Numerous references to Rawls could be made. My own personal way into his thinking was via Samuel Freeman's 'Cambridge Companion to Rawls, (Freeman 2003).
3. It could be argued that in UK law, this is the principle inherent in the 1936 'Duke of Westminster' case: *Inland Revenue Commissioners v. Duke of Westminster* [1936] A.C. 1; [1] 19 TC 490 http://www.bailii.org/uk/cases/UKHL/1935/4.html.
4. The UK's HM Revenue & Customs estimate tax evasion to cost GBP 4.6 billion a year in the UK (HMRC 2020b). Others, e.g., Murphy (2014), think it much higher.
5. *Partington v. Attorney-General* (1869), L.R. 4 E. & I. App. 100, per Lord Cairns at p. 122.

now popular with tax authorities in many tax jurisdictions such as that adopted in the UK in 2013.[6] Absolutes have been abandoned: judgment is substituted, at least to some degree, and meaning is sought within the law.

In fairness, this idea is now new. The Australian Acts Interpretation Act of 1901 said:[7]

> In interpreting a provision of an Act, the interpretation that would best achieve the purpose or object of the Act (whether or not that purpose or object is expressly stated in the Act) is to be preferred to each other interpretation.

There is in that case an ethic in interpreting the law, after all. It is not a case of 'black and white' in many, if not most countries, as some would like to claim.

For one group it has never been that. For the tax justice campaigner, and those others with a political interest in the role of tax in society, tax is not an issue that relates solely (if at all, in some cases) to raising tax revenue. There are, instead, for such groups multiple reasons to tax, which includes (Murphy 2015, Chapter 3) redistributing income and wealth, repricing goods and services; and reorganising the economy through fiscal policy. These too are all issues with an ethical foundation. The result is that tax does in that case require an ethical foundation that can embrace all these conflicting goals.

That too is in practice likely to be the case for the vast majority of taxpayers and tax professionals of whom the above caricatures are not fair. What they seek to find is a path through the extremes that some seek to justify. This might be defined as seeking tax compliance, which can be described as seeking to pay the right amount of tax (but no more) in the right place at the right time, where right means that the economic substance of the transactions undertaken coincides with the place and form in which they are reported for taxation purposes (Murphy 2010). It is suggested that this is the approach that should be adopted when seeking to create an inclusive code of ethics for taxation.

It may well be that tax authorities already share the view. In the aftermath of the G7, Finance Minister's announcement of a new tax deal to tackle multinational company tax abuse in June 2021 a UK Treasury spokesperson was noted to say (Inman and Partington 2021):

> The deal makes sure that the system is fair, so that the right companies pay the right tax in the right places.

The similarity in language to that noted with regard to tax compliance is apparent.

The question to answer in that case is what is 'right'? That then leads to the question as to whether it is possible to suggest a mechanism that might make it possible to deliver this ethical approach to tax on a universal basis, in the process creating a public good that by definition should be operated for the benefit of all in society?

---

6. UK Finance Act 2013, Part 5.
7. http://www8.austlii.edu.au/cgi-bin/viewdoc/au/legis/cth/consol_act/aia1901230/s15aa.html.

§16.02 THE PROBLEMS WITH TAX ETHICS

Examples suggest why there are problems with what might best be described as contextual approaches to tax ethics. Both are drawn from the UK for the sake of consistency

The first of these approaches comes from the guidance issued by the various professional institutes (excluding lawyers) that represent tax agents and those advising taxpayers in the UK. Unusually, they have cooperated in issuing this guidance, which is welcome in itself when professional rivalry usually prevents such cross-working. The guidance, which is described as relating to Professional Conduct in Relation to Taxation (PCRT) makes clear its scope (ICAEW 2019):

> The purpose of Professional Conduct in Relation to Taxation (PCRT) is to assist and advise members on their professional conduct in relation to taxation, and particularly in the tripartite relationship between a member, client and HM Revenue & Customs.[8]

Why it is thought that a different relationship might exist if working with a different tax authority is not clear. In itself, this might indicate a limitation in scope implicit in this Code. It is however welcome that the Code is considered to apply to all the members of the professional institutes that issued it, even if they do, for example, work for HM Revenue & Customs (HMRC) (as is the case for some to whom it applies). However, what the Code then says is that:

> Ethical behaviour in the tax profession is critical. The work carried out by a member needs to be trusted by society at large as well as by clients and other stakeholders. What a member does reflects not just on themselves but on the profession as a whole.

It then adds:

> A member must comply with the following Fundamental Principles:
>
> ***Integrity***
>
> *To be straightforward and honest in all professional and business relationships.*
>
> ***Objectivity***
>
> *To not allow bias, conflict of interest or undue influence of others to override professional or business judgements.*
>
> ***Professional competence and due care***
>
> *To maintain professional knowledge and skill at the level required to ensure that a client or employer receives competent professional service based on current developments in practice, legislation and techniques and act diligently and in accordance with applicable technical and professional standards.*

8. The UK's tax authority.

Confidentiality

To respect the confidentiality of information acquired as a result of professional and business relationships and, therefore, not disclose any such information to third parties without proper and specific authority, unless there is a legal or professional right or duty to disclose, nor use the information for the personal advantage of the member or third parties.

Professional behaviour

To comply with relevant laws and regulations and avoid any action that discredits the profession.

These are the principles which, it is suggested tax professionals should use in their work.

These principles are based on the International Code of Ethics for Professional Accountants (IFAC 2020) says that its overriding concern is (IFAC 2020, page 13):

> A distinguishing mark of the accountancy profession is its acceptance of the responsibility to act in the public interest. A professional accountant's responsibility is not exclusively to satisfy the needs of an individual client or employing organization. Therefore, the Code contains requirements and application material to enable professional accountants to meet their responsibility to act in the public interest.

This Code is promoted by the International Federation of Accountants (IFAC)[9] and is stated to be applicable to the work of all professional accountants in whatever activity they are engaged in.

That such a Code exists is welcome. The problem with the Code's five points of principle is that they appear to contain no obvious references to the supposed obligation to act in the public interest, which is not mentioned in them. Instead, obligations implicit in contractual relationships are the basis for those principles. In particular, the obligation to not breach the law or regulations noted in the fifth principle, which is the only part that might be suggested to refer to the public interest, is seemingly framed as a requirement to not discredit the tax profession. There is as a consequence no reference to a duty to the public at large.

In that case, it is not clear that either this code for taxation or the broader code for professional accountants on which it is based relate to ethics. They are instead codes of conduct, which are something quite different. At best it can be suggested that these codes promote a contextual ethic. That context is the particular duty of the accountant to the client within the context of not bringing the broader profession of which they are a part into disrepute. This represents a form of moral relativism that seems inappropriate when the obligation that these self-regulating professional institutes have appeared to accept is to create an ethic based on the moral imperative to act in the broader public interest.

This moral imperative is clearly necessary when considering the relationships that exist between the identified parties to taxation, namely, the government, the

9. https://www.ifac.org/.

taxpayer, the tax agent and civil society who are impacted by their behaviour whether within or beyond the jurisdiction in which tax is actually due. This last point is especially important within the context of tax spillovers, which describe the possibility that exists within all tax systems for one measure to undermine another, either within or beyond the jurisdiction to which it relates (Baker and Murphy 2019).

This concept of spillover should be of concern to a tax authority. The way that the behaviour of tax agents impacts the operation of the tax system is vital to its effectiveness. The UK's tax authority, HMRC, has a code of conduct which is its own best approximation to a code of ethics. This it describes as a Charter (HMRC 2020a) which it is required to publish by law, which law says that it:

> must include standards of behaviour and values to which Her Majesty's Revenue and Customs will aspire when dealing with people in the exercise of their functions.

The resulting Code does recognise the public interest. It says in the preamble:

> HMRC is here to collect the tax that pays for the UK's public services.[10]
>
> We'll help you meet your tax responsibilities and make sure you get any benefits, tax credits, refunds or other support you can claim. However, we will take firm action against the small minority who bend or break the law.

It then sets a standard that it says it aspires to:

> We'll give you accurate, consistent and clear information. This will help you meet your obligations, and understand your rights and what you can claim. When we ask for information, we rely on you to give us full, accurate and timely answers. If you disagree with us, we'll tell you about options available to you and work with you to reach an appropriate outcome quickly and simply.

What is very apparent is that there is duality or reciprocity of required action implicit in this standard: appropriate behaviour is required of both the taxpayer and tax authority. However, in none of the elaboration that follows is an ethic developed: what is suggested to exist is a legal obligation that must be fulfilled. This Charter does not, in that case, represent a code of ethics. Once more it is little more than a code of conduct.

The possible exception is with regard to tax agents, where HMRC has its own code of conduct (HMRC 2018). In that Code, HMRC recognizes that this code is a new area of work for them, their consideration of it having only begun in 2016, and more recently still with regard to tax planning and money laundering related issues, which are not being considered here. Importantly, they recognise the principles for professional accountants already noted, above. They state that if a person complies with the first three of those principles (integrity, professional competence and due care and professional behaviour) then compliance will also have been achieved with the expectations of HMRC. The last two are ignored by HMRC as they relate to the client relationship, and so are beyond its remit. Since it is only these last two aspects that do,

10. This is by no means the sole function of taxation. See Murphy, R (2015, Chapter 3).

however, have a public interest remit within them HMRC seem, as a consequence, to take this out of their area of concern. As with the profession, their horizon is decidedly limited and moral relativism appears to be the limit of their ambition, set within the context of their own particular needs from this relationship, which is, they say, that:

> HMRC requires all tax agents to maintain high standards that promote tax compliance.

What is especially surprising in this case is that they make no apparent effort to define what they mean by tax compliance within this code. Nor do they do so in their publications on the UK tax gaps, in which they refer to the term on many occasions. The closest that they get to a definition of tax compliance in that tax gap analysis is to define compliance activity on their part as (HMRC 2020b):

> An intervention by HMRC, such as a direct tax enquiry, employer compliance review or VAT assurance visit, designed to ensure that the correct amount of tax is being accounted for and paid.

This is a use of the term that is hard to reconcile with the use of the term tax compliance in their code for tax agents, who are expected to promote compliance without any intervention from the tax authority being required.

The Organisation for Economic Cooperation and Development (OECD), which is responsible for establishing many of the norms within international taxation, are of little greater assistance. In their glossary of taxation they define tax compliance as (OECD 2021):

> Degree to which a taxpayer complies (or fails to comply) with the tax rules of his country, for example by declaring income, filing a return, and paying the tax due in a timely manner.

Just as in the case of HMRC's definition of compliance within the context of the tax gap this definition appears to fall short of that required to match the use of the term tax compliance in association with professional ethics. What is apparent is that there is a gap as to what this ethic might be. A review suggests that the UK is not alone in suffering this deficit; for example, the Internal Revenue Service of the United States of America does have codes of ethics (IRS 2020), but they focus on employee conduct and not the broader public duty that a principle-based ethic on tax might embrace.

§16.03 TOWARDS A CODE OF TAX ETHICS

Tax is a public good. A public good is a service that is provided without profit to benefit all members of society. While few pay tax with enthusiasm, most appreciate just how important it is that tax is paid. It is this appreciation that would underpin a code of ethics for taxation and that justifies its creation. If the value of this overall public good is enhanced by such a code, with the benefit to society increasing as a result, then this would constitute a societal wide net welfare gain. That is why a code of ethics for taxation should be created.

In the absence of any clear guidance from professional bodies, tax authorities, or international agencies on the issue of what might be included in an appropriate inclusive code of ethics for taxation some suggestions need to be made as to the required content of such a code if it is to be inclusive, as is suggested to be essential.

This first requires a consideration of what inclusiveness might mean in this context. A number of qualities would seem to be embraced by the term. The term clearly relates to fair and equal treatment.[11] However, passive statements of intent are no longer seen as sufficient on such matters. Proactive statements of meaning are required as evidence of commitment to a policy. For example, in his 2019 book 'How to be an anti-racist', Ibram X. Kendi (2019) argued that not being a racist was insufficient: what was required was that a person be anti-racist. It is suggested within the context of a code of ethics for taxation that this is true of inclusivity. Saying that a policy of inclusivity exists is no longer enough: there must be clear evidence of intent that it will actually include those, most particularly, who have been excluded before its adoption. So, for example, it might ensure that those who have been excluded, for instance, because of their race, gender, sexuality, or disability, or for other factors such as their geographic remoteness, inability to communicate with ease, use of a second language or location outside a jurisdiction but who are nonetheless subject to its taxation, should now be covered by such a policy.[12] It is this approach to inclusivity that is adopted here.

Second, inclusivity also embraces the idea of comprehensiveness. This naturally follows from the idea that tax is a public good. This is a quality absent from the codes that have been reviewed. Comprehensiveness would require that all the stakeholders of a tax system be considered by a tax code of ethics. In recent work with Prof Andrew Baker for the Global Initiative for Financial Transparency (Baker and Murphy 2020) we argued that those stakeholders are:

- The government of a jurisdiction.
- The legislators of that jurisdiction, particularly those outside the government or members of the opposition.
- The tax authority of a jurisdiction.
- The electorate and the residents of that jurisdiction.
- Individual taxpayers within a jurisdiction, whether they are within the electorate, or not, and their agents.
- The businesses that trade within a jurisdiction, whether incorporated or not.
- Researchers, whether they are academics, journalists, civil society or those from other backgrounds.
- International agencies and actors in other countries, including those thinking of investing in the jurisdiction.

These are the audiences that a code of tax ethics should address if it is to be inclusive.

11. https://dictionary.cambridge.org/dictionary/english/inclusiveness.
12. https://www.merriam-webster.com/dictionary/inclusive.

Third, the range of activity to be considered then has to be addressed if inclusivity is to be achieved. This demand recognises that there is a wide range of activity within the tax arena, including:

- creating tax legislation;
- creating budgets for tax revenues;
- enforcing tax legislation, including the recovery of tax owing from taxpayers whilst respecting their individual circumstances and their right to appeal contested liabilities;
- the prevention of fraud within the tax system;
- ministerial conduct with regard to taxation;
- expected taxpayer conduct;
- the expected conduct of tax agents;
- international relations concerning taxation;
- the accountability of governments for tax revenues received.

The limited horizons of the codes of conduct already noted can be compared with this broad range of scope.

Fourth, it is important to recognise those qualities that the code of ethics is seeking to promote that are likely to assist the achievement of its goals. It is suggested that these include transparency, accountability, equality, justice, reciprocity, and honesty. More precisely, transparency, so that all account appropriately for the tax that is due; accountability, so that those with responsibility acknowledge it; equity, so that all are treated equally; justice, so that all have a right to fair treatment when there is a disagreement as to meaning or conduct; reciprocity, ensuring mutuality of obligation; and finally honesty, including accountability for breaches.

§16.04 DEVELOPING A CODE OF ETHICS

Based upon the principles noted a code of ethics can be developed. In the interests of effectiveness, this has to be as brief as possible. This goal is assisted by the fact that as this is a code of ethics it is principle based. That means it is not a set of rules. It is instead a code against which behaviour can be appraised, and failings assessed. What it seeks to inform are, for example, the codes of conduct already noted by providing these with a purpose that they otherwise lack.

A suggested code is attached to this chapter as an appendix.[13] It is suggested that this code of ethics, detailed as it is, lays the foundation for an inclusive approach to the management of a tax system. It is deliberately comprehensive in its scope. It is intended to meet the needs of all stakeholders, from those of civil society for data; to those setting policy who require tax gap and tax spillover analyses; to the tax authority demanding tax compliance from taxpayers, which principle is clearly implicit in the required behaviour that the code sets out; to tax agents, where the principles in the existing codes are extended to really embrace the public interest in a way that existing

13. This draft code is based upon Murphy (2007).

codes do not; to the imposition of ethical requirements on those politically responsible for the tax system as a whole. It is explicit in its requirement that discrimination on a wide range of bases be eliminated from the management of the tax system. The concept of tax being due in the right place is explicitly embraced, as is an underlying principle of transparency as the foundation for the public good inherent in a well-functioning tax system.

In that case, there remains a question to answer, which is whether there is the political will to adopt such a code of conduct? That is for others to answer.

§16.05 APPENDIX

A Code of Conduct for Taxation

Objective

This Code of Conduct relates to the management and payment of taxes due to a State or any appropriate authority designated by it.

Scope

This Code applies to:

1. Governments and their agencies in their role as managers of a national economy, tax legislators, assessors and collectors;
2. Governments and their agencies in other jurisdictions with whom a government and its agencies might have to deal when determining tax liabilities owing whether within their own jurisdiction or in another place;
3. Those holding office in government with responsibility for taxation;
4. Taxpayers, whether individuals, corporate bodies or otherwise;
5. Tax agents, whether they are undertaking tax planning or assisting taxpayers with tax compliance;
6. Those other parties, collectively termed civil society, whether within the jurisdiction or outside it.

Application

It is intended that this Code be voluntarily adopted by States and should be used to guide the conduct of governments, ministers, tax authorities, taxpayers, tax agents and others who engage with the tax system of a State that has adopted the Code.

The Code

The Code is divided into eight sections, each of which includes a number of statements of principle.

1. Government legislation

The overriding principle with regard to tax legislation is that it shall be lawfully created, freely available, readily interpreted and transparent as to purpose to assist those with an obligation to settle tax in accordance with the law. To further these objectives a government shall:

(a) only collect taxation in accordance with legislation approved in accordance with its law;
(b) ensure all tax legislation is made available free of charge to all those who might have a responsibility to comply with it;
(c) not change legislation without consultation, excepting changes relating to tax rates and allowances;
(d) to the extent that judicial decisions impact the interpretation of tax legislation ensure that those decisions shall be made available free of charge to all who have a responsibility to comply with tax law;
(e) have an obligation to publish its interpretation of any tax statute that it intends to use so that those with a responsibility to pay tax might know what the government expects of them;
(f) offer interpretation to those seeking clarification on the purpose of tax legislation if that is not otherwise available from the government;
(g) where there is a dispute as to the meaning of the law create a mechanism for the speedy resolution of the resulting uncertainty, with all such matters being resolved by independent third parties whether sitting as a court, tribunal or otherwise, with those taxpayers without the means to access such facilities being provided with access to the means to do so.

2. International relations and taxation

The overriding principle with regard to international relations and taxation is that a government shall offer cooperation to all governments seeking assistance to collect tax legally due by those subject to tax charges within their jurisdiction and shall expect the same cooperation in return. To further these objectives a government shall:

(a) not offer incentives whether by way of legislation, conduct or administrative practice that might encourage the artificial relocation of international or interstate transactions;
(b) provide support to other countries and tax authorities to assist the collection of tax due to them;
(c) provide full cooperation to international agencies in the development of mechanisms to facilitate these goals.

3. Ministerial conduct

The overriding principle with regard to the conduct of ministers is that of accepting responsibility for the tax system as a whole whilst refraining from engagement in the affairs of any taxpayer. To further these objectives:

(a) ministers[14] with responsibility for taxation shall be accountable to the legislative assembly that appoints them for their actions;
(b) those ministers must direct their tax authority about the actions required of their tax authorities, but must not engage with that authority on the tax affairs of any taxpayer;
(c) the ministers in question should be required to publish their own tax returns to demonstrate that their own tax conduct is beyond reproach.

4. Government accountability

The overriding principle with regard to government accountability for the tax system requires that the budget for taxes to be collected and accounts for revenues actually received should be published, with a reconciliation between them being provided. To further these objectives:

(a) governments shall publish budgets setting out their taxation plans in advance of those revenues being raised, which budgets shall require approval by the appropriate legislature. Those budgets shall be in sufficient detail to appraise which tax is being charged, at what rate, on how many taxpayers, with which allowances and reliefs being permitted for offset so that it might be possible to appraise the impact of tax paid across society as a whole, how tax expenditures are allocated and to whom, and with what expected net taxation due. Sufficient narrative shall be supplied to explain the logic inherent in the budget process for each tax, tax rate, allowance and relief so that all stakeholders might understand the reasons for the tax charges being made;
(b) governments shall account on a regular and timely basis for the taxation revenues it has raised, reporting in the same format and detail as is required in its budget statement so that outcomes may be compared to expectations, with the differences being highlighted in the accounting provided with a narrative explanation of notable variances to ensure accessibility for all stakeholders to this information;
(c) a government should publish an annual tax gap analysis explaining the difference[15] with the resulting tax gaps being explained by a tax spillover analysis[16];

14. The term minister would embrace those holding other titles appointed by any legislature or authority to have responsibility for the administration of taxation within a jurisdiction.
15. An explanation of desirable tax gap methodologies is available in Murphy (2021).
16. For an explanation of tax spillovers, *see* Baker and Murphy (2019).

(d) an independent audit agency should appraise the truth and fairness of the government's tax accounting, including its tax gap reporting and tax spillover analysis so that the stakeholders of the tax system might rely on this information for decision-making purposes.

5. Tax authority management

The overriding principle with regard to the management of a tax authority is to require that it treats each taxpayer fairly and without bias in the relationships it has with them in determining the tax liabilities that might be due while making available to them all that information and those explanations that they might require to assist with this process and to explain their rights, responsibilities and payments owing, as well as their right to appeal if they think that appropriate. To further these objectives:

(a) all taxpayers shall be treated equally by the tax authority. This requires that none shall suffer discrimination for reason of their race, ethnicity, nationality, national origin, gender, sexual orientation, disability, legal structure or taxation residence; and nor shall discrimination occur for the reason of income, age, marital or family status unless legally approved social policy shall suggest it appropriately. In addition, a taxpayer must not suffer discrimination because of the place where they might be located, or their use of a language other than those which are officially recognized by the State, or their inability to read or to access digital communication;
(b) the tax authority shall clearly notify a taxpayer of their obligations to pay tax, accepting that public notification as legally provided for shall be sufficient in respect of general obligations to report the potential that a labiality might be due;
(c) the tax authority shall provide an opportunity for taxpayers to seek advice with regard to their affairs so that matters of uncertainty that they might have can be resolved and the tax authority shall be bound to accept that proper disclosure has been made if the taxpayer follows the advice given;
(d) the tax authority shall not enter into agreements as to tax liabilities owing other than on bases provided for in law or published practice generally available to all taxpayers at the time that the arrangement is made;
(e) the tax authority shall operate a complaints procedure with regard to the failure of their staff to act appropriately with regard to any taxpayer's affairs and shall investigate all such complaints in a timely fashion;
(f) the tax authority shall draw attention to the right to both complain and appeal when dealing with taxpayers.

6. Taxpayer conduct

The overriding expectation with regard to taxpayer conduct within the tax system is that they should conduct themselves openly, honestly and accountably. To further these objectives taxpayers should:

(a) act in good faith at all times with regard to the management of their taxation liabilities;
(b) register for all taxes as required by law;
(c) disclose all sources of income, profit and gains and arising to them as required by law;
(d) be open as to the ownership and control of any legal entities, partnerships, trusts and other such entities that they might use to manage their affairs so that they might be held accountable for any resulting tax liabilities owing;
(e) record their transactions if they shall have an impact in more than one location in that place where the economic substance of the transaction arises;
(f) settle all obligations due by them at the time they are due for payment;
(g) act respectfully towards the tax authority and those who work for it;
(h) make full disclosure of their affairs to any tax agent or adviser who they might engage to act on their behalf;

7. Tax planning

The overriding expectation with regard to tax planning is that it takes place within the spirit of the law. To further these objectives taxpayers should:

(a) seeks to ensure that their tax planning complies with the spirit as well as the letter of the law;
(b) only appoint tax advisers who undertake to work in accordance with this principle;
(c) ensure that any tax planning that they undertake reflects the economic substance of the transactions actually undertaken;
(d) make sure that no steps are added into any into a transaction solely or mainly to secure a tax advantage;[17]
(e) not change the location in which a transaction is recorded for the purpose of securing a tax advantage;
(f) disclose full details of arrangement entered into with the intention of securing a tax advantage to all tax authorities that might need to be aware of it.

8. Tax agents

The overriding expectation with regard to tax practice is that it complies with both the letter and the spirit of the law. To further these objectives tax agents should:

17. A tax advantage is defined as any reduction in a tax liability that would not otherwise arise.

a. act with integrity, requiring that they be straightforward and honest in all professional and business relationships;
b. be objective meaning that they do not allow bias, conflict of interest or undue influence of others to override professional or business judgements
c. act within their professional competence and undertake all due care to maintain their professional knowledge and skill at the level required to provide the services that they have undertaken to supply;
d. respect the confidentiality of information acquired as a result of professional and business relationships and, therefore, not disclose any such information to third parties without proper and specific authority, unless there is a legal or professional right or duty to disclose, nor use the information for the personal advantage of the member or third parties.
e. comply with relevant laws and regulations, and avoid any action that discredits the profession;
f. always act within the spirit of the law in recognition of their professional duty to act in the public interest;
g. never act on behalf of a client who will not make full disclosure of their tax affairs on a timely basis to all tax authorities who have a right to know about them;
h. never induce, encourage, advise or otherwise permit their client to submit an uncertain filing position[18] to a tax authority if they have encouraged or advised that such a position be adopted;
i. always advise a tax authority if an uncertain tax position exists within a client filing to a tax authority through no fault of their own e.g. because there is genuine uncertainty as to the tax status of a transaction where an opinion is being sought as to the correct filing to be made;
j. deal with all enquiries from a tax authority on a timely, efficient, and open basis.

Bibliography

Baker, A and Murphy, R. (2019). *The Political Economy of Tax Spillover: A New Multilateral Framework*. Global Policy 10(2): 178-192.

Baker, A and Murphy, R. (2020). *Making Tax Work: Consultation Draft*. Washington DC, USA: Global Initiative for Financial Transparency. https://fiscaltransparency.us12.list-manage.com/track/click?u=a98689428233f5de5539eb8f5&id=faeca31299&e=aef714549c.

Freedman, J. (2006). *Defining Taxpayer Responsibility: In Support of a General Anti-Avoidance Principle*. London, UK: British Tax Review.

Freeman, S. (2003). *The Cambridge Companion to Rawls*. Cambridge, UK: Cambridge University Press.

18. An uncertain filing position is defined by David (now Clair) Quentin as 'uncertainty as to the outcome in the event of a tax authority challenge'. (Quentin 2014)

Gunnarsson, Å. (2020). *World Tax Summit - TaxCOOP2020, Ethics, Inclusiveness and Other Issues*, Montreal (online), October 14, 2020.

HMRC (2018). *HMRC: The Standard for Agents*. London, UK: HM Revenue & Customs https://www.gov.uk/government/publications/hmrc-the-standard-for-agents/hmrc-the-standard-for-agents.

HMRC (2020a). *The HMRC Charter*. London, UK: HM Revenue & Customs https://www.gov.uk/government/publications/hmrc-charter/the-hmrc-charter.

HMRC (2020b). *Measuring Tax Gaps, 2020 edition*. London, UK: HM Revenue & Customs https://assets.publishing.service.gov.uk/government/uploads/system/uploads/attachment_data/file/907122/Measuring_tax_gaps_2020_edition.pdf.

ICAEW (2019). *Professional Conduct in Relation to Taxation*. London, UK: The Institute of Chartered Accountants in England and Wales. https://www.icaew.com/-/media/corporate/files/technical/tax/pcrt/pcrt.ashx.

IFAC (2020). *Handbook of the International Code of Ethics for Professional Accountants*. New York, USA: International Federation of Accountants. https://www.ifac.org/system/files/publications/files/IESBA-English-2020-IESBA-Handbook_Web-LOCKED.pdf.

Inman, P and Partington, R. (2021). *UK Pushes for City of London to Be Exempt from G7 Tax Plan*. London, UK, The Guardian. https://www.theguardian.com/business/2021/jun/09/uk-city-of-london-exempt-g7-tax-plan-chancellor-financial-services-global-corporation.

IRS (2020). *Ethics and Conduct Matters*. Washington DC, USA: Internal Revenue Service https://www.irs.gov/irm/part6/irm_06-735-001.

Kindi, I.X. (2019). *How to Be an Anti-racist*. London, UK: Bodley Head.

Murphy, R. (2007). *A Code of Conduct for Taxation*. Basildon, UK. The Association for Accountancy and Business Affairs and the Tax Justice Network https://www.taxjustice.net/cms/upload/pdf/AABA-TR-Code_long.pdf.

Murphy, R. (2010). *Why Do We Need a General Anti-avoidance Principle*? London, UK: The Trades Union Congress https://www.tuc.org.uk/research-analysis/reports/general-anti-avoidance-principle.

Murphy, R. (2014). *Tax Evasion in 2014*. London: Public & Commercial Services Union. http://www.taxresearch.org.uk/Documents/PCSTaxGap2014Full.pdf.

Murphy, R. (2015). *The Joy of Tax*. London: Transworld Publishers.

Murphy, R. (2021). *Reappraising the Tax Gap*, Chapter 4 in Unger, B, et al (eds) *Combating Financial Fraud and Empowering Regulators*. Oxford, UK: Oxford University Press https://oxford.universitypressscholarship.com/view/10.1093/oso/9780198854722.001.0001/oso-9780198854722-chapter-4.

OECD (2021). *Glossary of Tax Terms*. Paris, France: The Organisation for Economic Cooperation and Development https://www.oecd.org/ctp/glossaryoftaxterms.htm.

Olson, N. (2020). *World Tax Summit - TaxCOOP2020, Ethics, Inclusiveness and Other Issues*, Montreal (online), October 14, 2020.

Quentin, D. (2014). *Risk-Mining the Public Exchequer*. London: self-published. http://www.davidquentin.co.uk/Risk-Mining_The_Public_Exchequer.pdf.

Van Parijs, P. (2020). *World Tax Summit - TaxCOOP2020, Ethics, Inclusiveness and Other Issues*, Montreal (online), October 14, 2020.

Conclusion

Louise Otis, Brigitte Alepin & Lyne Latulippe

More than ever, coordination and cooperation have become the pillars of tax policies in the 21st century. While each chapter of this book approaches tax policy from a different angle, they all concur that tax cooperation and tax coordination are necessary to achieve significant tax reforms. Above all, in the laborious process of negotiating new taxation legislation, democratically elected governments must have the audacity to stand together to face the power of capital exacerbated by globalization and digitalization. Based on the intention of governments, policymakers must draft clear and precise rules, in line with the internationally coordinated standards and norms to limit loopholes and misinterpretation and leave no room for legal tax avoidance strategies.

The COVID-19 pandemic has been an important trigger for the advanced step we are pursuing today in international taxation. COVID-19 has shown that globalization and fierce competition between countries do not always yield benefits for the world. The world's richest have become wealthier during the pandemic, as social and economic inequality worsened in almost all nations. This electroshock abruptly revealed to the world that it is too late to rely on endless discussions held yearly in summits. Now is the time to move towards bigger changes.

The great leaders in international taxation have seized this momentum to move forward on the road to the modernization of tax systems for the common good. The TaxCOOP2020 World Summit, which inspired this book, was a unique major global tax meeting held during the COVID-19 pandemic. During four days, the greatest leaders in taxation opened their minds and hearts while sharing their precious thoughts on the urgency of reforming international taxation to face current and future major challenges.

This book also shows that we cannot modernize our tax regimes without taking into consideration the vital needs of all countries. Moreover, we must pay close attention to the world's young citizens. This requires listening carefully to their opinions and recognizing their contribution because ultimately the global reform of taxation will be their heritage. We must acknowledge the important role of young tax leaders and encourage collaboration with great thinkers of tax policy if we want to achieve successful reforms.

Now that we are moving forward with the modernization of global and domestic tax systems—which will entail a fair share of taxes by large corporate groups—let us envision some of the necessary steps down that road.

First and foremost, a new tax regime must take into account the world's most critical challenge of our time: global warming. Recent developments, such as agreeing to a global minimum tax rate, have shown that what seems impossible can be achieved. These advances provide a renewed strength and confidence to governments about tax policy choices that should inspire other steps to protect our planet. In 2019, at the COP25 in Madrid, TaxCOOP put forward the unavoidable necessity of redefining taxation systems in order to gather funds for responding promptly and efficiently to the alarming situation that afflicts our planet.

Second, there will soon be nearly 3,000 billionaires in the world with close to USD 15 trillion in assets. Documented evidence shows that most of them do not pay their fair share of taxes. No sound reason can justify this indifference to the global common good. Therefore, future reforms should focus on reestablishing a more balanced contribution by the world's billionaires. The legislation governing so-called philanthropic foundations should also be reviewed as those foundations are often used for tax avoidance purposes despite their ostensible charitable aims.

Third, the time has come to introduce more powerful ways to reach global consensus such as high-level mediation carried on by international experts. We no longer have the luxury of lengthy formulaic negotiations of the kind we carried out for decades. We need to include neutral third parties who are impartial and independent to guide, activate, and accelerate the negotiations. This is how coordination and cooperation would achieve significant tax reforms.

Global challenges such as the pandemic reveal the necessity of protecting the foundations of our democracies and preserving the financial resources of our governments, which, in the end, are those of each and every one of us.

SERIES ON INTERNATIONAL TAXATION

1. Alberto Xavier, *The Taxation of Foreign Investment in Brazil,* 1980 (ISBN 90-200-0582-0).
2. Hugh J. Ault & Albert J. Rädler, *The German Corporation Tax Law with 1980 Amendments,* 1981 (ISBN 90-200-0642-8).
3. Paul R. McDaniel & Hugh J. Ault, *Introduction to United States International Taxation,* 1981 (ISBN 90-6544-004-6).
4. Albert J. Rädler, *German Transfer Pricing/Prix de Transfer en Allemagne,* 1984 (ISBN 90-6544-143-3).
5. Paul R. McDaniel & Stanley S. Surrey, *International Aspects of Tax Expenditures: A Comparative Study,* 1985 (ISBN 90-654-4163-8).
6. Kees van Raad, *Nondiscrimination in International Tax Law,* 1986 (ISBN 90-6544-266-9).
7. Sijbren Cnossen (ed.), *Tax Coordination in the European Community,* 1987 (ISBN 90-6544-272-3).
8. Ben Terra, *Sales Taxation. The Case of Value Added Tax in the European Community,* 1989 (ISBN 90-6544-381-9).
9. Rutsel S.J. Martha, *The Jurisdiction to Tax in International Law: Theory and Practice of Legislative Fiscal Jurisdiction,* 1989 (ISBN 90-654-4416-5).
10. Paul R. McDaniel & Hugh J. Ault, *Introduction to United States International Taxation* (3rd revised edition), 1989 (ISBN 90-6544-423-8).
11. Manuel Pires, *International Juridicial Double Taxation of Income,* 1989 (ISBN 90-6544-426-2).
12. A.H.M. Daniels, *Issues in International Partnership Taxation,* 1991 (ISBN 90-654-4577-3).
13. Arvid A. Skaar, *Permanent Establishment: Erosion of a Tax Treaty Principle,* 1992 (ISBN 90-6544-594-3).
14. Cyrille David & Geerten M.M. Michielse (eds), *Tax Treatment of Financial Instruments,* 1996 (ISBN 90-654-4666-4).
15. Herbert H. Alpert & Kees van Raad (eds), *Essays on International Taxation,* 1993 (ISBN 90-654-4781-4).
16. Wolfgang Gassner, Michael Lang & Eduard Lechner (eds), *Tax Treaties and EC Law,* 1997 (ISBN 90-411-0680-4).
17. Glória Teixeira, *Taxing Corporate Profits in the EU,* 1997 (ISBN 90-411-0703-7).
18. Michael Lang et al. (eds), *Multilateral Tax Treaties,* 1998 (ISBN 90-411-0704-5).
19. Stef van Weeghel, *The Improper Use of Tax Treaties,* 1998 (ISBN 90-411-0737-1).

20. Klaus Vogel (ed.), *Interpretation of Tax Law and Treaties and Transfer Pricing in Japan and Germany,* 1998 (ISBN 90-411-9655-2).
21. Bertil Wiman (ed.), *International Studies in Taxation: Law and Economics; Liber Amicorum Leif Mutén,* 1999 (ISBN 90-411-9692-7).
22. Alfonso J. Martín Jiménez, *Towards Corporate Tax Harmonization in the European Community,* 1999 (ISBN 90-411-9690-0).
23. Ramon J. Jeffery, *The Impact of State Sovereignty on Global Trade and International Taxation,* 1999 (ISBN 90-411-9703-6).
24. A.J. Easson, *Taxation of Foreign Direct Investment,* 1999 (ISBN 90-411-9741-9).
25. Marjaana Helminen, *The Dividend Concept in International Tax Law: Dividend Payments Between Corporate Entities,* 1999 (ISBN 90-411-9765-6).
26. Paul Kirchhof, Moris Lehner, Kees van Raad, Arndt Raupach & Michael-Rodi (eds), *International and Comparative Taxation: Essays in Honour of Klaus Vogel,* 2002 (ISBN 90-411-9841-5).
27. Krister Andersson, Peter Melz & Christer Silfverberg (eds), *Liber Amicorum Sven-Olof Lodin,* 2001 (ISBN 90-411-9850-4).
28. Juan Martín Jovanovich, *Customs Valuation and Transfer Pricing: Is It Possible to Harmonize Customs and Tax Rules?,* Second Edition, 2018 (ISBN 978-90-411-6134-5).
29. Stefano Simontacchi, *Taxation of Capital Gains under the OECD Model Convention: With Special Regard to Immovable Property,* 2007 (ISBN 978-90-411-2549-1).
30. Michael Lang, Josef Schuch, & Claus Staringer (eds), *Tax Treaty Law and EC Law,* 2007 (ISBN 978-90-411-2629-0).
31. Duncan Bentley, *Taxpayers' Rights: Theory Origin and Implementation,* 2007 (ISBN 978-90-411-2650-4).
32. Sergio André Rocha, *Interpretation of Double Taxation Conventions: General Theory and Brazilian Perspective,* 2008 (ISBN 978-90-411-2822-5).
33. Robert F. van Brederode, *Systems of General Sales Taxation: Theory, Policy and Practice,* 2009 (ISBN 978-90-411-2832-4).
34. John G. Head & Richard Krever (eds), *Tax Reform in the 21st Century: A Volume in Memory of Richard Musgrave,* 2009 (ISBN 978-90-411-2829-4).
35. Jens Wittendorff, *Transfer Pricing and the Arm's Length Principle in International Tax Law,* 2010 (ISBN 978-90-411-3270-3).
36. Marjaana Helminen, *The International Tax Law Concept of Dividend,* Second Edition, 2017 (ISBN 978-90-411-8394-1).
37. Robert F. van Brederode (ed.), *Immovable Property under VAT: A Comparative Global Analysis,* 2011 (ISBN 978-90-411-3126-3).
38. Dennis Weber & Stef van Weeghel, *The 2010 OECD Updates: Model Tax Convention & Transfer Pricing Guidelines - A Critical Review,* 2011 (ISBN 978-90-411-3812-5).
39. Yariv Brauner & Martin James McMahon, Jr. (eds), *The Proper Tax Base: Structural Fairness from an International and Comparative Perspective— Essays in Honour of Paul McDaniel,* 2012 (ISBN 978-90-411-3286-4).
40. Robert F. van Brederode (ed.), *Science, Technology and Taxation,* 2012 (ISBN 978-90-411-3125-6).

41. Oskar Henkow, *The VAT/GST Treatment of Public Bodies*, 2013 (ISBN 978-90-411-4663-2).
42. Jean Schaffner, *How Fixed Is a Permanent Establishment?*, 2013 (ISBN 978-90-411-4662-5).
43. Miguel Correia, *Taxation of Corporate Groups*, 2013 (ISBN 978-90-411-4841-4).
44. Veronika Daurer, *Tax Treaties and Developing Countries*, 2014 (ISBN 978-90-411-4982-4).
45. Claire Micheau, *State Aid, Subsidy and Tax Incentives under EU and WTO Law*, 2014 (ISBN 978-90-411-4555-0).
46. Robert F. van Brederode & Richard Krever (eds), *Legal Interpretation of Tax Law*, 2014 (ISBN 978-90-411-4945-9).
47. Radhakishan Rawal, *Taxation of Cross-border Services*, 2014 (ISBN 978-90-411-4947-3).
48. João Dácio Rolim, *Proportionality and Fair Taxation*, 2014 (ISBN 978-90-411-5838-3).
49. Paulo Rosenblatt, *General Anti-avoidance Rules for Major Developing Countries*, 2015 (ISBN 978-90-411-5839-0).
50. Gaspar Lopes Dias V.S., *Tax Arbitrage through Cross-Border Financial Engineering*, 2015 (ISBN 978-90-411-5875-8).
51. Geerten M.M. Michielse & Victor Thuronyi (eds), *Tax Design Issues Worldwide*, 2015 (ISBN 978-90-411-5610-5).
52. Oktavia Weidmann, *Taxation of Derivatives*, 2015 (ISBN 978-90-411-5977-9).
53. Chris Evans, Richard Krever & Peter Mellor (eds), *Tax Simplification*, 2015 (ISBN 978-90-411-5976-2).
54. Reuven Avi-Yonah & Joel Slemrod (eds), *Taxation and Migration*, 2015 (ISBN 978-90-411-6136-9).
55. Alexander Bosman, *Other Income under Tax Treaties: An Analysis of Article 21 of the OECD Model Convention*, 2015 (ISBN 978-90-411-6610-4).
56. John Abrahamson, *International Taxation of Manufacturing and Distribution*, 2016 (ISBN 978-90-411-6664-7).
57. Frederik Boulogne, *Shortcomings in the EU Merger Directive*, 2016 (ISBN 978-90-411-6713-2).
58. Angelika Meindl-Ringler, *Beneficial Ownership in International Tax Law*, 2016 (ISBN 978-90-411-6833-7).
59. Andreas Waltrich, *Cross-Border Taxation of Permanent Establishments: An International Comparison*, 2016 (ISBN 978-90-411-6832-0).
60. Sergio André Rocha & Allison Christians (eds), *Tax Sovereignty in the BEPS Era*, 2017 (ISBN 978-90-411-6707-1).
61. Peter Antony Wilson, *BRICS and International Tax Law*, 2018 (ISBN 978-90-411-9435-0).
62. Louise Otis, Brigitte Alepin & Blanca Moreno-Dodson (eds), *Winning the Tax Wars: Tax Competition and Cooperation*, 2018 (ISBN 978-90-411-9460-2).
63. Marta Castelon, *International Taxation of Income from Services under Double Taxation Conventions: Development, Practice and Policy*, 2018 (ISBN 978-90-411-9594-4).

64. D.M. Broekhuijsen, *A Multilateral Tax Treaty: Designing an Instrument to Modernise International Tax Law*, 2018 (ISBN 978-90-411-9872-3).
65. John Abrahamson, *International Taxation of Energy Production and Distribution*, 2018 (ISBN 978-90-411-9101-4).
66. Leopoldo Parada, *Double Non-taxation and the Use of Hybrid Entities: An Alternative Approach in the New Era of BEPS*, 2018 (ISBN 978-90-411-9991-1).
67. Richard Snoeij, *International Tax Aspects of Sovereign Wealth Investors: A Source State Perspective*, 2018 (ISBN 978-90-411-9431-2).
68. Aleksandra Bal, *Taxation, Virtual Currency and Blockchain*, 2019 (ISBN 978-94-035-0103-1).
69. Werner Haslehner, Georg Kofler, Katerina Pantazatou & Alexander Rust (eds), *Tax and the Digital Economy: Challenges and Proposals for Reform*, 2019 (ISBN 978-94-035-0361-5).
70. Eva Escribano, *Jurisdiction to Tax Corporate Income Pursuant to the Presumptive Benefit Principle: A Critical Analysis of Structural Paradigms Underlying Corporate Income Taxation and Proposals for Reform*, 2019 (ISBN 978-94-035-0640-1).
71. Jérôme Monsenego & Jan Bjuvberg (eds), *International Taxation in a Changing Landscape: Liber Amicorum in Honour of Bertil Wiman*, 2019 (ISBN 978-90-411-9234-9).
72. Kasper Dziurdź, *Non-discrimination in Tax Treaty Law and World Trade Law: The Impact of Formal, Substantive and Subjective Approaches*, 2019 (ISBN 978-94-035-0904-4).
73. Félix Daniel Martínez Laguna, *Hybrid Financial Instruments, Double Nontaxation and Linking Rules*, 2019 (ISBN 978-94-035-1074-3).
74. Jan Gooijer, *Tax Treaty Residence of Entities*, 2019 (ISBN 978-94-035-1301-0).
75. John Abrahamson, *International Taxation of Banking*, 2020 (ISBN 978-94-035-1094-1).
76. Richard Krever & François Vaillancourt (eds), *The Allocation of Multinational Business Income: Reassessing the Formulary Apportionment Option*, 2020 (ISBN 978-94-035-0614-2).
77. Ajit Kumar Singh, *Exploring the Nexus Doctrine in International Tax Law*, 2021 (ISBN 978-94-035-3363-6).
78. Galya Savir, *Regulation and Tax in Space*, 2021 (ISBN 978-94-035-3393-3).
79. Rita Julien, *Credit Method Compatibility and Constraints under EU Law: An Analysis of the Case Law of the CJEU*, 2021 (ISBN 978-94-035-2363-7).
80. Sergio André Rocha & Allison Christians (eds), *A Multilateral Convention for Tax: From Theory to Implementation*, 2021 (ISBN 978-90-411-9428-2).
81. Brigitte Alepin, Lyne Latulippe & Louise Otis (eds), *Coordination and Cooperation: Tax Policy in the 21st Century*, 2022 (ISBN 978-94-035-3740-5).

www.ingramcontent.com/pod-product-compliance
Lightning Source LLC
Chambersburg PA
CBHW071242230926
51849CB00001B/203
9789403537405